# DISASTER RESPONSE
# AND PLANNING
# FOR LIBRARIES

# DISASTER RESPONSE AND PLANNING FOR LIBRARIES

THIRD EDITION

*Miriam B. Kahn*

AMERICAN LIBRARY ASSOCIATION
Chicago   2012

**Miriam B. Kahn,** founder of MBK Consulting, helps libraries, archives, corporations, and cultural institutions plan for, recover from, and prevent disasters that interrupt services. Since 1989, she has worked in the field of preservation, consulted on disaster response, and offered hands-on assistance during disasters. She is the author of Disaster Response and Planning for Libraries, second edition, and Protecting Your Library's Electronic Resources (both published by ALA Editions). She is a popular presenter and teacher, offering courses at Kent State University's Graduate School for Library and Information Science and throughout the Midwest. She holds an MLS from Queens College, CUNY, and a PhD from Kent State University.

Printed in the United States of America

16   15   14   13   12      5   4   3   2   1

While extensive effort has gone into ensuring the reliability of the information in this book, the publisher makes no warranty, express or implied, with respect to the material contained herein.

ISBNs: 978-0-8389-1151-8 (paper); 978-0-8389-9419-1 (PDF). For more information on digital formats, visit the ALA Store at alastore.ala.org and select eEditions.

**Library of Congress Cataloging-in-Publication Data**

Kahn, Miriam (Miriam B.)
    Disaster response and planning for libraries / Miriam B. Kahn.—Third edition.
        pages   cm
    Includes bibliographical references and index.
    ISBN 978-0-8389-1151-8
    1. Libraries—Safety measures. 2. Library materials—Conservation and restoration.
3. Libraries—Safety measures—Planning. 4. Library materials—Conservation and restoration—Planning. I. Title.
    Z679.7.K38 2012
    025.8'2—dc23                                                                                      2011043703

Cover design by Casey Bayer. Cover image © Tom Grundy/Shutterstock, Inc.
Text design in Classic Round by Karen Sheets de Gracia and Dianne M. Rooney

♾ This paper meets the requirements of ANSI/NISO Z39.48-1992 (Permanence of Paper).

*For all those who respond to disasters without hesitation*

# Contents

## Appendix **A** **Checklists and Forms** **93**

Appendix **B**  **Associations, Organizations, and Companies**  **135**

THIS IS THE THIRD TIME I HAVE REVISED THIS BOOK IN AN EFFORT TO HELP librarians, archivists and museum curators deal with disasters, large and small. Since 2002, libraries, archives, historical societies, museums, record centers, courthouses, and all types of businesses and innumerable individuals have dealt with disasters. Time after time, we realize that disasters come in all shapes and sizes, from Hurricanes Katrina, Rita, and Wilma in 2004–2005 and Hurricane Irene in 2011 to tsunamis in Asia in 2006 and 2011, from the earthquakes in Haiti and Chile in 2010 and on the east coast of North America in the summer of 2011 to the collapse of the archives in Cologne in 2009. In the past ten years, rivers flooded, dams broke, roofs collapsed, fires erupted—disasters too numerous to mention here. Still, libraries, archives, historical societies, museums, and other cultural institutions need this basic book on disaster response to help respond to and plan for the inevitable crisis that is too large for a mop or wet vac.

There is an increased awareness that cultural institutions need a disaster response plan that includes physical and virtual collections, services, administration, and cash flow. Disaster response plans must include advice for dealing with computers, individuals, and their families. The focus of this book continues to emphasize restoration of services to our patrons. We must think beyond the standard bricks and mortar of our buildings to the people and organizations we serve. We must respond to disasters quickly and efficiently, helping others regain some semblance of their previous lives, reconnect with families and jobs, and get back on their feet. That's too large a task for this book, well beyond what cultural institutions do, yet our services are now intertwined with the lives of our patrons.

We must respond quickly and efficiently to restore services. That is the focus of this book. To help cultural institutions respond to and recover from disasters, to plan and prepare for disruption of services and dislocation from their normal routines.

Large and small, public and private, all types of institutions and businesses need to plan for disasters. Disasters come whether or not we are prepared.

Changes since the last edition:

- The field of disaster response is international. We hear about natural and man-made disasters as they occur and respond with physical and financial assistance as quickly as possible. The news keeps all of us informed almost instantaneously, especially when disasters strike. Conservators and preservation professionals travel to disaster sites, providing information and assistance aimed at restoring access to collections in cultural institutions.

■ Social networking is ubiquitous, so we need to consider the implications for communications and public relations. Facebook pages, Twitter feeds, wikis, and blogs are everywhere. They seem to spring up instantaneously when a disaster occurs. Cell phones and digital cameras connect us seamlessly with one another and the world around us, bringing voices and images of disasters to the institution and to the public. We must plan how to limit unofficial information about disasters, because our staff members will disseminate news with or without our permission and oversight.

■ Grief counseling is now an integral part of any disaster response plan, no matter what the type of disaster or crisis. Although this topic is beyond the scope of this publication, it is necessary to consider how and when your institution will provide grief counseling. In the immediate aftermath of a disaster, institutions must provide counseling to staff members to help them cope with the stress.

■ Mission statements and collection development policies are essential guidelines for prioritizing the recovery of damaged materials. They are even more important now that so many of our resources are electronic and digital. The rate of recovery and the order of recovery of services and materials, both print and electronic, depends upon the patron base and the scope of the disaster, what is affected, the type of resources, and the needs of your organization.

■ Preparedness serves two purposes: prevention of the disaster in the first place, and preservation and security of collections during and after the disaster.

Each section of this book pertains to all types of cultural institutions, from one-person programs to complex institutions with hierarchical management and administration; from one room to multiple buildings or campuses; from physical objects to digital or virtual. Use the parts of this book that pertain to the size of your institution, and adapt the rest to meet the crisis you face. This publication continues to emphasize the recovery of physical objects, while discussing the importance of backup and remote sites for data and electronic resources.

The events of September 11, 2001, continue to echo in my mind. It is a date and event that changed disaster response forever. The events of that day reinforced the need for each and every business, cultural institution, organization, and government agency to plan for disasters. Since then, disaster response and all its related fields are more visible and more important to all of us. Heightened awareness of security issues, contingency plans, disaster response plans, and many other buzzwords are in the news and professional literature of almost every industry. In the wake of those attacks and of subsequent terrorist scares and natural and manmade disasters, the revision of this book is important. Even so, the primary focus of this publication is still damage to tangible collections in libraries and archives, historical societies and museums. In the light of past events, library disaster response plans must be integrated into disaster response and emergency plans of cultural institutions and communities at large.

Disaster response and emergency plans are integral to the survival of universities, museums, cities, counties, and states. Each crisis reminds us that preparing for small disasters is just as important as planning for the worst, or the unforeseen. Planning for disaster is an attempt to minimize the loss of information to clientele and decrease the loss of access to and closure of collections. Without planning, the chances of survival of a business, information center, library, archives, or museum are next to impossible. Some planning will ensure that part or all of the institution will survive to rebuild itself in a new and stronger manner.

Disasters, emergencies, and crises can occur in many forms, from fire, water, tornado, and loss of power and phones to the destruction of buildings and collections. Disasters occur when we lose a key employee, discover the theft of rare items in our collections, and deal with disruptive patrons. The disaster response team responds to each disaster taking into account its scope and circumstances. Preparation is key for a successful recovery.

While this publication addresses only physical disasters, keep in mind that many other events are disastrous for your institution, including bomb threats, major thefts, and disruptive patrons.

This publication is designed to help libraries and archives, historical societies, record centers, and museums respond to and recover from disasters. The materials and suggestions will assist in the design of disaster response plans. Adapt the plans and procedures to your institution's needs.

The plans and procedures in this publication are generic for all types of cultural institutions and organizations. If you place this book on the shelf without taking the time to modify its procedures to your institution's needs, you did not write a disaster response plan for your own organization. In the worst-case scenario, there are sections designed to be used as situations warrant. Moreover, designing and completing any plan do not guarantee that your institution will survive a disaster. It is merely one step in considering all the risks and preventing them. Planning for disasters will accomplish two things: increase the chances for you and your library to survive a disaster and decrease the impact afterward.

Store copies of the disaster response plan and computer backup data off-site at home, in record storage centers, or in banks. Place digital copies on remote servers and in digital repositories. Keep at least one hard copy of the plan in each department and building. Update the plan whenever there are changes in personnel, hardware and software, or in the physical layout of the institution.

# Arrangement and Purpose

THIS PUBLICATION IS DIVIDED INTO FIVE SECTIONS, TWO APPENDICES, AND A BIBliography. There is one section for each of the four phases of disaster response planning. The fifth section contains procedures for stabilization and basic treatment of some collections once the recovery process is in full swing. The first appendix contains checklists and forms to organize and coordinate various activities during the response and planning phases. The second appendix lists different organizations, companies, and suppliers of disaster response services, consultation, and assistance. A current selective bibliography is appended to this work for consultation and for in-depth information about some of the more complex issues.

This work provides practical, down-to-earth information and advice for dealing with disasters and planning for their eventual occurrence. There are quite a number of books in the field of disaster response and preparedness that cover theories of planning and recovering print and nonprint materials. Some ideas from those books are included, but the theory contained within is minimal and will mainly be found in the fifth section of this book.

As the focus is practicality, this publication begins with the most important aspect of a disaster response plan, "Response." This section comes first, just in case a reader needs to implement a response before there is an opportunity to put an actual plan together. This first section contains information on small jobs and how to handle them in-house with the institution's own staff and suggestions for hiring out the labor and supervising staff. The goal is to get back to normal as soon as possible.

Computers play an integrated part in libraries, archives, and information centers. Catalogs, circulation systems, collections, and finding aids are located and preserved on these computers. So we must create disaster response plans for recovery of lost data and resumption of services. Plans that revolve around computers are usually called "contingency plans" and focus on restoring the programs and data carefully backed up every hour, day, or week. The specifics of planning for recovery of computer systems go beyond the scope of this publication. But I would be remiss to ignore the computers, so basic information and references about where the computer disaster response plan should be added or inserted will be included throughout. Some publications on the subject will be found in the bibliography.

The second section is "Recovering Collections and Restoring Operations," which discusses the resumption of services and operations. It includes guidelines for what to do when the institution is no longer in disaster mode, including evaluating the effectiveness of the plan and modifying it as needed with additional staff training in the weak spots.

For the sake of simplicity, this book deals with response and recovery separately. However, as Camila Alire points out in the *Library Disaster Planning and Recovery Handbook,* "the reality is that both activities [disaster response and recovery] can be operating at the same time."[1]

"Prevention," the third section, is closely tied in with the fourth section, "Planning." Prevention can stand alone and be accomplished without a formal disaster response plan.

"Planning," the fourth section, lists all responsibilities suggested for the team members; prioritizes the order of recovering damaged collections; and provides suggestions for staff training. This section is rounded out with information on how to plan for loss of computer services.

The fifth section, "Response and Recovery Procedures," includes information on handling, packing, drying, and cleaning print and nonprint, paper and nonpaper materials. There is information about dealing with mold and what effects ozone has on collections. Some of this section is taken from information collected by the author and distributed at seminars for libraries, archives, historical societies, and disaster response companies.

There are two appendices. The first, "Checklists and Forms," contains checklists and forms for use during all the phases of disaster response planning. They are fairly generic and so should be adapted for use at your institution. The second appendix, "Associations, Organizations, and Companies," contains a selected list of organizations, companies, and suppliers who can and will assist during disaster response, recovery, and planning. Not every organization or company is listed, mostly the large or national ones. Add your local contacts to make this plan your own.

The bibliography is divided into three parts. The first is a basic bibliography of books and articles that contain the basics of planning and response. The second part lists publications by topic and is designed to assist with specialized planning and recovery needs. The third part is a general bibliography containing additional readings that cross topic lines. The books, articles, and journals included in the bibliography are only some that are available in this flourishing field. Some citations refer to other bibliographies. Use the citations to educate the disaster response team and staff members of your institution.

While your plan is in draft form and when it is completed, place basic response procedures with phone numbers in the front of your disaster response manual for easy reference and contact. Post the daytime numbers for the disaster response team at phones for a swift response.

## NOTE

1. Camila Alire, *Library Disaster Planning and Recovery Handbook* (New York: Neal-Schuman, 2000), 12.

# Acknowledgments

THANKS FOR THIS THIRD EDITION GO TO CLARK SEARLE, WHO HELPED ME UPDATE the topics of mold and insurance and the issues of responsible record keeping during the response and recovery phases. Julie Callahan for helping me address the needs of public and academic libraries. Kirk Lively, who provides information on current disaster response companies, their specialized services, and mold removal. To my colleagues, Nancy Birk, Karen Gracy, and Margaret Maurer, thanks for listening to my new ideas and helping me form them into coherent concepts. To my students, who listened to my numerous lectures about disaster response and shared their own stories about water, fire, and mold. To Vic Fleischer, whose request to review his disaster response plan jump-started the long-stalled revision of this book. To the librarians, archivists, records managers, and book collectors who called for help with mold removal and drying water-damaged books. To Nan Garrison, colleague and friend, who fed me and listened to my complaints about yet another mold consultation. Thanks to my editor Michael Jeffers for his encouragement during the slow and difficult spots. And, as always, thanks to my family for their support. The ideas and techniques in this book are the result of my experiences, feedback from earlier editions, and from my workshops. Any errors and omissions are mine alone.

# Introduction

Disasters happen. You plan for them, work to prevent them, or turn a blind eye and hope one will never occur. Sooner or later, you must deal with one. Disasters come in all sizes. Sometimes disasters affect a small part of your building, sometimes the entire building, and in the most extreme and tragic times the entire area. Since you do not know when or how extensive the disaster will be, you can only be prepared.

If this is the case, then why write about disasters at all? Well, in the twenty-odd years I have been dealing with disasters, I know they will come, that we are never truly prepared, and that we will respond, recover, and go on to rebuild even better cultural institutions. To respond quickly and efficiently, you must plan and prepare for whatever comes your way. Plan for the small disaster and the rest will begin to fall into place.

So where do you start? This book provides guidelines for responding to disasters and recovering operations, materials, and resources, including staff and income. From there you start the process all over again, by planning and preventing the next disaster. Notice I started the process with response and not planning. The sad but true fact is that most institutions, most businesses, most people never plan for disasters. They respond to disasters and, in doing so, recover all they can, pick up the pieces, and plan for the next one. The logical place to begin is with response and a determined, coordinated effort to restore access to collections and resources, physical and digital.

When disaster strikes, your first reaction must be response. It is very important to follow your plan and carry out the steps and policies you created. So if you have a plan, activate it. If you don't have a plan, all is not lost.

Respond using your knowledge of the institution and its needs, mission, and collection development policies. Respond with a sense of priorities based upon those needs and your patron base. Respond with the goal of recovering access to services and resources as quickly and painlessly as possible. Respond, don't ignore the disaster, and don't expect others to do it for you.

Common sense tells us to evacuate a building in the case of fire, smoke, and sometimes severe weather. For tornados, find the tornado shelter in the building. Now is not the time for heroics. Pull a fire alarm, call 911, and evacuate the building. Response is part of making certain all the people are safe.

Disasters come in various sizes and levels of seriousness. They strike departments, buildings, institutions, communities, and regions. Fire, flood, and broken water pipes are just as serious and stressful as hurricanes, tornados, earthquakes, and blizzards. They wreak havoc on our institutions, our routines, and our lives. Bomb threats, hazardous waste contamination, and epidemics may be beyond our control but we can plan for them. Power and phone outages, loss of Internet, wireless, and e-mail access can cripple an institution and reference services if we don't plan for them. That's what disaster response is all about. Consider the various crises that can strike, large and small. Plan your response. Follow your plans. Ask for help. When it is all over, revise your plans so you are ready when the next disaster occurs.

This book provides guidance, suggestions, plans, and checklists for responding to and recovering from disasters. Planning is the key, planning for your response is the best insurance for surviving each disaster whenever it happens.

For the readers who don't have time to design a plan or read this book, this introduction provides guidance for responding to disasters.

## Why Write a Disaster Response Plan?

Disaster response and prevention policies are essential for the continuation of libraries, archives, historical societies, and museums. Our patrons expect that we are open for business at all hours and accessible when they want information. With the proliferation of computers and our dependence upon data and online services, downtime and lack of accessibility are detrimental to quality service and our reputation. So what is to be done? First, thinking about disasters, or "the worst," is the best first line of defense and prevention. If nothing ever went wrong, then disaster plans would be a waste of time. Sadly, this is not the case. Every day we read about floods, mold infections, and fires that cause irreparable harm to library and archival collections. Even a slowdown of service or power outage has untold repercussions in quality of service and the ability to provide information in a timely manner.

In the aftermath of the destruction of the World Trade Center on September 11, 2001, financial institutions immediately activated the contingency plans for their computer systems. Through careful planning and testing, mandated by the federal government, they were able to restore operations quickly. Those businesses that did not have plans or data backed up in remote locations struggled to get their operations up and running. In some cases, all documents and data were lost forever.

After Hurricane Katrina, libraries and archives, universities and businesses scrambled to provide safe work space for staff and recover collections as quickly as possible. Restoration of service, access to e-mail and the Internet were key to providing benefits to the displaced and a communication lifeline to residents of Louisiana and Mississippi.

After the earthquakes in Haiti and Chile, cultural institutions provided information and e-mail access to individuals who lost homes and businesses, and helped reunite families. We don't always think about the roles libraries and archives play during a disaster. Libraries are safe havens from the chaotic storm of displaced lives. They are the information hub of our information-hungry society. If we don't plan for response to disasters and quick restoration of services, libraries and archives are not available for our patrons to use to resume their lives and contact with the outside world.

While dealing with the enormity of the human tragedy, disaster response teams plan to recover effectively and efficiently from the worst and to provide access to our resources as quickly as possible. While we cannot necessarily plan for every contingency, we can plan how we will restore services as quickly as possible. After each disaster, the library and archives community is reminded of the importance of foresight and planning for the loss of collections and data, services and information.

## What Is a Disaster Response Plan and Why Is It Important?

Disaster response is the procedures and processes whereby a team of trained individuals responds to a disaster and determines how to best recover the damaged materials so that "business as usual" can resume as quickly as possible. It is best if the response and recovery procedures are worked out ahead of time. This will enable the disaster response team to implement response and recovery procedures as quickly as possible based upon well-thought-out priorities and techniques.

During the disaster response phase of the operation, volunteers, outside consultants, and contractors are often called in to assist with the recovery of damaged materials. It is important to consider the role of outside or volunteer assistance, where their services can best be used, how they can relieve physical and emotional stress from full-time staff, and how their services can be used to perform many of the labor-intensive procedures. A well-thought-out disaster response plan will decrease the amount of time it takes to implement disaster recovery procedures and should decrease the loss of materials and contents and increase the recovery rate.

In the planning phase, select the disaster response team. Team members are responsible for directing the activities during the response and recovery phases. The disaster response team allocates responsibilities and assists with recovery prioritization decisions. The team should be involved with training for themselves and any staff and volunteers who will work on recovering the collections and facility from the disaster.

Preparation, or preparedness, is the phase during which the disaster response team surveys the building and its collections for potential hazards and the identification of previous water leaks, and so on. During this phase, the team creates simple floor plans showing where collections are located and what is in various rooms. Identify the location of fire alarms, fire escapes and emergency doors, and fire extinguishers and mark floor plans accordingly. Disaster response planning and prevention, or preparedness, are performed when all is sane and quiet, and decisions are made in a rational, carefully considered manner.

On the flip side of the process, disaster response and recovery plans are activated when all is chaos, amidst conflicting demands to restore services, collections, and access to the building. There is often a tension between the disaster response team and the director, administrators, and patrons. The response phase concentrates upon doing just that, responding to the news that a "disaster" has occurred, assembling the appropriate staff, outside assistance, and supplies, while recovering the collection and the facility. The recovery phase concentrates on restoring the collection to a usable form and resuming services in a timely, efficient, and cost-effective manner.

Taken as a whole, a disaster response plan is essential to the continuation of the institution, retention of patrons, and fast and efficient resumption of services to patrons and staff.

## Response

*At the worst possible moment,* the phone rings or your e-mail pings with news of a disaster in your institution. You are heading out the door to an important meeting, vacation, or just for the weekend. Your adrenaline surges as you call the disaster response team and race to the scene. Take a deep breath as you respond to the situation based upon the careful planning and heated discussions of the past months and years. All the planning and preparation finally pays off. It is time to put your plan into action.

There are three basic stages of response:

1. Respond to the disaster by assembling your team
2. Assess the scope of the damage
3. Begin recovery of services and collections

### Initial Response to the Disaster

First assemble your disaster response team. During the planning phase, you selected two or three possible places to meet, one near the building if the library or building is damaged, in a quiet location out of the weather somewhere nearby. In the case of a small, isolated disaster in the building, meet in a conference room. Assemble your team at the appropriate location. If you do not have a plan or a predetermined location, select a place where you can talk and synchronize response activities.

If you do not have a team, gather together department heads, administrators, and staff with preservation and/or disaster response experience. Include someone from the IT (information technology) department. From this group, select a team leader other than the director. The director has a separate set of responsibilities during a disaster, as does the head of IT or computer services.

The team leader should have enough authority to supervise staff and assign tasks without asking permission from someone else. In some institutions, the team leader is the head of facilities and maintenance, in other cases, the deputy director responsible for buildings and properties, in others, the head of preservation, archives, or special collections. For every institution, there is a logical person to be in charge. The only time the head of the disaster response team should be the director is if the library has only one staff member. If the disaster affects the entire institution or community, select a disaster response team member as liaison with the institutional or community emergency management team.

Once you have a disaster response team leader and team, then the director and the team leader should brief the team as to the scope of the disaster: what was damaged and what was affected. Was there a fire? A broken water pipe? Is there a power outage and are the phones and Internet affected? When can the team get access to the building(s)?

If the power is out, how long until the utility company can repair the damage and restore service? In the meantime, can your staff provide services such as reference and circulation without power? If so, implement manual circulation and reference procedures. If there are battery-operated computers with circulation capability, then use them.

Activate the IT disaster response plan to provide access to electronic services from a remote location or off-site. Move all public services operations to a remote location where some portable computers can provide access to electronic resources and circulation systems.

In these days of wireless access, instant communication, and remote accessibility to electronic collections, there is no excuse for loss of services to your patrons. Assign staff to provide reference from alternative locations while you restore services at your primary location.

If there was water or fire damage, consider closing the building until the scope of the damage to the collection can be ascertained.

If the structure of the building is damaged, from fire, flood, hurricane, tornado, or earthquake, a structural engineer should check the physical integrity of the building, ensuring it is safe to enter and work within. If not, then contact a firm that can remove the collections from the building and store them in a safe, secure, remote location. Discuss appropriate handling and packing procedures for this pack-out operation so materials do not sustain additional damage.

# Disaster Response Planning in a Nutshell

Consider the types of disasters most likely to happen or the crises that occur on a regular basis and plan for these, while keeping in mind disasters might destroy the entire building or collection.

When planning for disasters, consider what services would be most affected by loss of access to the building and its collections. Is it access to the specialized collections, microfilm, digital resources, and documents, or the loss of payroll and financial information that keeps the institution funded? What other services will be disrupted? Other issues to consider and record:

- Who has the authority to order and pay for supplies and services that are needed?

- Who can make such decisions as calling the insurance company in to assess the loss and asking the disaster response firm and consultants to determine the scope of loss and the amount of work needed to "restore" the collection?

- Who has the authority to designate staff to "other duties as assigned," hire temporary staff, or rent space and equipment to work? How does having a union at your institution change work procedures?

- Who is in charge of discussing the situation with the board of trustees or the director of the institution?

- Who will be the media spokesperson for the institution if there is no public information officer?

- Who is responsible for declaring a disaster for the computer systems? Where will they set up temporary operation? What firm or individual stores the backup tapes? How quickly can the online system get back up and running?

These are just some of the many issues to be considered when designing the response portion of a plan. If you have ever been involved in a disaster, then you are aware that making decisions on the fly is not best for the library's collection or its personnel. Everyone is working under a high adrenaline level and may find it difficult to make educated, rational assessments of the situation and the condition of the remaining collections. Important materials could be damaged by being overlooked or discarded accidentally. Recovery decisions need to be prioritized ahead of time, during the planning process. Disaster response planning takes time but is well worth the effort.

## What If the Disaster Happens before You Have a Plan?

If you don't have a plan and a disaster occurs, take the following seven steps.

1. Gather together key staff in a quiet place, either in the building or near it.

2. Assess the scope of the damage and potential disruption of primary services and functions. Review affected collections for importance within the library's mission and in terms of the magnitude of damage from water or fire.

3. Contact colleagues outside of the institution for assistance and recommendations for consultants and disaster response/drying companies.

4. Assign staff to recovery responsibilities:
   - Performing physical work
   - Acting as liaison with the administration and performing administrative work
   - Communicating with both internal and external organizations (with media and others outside of the institution)
   - Contacting your insurance agent (Ask about disaster response assistance and available funds.)
   - Working with disaster response companies and consultants
   - Locating alternative work areas and supplies

5. Meet again with key staff to coordinate the recovery operation.

6. Begin the recovery operation, starting with primary priorities and services.

7. Start phasing in the return of primary services and functions.

# Response

Disaster strikes! Suddenly everyone and everything goes crazy. Your adrenaline pumps and the disaster response team has to do something about the disaster! Hopefully, this is the moment you have been working toward, making plans and trying to prevent additional damage to collections.

Response comes about in two distinct parts: reacting to the disaster as it occurs, and dealing with the disaster as prelude to resuming operations. The safety of people always comes before the collections and the building, no matter what. Once a disaster occurs, the disaster response team needs to work together to ensure the swift recovery of the collections and resumption of services.

Inevitably, at colleges and universities, circulation desks are staffed in the evenings by students and paraprofessionals. It is essential these staff members be trained in disaster response procedures. It is even more important that they be given the authority to make decisions when confronted with an emergency or disaster. The disaster response team and administrators must trust that the decisions made when encountering a disaster were the correct ones at the time. Re-evaluate the immediate response procedures after the disaster is over and operations are running smoothly.

The first part, reacting to the disaster when it happens, should be simple because it entails evacuating the people from the building and calling for help. Make the procedures for evacuating the building simple. Call for help, evacuate the building, and activate the disaster response team. Take a deep breath. The disaster response team must work together to both resume services and recover the damaged collections. Take the time you need to gather your thoughts and review policies and procedures before wading into the crisis.

Some sample immediate response procedures are

- If there is a fire, pull the fire alarm and evacuate the building. Assemble the staff at the designated meeting place. Confirm that all staff left the building. Notify the police and fire department if there are missing staff members. Do *not* re-enter the building.
- If there is water from a broken pipe, sprinkler system, or restroom, call the facilities maintenance department. Get the water shut off immediately. Evacuate the building

as needed. Notify the disaster response team and arrange to have standing water removed from the building.

- In case of natural disasters, follow the directions from the emergency management agency announcements. For tornados, proceed quickly to tornado shelters in basements and ground-floor rooms without windows. In the case of hurricanes and flooding, there are usually warnings issued ahead of time, so board up the windows, turn off computer systems, make certain data backup is complete and stored off-site away from the potential disaster area, and staff know where to report when the hurricane or flood has passed. If you cannot leave safely, go to the shelters and wait for the storm to pass.

- For blizzards and ice storms, stay indoors and wait for the storm to pass. Tornado shelters are supposed to be stocked with nonperishable food, potable water, flashlights, radios, and other emergency supplies. If trapped by the storm, move patrons and staff to the shelters and call for help.

- In the case of bomb threat, get a staff member to call the police and evacuate the building. Calmly try to get information about the explosive. The same for people wielding guns and knives; call for help and evacuate the building as quickly and quietly as possible.

No matter what, call for help and evacuate the building or the area quickly, then call the disaster response team. Follow the plan and work together toward a swift recovery. Do not throw all that hard work and planning away. After the disaster is over, then take the time to evaluate how the procedures worked and to modify your plan accordingly.

Although this part of disaster response seems straightforward, it does require some forethought. Questions to consider during the planning and prevention phase are: Do your student workers know what to do in the event of a disaster? Where should all staff meet? What are the institution's policies for evacuation during inclement weather? What types of emergency supplies are stocked in tornado shelters? How many people can the shelters house? Are there enough supplies for a day or two? and finally, Who is responsible for checking and updating the supplies?

During the planning phase, investigate the various emergency policies with health and public safety personnel, facilities and maintenance staff, risk management officers at your institution, the city or county emergency management agency, and the city or county fire and police departments. What are their procedures and policies, and how does the library fit into the plan? The smaller your institution, the more important it is to work with local fire, police, and emergency personnel to coordinate your response plan with their procedures.

The second part of disaster response, working to resume services and operations, comes in three phases:

1. Responding to notification of the disaster
2. Assessing the situation and damage
3. Beginning to rescue and recover collections and restore services

Of course, you need to restore services quickly and, in some cases, even before you assess the scope of the disaster. Maintaining services during a disaster may be part of your institution's emergency response plan. If that is the case, then during the planning phase, determine where the library/archives fits and what roles you can provide. It is almost impossible to write about response and recovery activities at one time and cover everything logically. This chapter covers response and the various activities associated with it. The next chapter deals with recovery operations.

You may find it necessary to divide your disaster response team to deal with recovery of operations and services while assessing the damage to the structure and collections. If this is the case, active communication and coordination of activities is fundamental for a successful resumption of services and recovery of collections.

## Phase One: Responding to Notification of the Disaster

First, assemble the disaster response team. During the planning phase you selected a place to meet outside the building if the entire library or building was damaged. That place should be quiet and away from the emergency vehicles. If the building is intact and accessible, meet in a conference room inside the building. If there is no disaster response team in place, gather together department heads, the preservation or rare books/special collections librarian, the library/archives director, and the head of technical services. Contact someone from the facilities maintenance department for assistance with removal of water, mud, and debris.

This is a very chaotic time and place. Many people with varying levels of authority and responsibility are trying to get the situation under control. Stay calm and work together. Take the time to decide who you need to call, what supplies you might need, and whether other staff members should report to the alternative location.

Find out who is in charge of the building or area and ask to be notified when you can enter the building. You might need some type of identification to confirm that the disaster response team leader is in charge of the response operation. During the planning phase, create identification cards that show you are members of the disaster response team ("DRT"). Consider obtaining vests or T-shirts with "Library/Archives DRT" to identify team members to the other people in the area. It is very possible that this is the first time you will come in contact with the facilities maintenance staff and with safety and security personnel.

The disaster response team should select a team leader from this group if none was selected during the planning phase. Don't forget to include the head of information systems in your discussions, because this department may have special needs for the implementation of its part of the disaster response plan. The disaster response team leader should not be the library director unless you are a one-person library. The library director has many other responsibilities and will be busy communicating with administration, insurance companies, and even the disaster response companies. In some institutions, the head of facilities is the disaster response team leader (more on this in section 4, "Planning") because this department deals with small disasters on a regular basis and has contacts with companies that provide water removal, cleanup, and emergency maintenance.

Next, the disaster response team leader should brief the disaster response team about the situation. Review the responsibilities of the team and call in additional staff as needed. The disaster may be caused by water, fire (which will leave you with water afterward), or loss of power, phones, and Internet access. If it is the latter, implement procedures to provide services manually and contact the utility company. At this point, the information services or computer disaster response team should activate their plan to operate from a remote location and provide assistance to check collections in and out using the backup circulation system, if any. If the power or phones will be out for an extended period of time,

then determine how to provide access to various library services, including reference and electronic resources, from a remote location or by referral. Today's social networking tools are great for reference staff who offer ready reference and referral services. During the planning phase, consider how you will integrate social media into your disaster response plan.

During this initial phase of disaster response, take the time necessary to gather your thoughts. Review the disaster response plan and coordinate the next phase of the response plan. The disaster response team needs to be working together to resume operations and recover collections quickly and safely.

The following response procedures pertain primarily to damage from fire and water:

- Close the building or the damaged area to the public.
- Shut the water off and find out if the other utilities are on or should be turned off.
- Start the response operations by activating the basic internal communications policy and alerting the disaster response team, consultants, or contractors.

## Phase Two: Assessing the Situation and Damage

This next phase of the disaster response plan begins when the building or area is safe to enter.

First, the disaster response team needs to assess the damage. Walk through the damaged area to see what really happened. Make a list of the areas that require pack-out, cleanup, or removal to storage. Check the damaged collection against the "Prioritization for Recovery Checklist" (see appendix A.16). Now is not the time to weed the collection. If you did not prioritize the recovery of collections during the planning phase, call in the subject specialist or bibliographer to make up a basic prioritization list, based upon recovery time lines for water-damaged materials.[1] (See appendix A.18.) If your library has a small staff, contact the local library/archives consortium, the state library, the regional library consortium, or the Regional Alliance for Preservation for assistance.

In addition to the disaster response team, the information systems team should be called in to determine the extent of damage to the online public access catalog (OPAC), circulation systems, website, and all electronic resources. Coordinate the use of personnel and resources during the phases of recovery of data and reintegration of systems. Be certain to continue to include the liaison from the information systems' disaster response team in all meetings.

Next, brief the director of the library/archives or the head of the institution about the situation. Activate the external communications plan. Decide if the building or area needs to remain closed, and if so, estimate for how long.

Finally, contact the appropriate outside assistance, consultants, and drying or disaster response company. Call in additional staff to assist with the recovery operation. Reallocate staff as needed to other areas of the library, the campus, or the area. Assemble the necessary supplies to begin recovery and cleanup.

## Phase Three: Beginning to Rescue and Recover Collections

Talk with facilities maintenance staff, or with the disaster response/drying company if they will be performing this service, and remove the standing water.

Start to pack out the water-damaged and smoke-damaged items for freezing or air drying. A good rule of thumb is, between 100 and 300 volumes can be air dried locally if you have the manpower, otherwise freeze all the wet books. Keep in mind, air-dried books will swell and distort while drying and may need to be rebound professionally before returning them to the shelves. Freezing books buys time to dry and clean the building and assess the scope of damage and loss of collections. Vacuum freeze-dry all frozen books and papers. Do not defrost before drying.

Next, move the dry and undamaged items into storage or a temporary access area if a large portion of the area or building was damaged. This will prevent secondary damage from increased levels of moisture and relative humidity. If it is impractical to move the undamaged items to another location, then set up fans and drop the temperature in the damaged area. Air movement and decreased temperature will lower the chance for a mold outbreak.

Then, discard irreparably damaged items and debris so they no longer contribute moisture to the building and other materials. This includes wet ceiling tiles and loose carpet squares. Remove wet curtains, area rugs, and furniture to decrease the moisture in the area. Professionally clean and dry these furnishings and store them in a safe place until the environment (temperature and relative humidity) is stabilized and the building is clean and dry. This will decrease the chance for a mold outbreak.

Set up fans to move the air and adjust the HVAC (heating, ventilating, and air-conditioning) system to dry the air and stabilize the environment.

Now you are ready to concentrate on the recovery phase. This begins after the immediate crisis, actions, and emotions are under control. Recovery will be covered in section 2.

Remove all damaged or wet computer equipment for cleaning, repair, and recertification. Move any undamaged computer equipment to a safe location, remote storage, or off-site operations center. Coordinate with information systems' disaster response plan.

## Call for Outside Assistance

During the response phase, it is important to ask for outside assistance, even if the disaster response team members think they can handle the situation alone. The only time you might not call for help is if the disaster is very isolated and has affected only a few volumes. Otherwise, you will want outside guidance and assistance for at least one or two days, until the situation is under control and the emotional stress has decreased.

It is important for the person or company providing assistance to be familiar with the collection and the institution's policies. The outside consultant or company is not emotionally tied to the collections and is therefore capable of presenting choices and options where the staff's emotions and attachment to materials may rule.

Consultants provide additional assistance by recommending disaster response/drying companies and others who specialize in conservation of the unique, fragile, and nonprint or nonpaper items in the collections. A consultant, working in conjunction with the disaster response team leader, relieves the director of the archives or library of the day-to-day stress of dealing with cleaning up, possibly with the help of temporary laborers hired to do much of the nonskilled physical labor. If necessary, the consultant and the disaster response team member responsible for working with volunteers should work with the disaster response company, demonstrating how to move books and pack boxes for shipment. One or both should be the liaison between the company and the library/archives.

If the facilities maintenance staff are available to dry and clean the building and move the collections, you still want a disaster response team member to act as liaison to answer questions. Provide some basic training and information about handling wet materials and packing boxes. Stabilizing the environment is the first priority. If facilities maintenance staff are also responsible for this task, provide guidelines and parameters for decreasing the temperature and relative humidity. This is counterintuitive, for most people assume you raise the temperature to dry a structure. Unfortunately, if you raise the temperature, you increase the risk of a mold infection in the building and HVAC system.

The director of the library/archives might wish to have the consultant prepare recommendations and bid specifications for specialized work. These recommendations provide guidelines for disaster response and drying companies. Ask the consultant to demonstrate procedures for cleaning books, packing boxes, removing dirt, and mold prevention and removal. Demonstrations of packing and cleaning are best practiced during the planning phase. A quick refresher in handling and packing wet books is essential for all personnel, employees, students, volunteers, and contractors. If your institution is small or the disaster is large in scope and damage, you could ask the disaster response consultant to assist with writing temporary policies for providing access to collections and services from a remote location. As a follow-up, ask the consultant to write recommendations for preventing future disasters.

## Damage Assessment

First, take out the "Prioritization for Recovery Checklist" (appendix A.16) and see the subsection "Prioritization Categories" under "Prioritization for Recovery" in section 4 and review the established criteria as well as the collection policy and mission statement for the institution. Do not change the criteria or prioritization at this time. Decisions made under stress and with adrenaline pumping, or when emotions are high, are not always rational and justifiable, or based upon the organization's mission statement. If no decisions were made prior to the disaster, ask for outside assistance from a consultant familiar with your collections and selection policies.

Now, walk through the damaged areas carefully. Document the damage with photographs or video to show the insurance adjuster. If the damage is extensive, ask the insurance company to send an adjuster who specializes in water damage claims. Checklists A.5–A.9 for documenting damage assessment are located in appendix A. It is not always necessary for the adjuster to be present when you begin the response and recovery phases of disaster response. The insurance company must be notified that the disaster occurred and that the disaster response team knows what can and cannot be done within the policy's terms. During the planning phase, the disaster response team should ask if there are procedures that must be followed for a successful claim. When contacting the insurance company, ask if there is anything special you must do in terms of documentation and proof of loss.

Check damaged collections against your checklist or the prioritization categories. List damage and recovery steps for specific parts of the collection. If the damage is extensive, you may need to identify undamaged materials for storage or relocation to a dry, secure section of the institution or even another building. Do not mix wet and dry materials in the same area.

Use copies of the floor plans to indicate the damaged locations and to prioritize recovery operations. Indicate the wet items to be removed for packing and where the packing area will be. Mark the dry collections, whether portions within the damaged areas will need to be moved, and to where.

Note the types of damage (water, soot, debris, etc.) to different areas of the collection and the types of cleanup necessary when the recovery phase begins.

If there is structural damage to the building, such as a hole in the roof, broken windows, or holes in doors and walls, list the damage. Get security to protect the building from unauthorized persons. Have facilities maintenance staff board up the windows and doors. Have a company come in to cover the holes in the roof. Make certain the roof covering is secure enough to withstand the rain or snow. It should have some type of drainage so the tarp does not fill with water and collapse into the building. Repair roof damage right away. This area is a prime candidate for additional damage to the structural integrity of the building and an avenue for mold infections. Decreasing secondary damage is essential for a successful recovery. You want to protect against a mold infection months after the building is dried and cleaned.

If it is possible to segregate the damaged area from the rest of the building, do that. Close off the space between the suspended ceiling and the true ceiling to keep dust and debris out of the HVAC system and thus the entire building. Begin to stabilize the environment in the remaining undamaged parts of the building. Both these activities will decrease additional damage to the collection and the chance of a mold infestation.

Consult with the information systems disaster response team and add their input into the assessment phase. Once the IS team has their crisis under control, ask when they expect circulation systems and electronic resources will be available for users. The sooner the circulation system is back in operation the better, especially if your manual circulation system entails writing out patron codes and bar codes for all borrowed books. Studies show that for every hour data input operations are down, it takes a day to re-input information, which is, of course, interspersed with regular, routine operations.

Coordinate with IS to catalog and identify damaged and destroyed computer equipment. Work with the IS disaster response team to prioritize the replacement of damaged equipment and the reconditioning of wet computer components. Check with the insurance adjuster to determine criteria for replacement of computers and restoration of service. Part of the IS disaster response plan should include a remote operating site, whether a hot site or mobile trailer. Discuss these procedures and hold a discussion of various recovery scenarios during the planning phase.

While assessing the scope of the damage, make a list of necessary supplies, equipment, and services. Have the disaster response team member responsible for supplies and pack-out requisition and collect the items. If no disaster response team member is assigned to do this, designate an appropriate staff member and obtain the authorization to spend money from the director.

When the survey of the damaged building is complete, review the list of work to be performed, using checklists A.10–A.13 found in appendix A. Divide the damaged area up among staff for supervision of activities. This is particularly important if more than one floor was affected by the fire or flood. If you don't have enough disaster response team members to go around, then use supervisory staff to assist you.

Begin recovery of the first-priority items unless you are unable to access that part of the building or institution. Remove standing water and debris. Remove the damaged items from the floor, then the shelves. After dealing with first-priority collections in each area of the building, move to the second-priority materials.

# Response to Different-Sized Disasters

Disasters come in all sizes, from wet carpet and ceiling tiles from a roof leak to the loss of buildings or communities from flood or tornado, from earthquake to tsunami, from wildfires or arson. Construction accidents are a major cause of disasters. If you haven't written a disaster response plan before renovation begins, now is the time to put something simple together. Create guidelines for dealing with fire or water damage, designate a liaison between the library/archives and the construction foreman. If you try to prepare for every type of disaster, you may never complete your plan. Review safety precautions with the construction crew. These precautions include no smoking on the premises to prevent fire, cleaning up and removing all food and drink at the end of each day to prevent insect infestation and mold, and securing all doors and windows to prevent theft and damage from inclement weather. Design your response procedures from possible scenarios and work your way up to large-scale disasters.

## Small Scale

Small-scale disasters usually require the disaster response team members, the department's staff, and facilities maintenance personnel. Collect supplies and equipment for cleaning up the disaster from in-house supplies. It may not be necessary to close the entire building to deal with a very small disaster, but consider closing the affected department until cleanup is complete.

Examples of small disasters include excessive condensation and dripping from the air-handling system or a sink or toilet that overflowed into the collection. The former is sometimes difficult to detect and may come to light when a mold infection is discovered. Water leaks from sinks, pipe joints, and toilets should be shut off or stopped as soon as they are discovered, the water leak repaired, and the collection and the area dried out. Watch for mold outbreaks afterward from water that was trapped in the walls, ceilings, or carpets. Monitor the relative humidity to confirm that the air-handling system is controlling the environment.

Treat mold outbreaks that affect books, even in a small, defined area, immediately. Isolate the materials and cover over all the air-handling ducts to prevent spreading the mold throughout the building. Drop the temperature and relative humidity to control the spread of mold. Remember, the best way to control or prevent mold is to keep the environment stable. Contact a consultant to help you deal with removing the mold. Advice from the consultant should include referrals to disaster recovery companies that handle mold and to industrial hygienists who will test the quality of the air and identify the types of mold present. If you contract with an industrial hygiene company, the disaster response/drying company must comply with their recommendations.

A small-scale disaster usually involves less than 300 damaged items (several stacks or ranges of books) or an isolated area of the collection. Two to six people should be sufficient to deal with the disaster and stabilize the area. If the "small" disaster is large enough to require the assistance of most of the staff, close the building until the immediate response is well under way. Depending upon the amount of damage caused by a "small" disaster, operations and services should return to normal within two to eight hours. Response steps should include removing the water and packing up damaged items in the collection for freezing and vacuum freeze-drying if more than 300 items are wet or for air drying if fewer than 100 items are damaged.

Don't forget to let staff in the building and the institution's administrators know about the disaster and how it was handled. Remember to look at the disaster response plan afterward and determine how it helped with cleanup and recovery. Revise those sections of the plan that were deficient or lacking.

## Large Scale or Wide Area

Large-scale and wide-area disasters constitute the more catastrophic situations that occur in libraries, archives, and historical societies. They usually involve a large portion of the building or the institution as a whole. A large-scale disaster involves at least 500 items in the collection. A wide-area disaster involves the entire institution, city, or county. Personnel to deal with the response and recovery aspects of the disaster include the disaster response team members, all staff,

facilities maintenance, security, and outside contractors (consultants or a disaster response/drying company or both).

Examples of large-scale disasters are a leak in the roof or a major water-pipe break that soaks a large portion of the collection or goes unreported overnight so that there are four to six inches of standing water on the floor. Other large-scale disasters include a collapsed roof, mud slide, sewage backup into the basement, and fire that engulfs the building. Wide-area disasters are usually caused by nature, such as a hurricane, tornado, earthquake, or flood, and involve an entire geographical area and disruption of utilities. There are wide-area man-made disasters, such as the destruction of the World Trade Center in New York City and the damage to the Pentagon in Washington, DC, on September 11, 2001, caused by bombs and explosives, the collapse of the Cologne Archives on March 9, 2009, due to underground construction adjacent to the structure, and the earthquake and tsunami in Japan in March 2011. In large-scale and wide-area disasters, the area's infrastructure is damaged or destroyed, necessitating the temporary relocation of the library/archives or at least reference, public service, and information operations of the institution. Activate your disaster response plans and contingency plans immediately and direct staff to alternate work locations pending assessment of the damage.

Both large-scale and wide-area disasters necessitate closing the building or operations for at least 24 to 48 hours or longer until the basic recovery operations are well under way and all the standing water and debris are removed. Damaged materials should be packed and moved to freezer storage pending shipment to a vacuum freeze-drying company for drying and cleaning. Supplies and equipment necessary to perform the response and recovery operations will initially be drawn from in-house supplies, then obtained from the outside sources identified during the planning phase.

If you need to relocate reference and public services, you need to work with the IS disaster response team to authorize IP addresses to service providers. Reference staff may need to run remote authentication software. Coordinate this phase of response and recovery with the IS disaster response team.

When the disaster occurs, activate the communications plan. Let staff know where to report and which staff should report at what time. Keep the institution's administration informed of the situation. Notify vendors and suppliers of any changes in location or phone numbers, and let them know how to get in touch with the institution. Release information to the press as to the scope of the disaster, how long you plan to be closed, how to contact the institution, and if donations or assistance are needed. The designated spokesperson or public relations officer from the institution should be the only person speaking directly with the media. Remind staff members that there is a spokesperson and all external communication should be limited to safety check-in. This is particularly important in today's age of instantaneous communication and social networking. Modify the scripts in your communications plan accordingly to reflect the severity of the disaster and the need for assistance. Don't forget to ask for donations. (Consult the subsection "Communications," in section 4, for details.) This information should also direct patrons and clients to alternative locations and services in the community. Basic information for dealing with the media follows in the very next part of this section.

When the response and recovery operation is under control, reopen the building. It might be necessary to keep the badly damaged areas closed. If so, determine how to get the undamaged materials to patrons while keeping them out of the damaged area. After the water, dust, soot, and debris are removed and the collection is "safe" again, open up the area. It may take weeks or months to get the damaged portion of the collection back on the shelves. In the meantime, set up a routine for checking the damaged areas for mold and standing water. Monitor the relative humidity and temperature of the damaged areas to confirm the HVAC system is keeping the environment stable.

In the case of a wide-area disaster, where the building or surrounding areas are destroyed or untenable, the library, archives, or information center needs to relocate to another branch or location altogether. If the library is part of a branch system, another library will have to take on the additional burden, with staff distributed throughout the system. If the library stands alone, then a new location will have to be found. Empty storefronts in shopping centers make excellent temporary locations for libraries and archives with abundant parking, easy access, and slab foundations that can hold the weight of bookshelves.[2] If the primary mission of the library is information retrieval and dissemination, as in a business library, then it should be possible to work from a remote location or from another business library for a short while, or even telecommute. Careful coordination with the information systems disaster response team is essential to get the information retrieval function of the library or archives back to normal.

As follow-up to the disaster, issue another press release informing the public that the situation is back to "normal," that operations and services have been restored, and what the residual damage is, if any. Contact vendors and suppliers and let them know the outcome of the disaster. Write about the disaster and its aftermath for professional publications. Discuss the disaster and its aftermath with staff, the disaster response team members, and outside contractors. Answer questions and evaluate the response plan for its strong and weak points. Modify the plan accordingly.

## Dealing with the Media

Once response efforts are under way, it is important to let people know what happened and what is needed, if anything. The communications portion of the plan should be activated. Provide the communications or public relations officer of your institution with an overview of the scope of the disaster and information about immediate needs for restoring the collection. Work out basic communication scripts during the planning phase.

■ Inform the staff as soon as the immediate disaster is discovered. Provide information about where and when to report to work.

■ Release information to the vendors and suppliers of products and services and to the media and the public at the same time.

■ Press releases should be mailed, faxed, and e-mailed to suppliers of services and products, giving them the temporary location, phone and fax numbers, contact person, and hours.

■ The designated spokesperson or public information officer for the institution should let the media and the public know what happened and what is being done to recover collections and resume services. If donations of time, supplies, collections, or money are desired, tell them what you want and who to contact. Be specific. Include the temporary location, phone and fax numbers, contact person, and hours. If items in circulation are out, let the public know where to return them or if they should hold on to the materials.

■ Distribute a press release to the local TV stations, radio stations, and newspaper. If there is a web page for the collections or institution, include temporary contact information on the page.

Remember, only one person should be designated to speak for the institution in order to avoid conflicting or negative accounts of the disaster.

## Working with Contractors

In the planning phase, the library/archives staff met with consultants and disaster response/drying companies. When the disaster occurs, contact the outside contractors for assistance with response and recovery. Provide a scope of work for the disaster response/drying company to follow. Discuss handling and security issues with the company, and designate a member of the disaster response team as liaison for questions and problems. No matter how experienced the disaster response company staff members are, they still require some supervision to prevent theft, damage to books, and to answer questions.

Keep a few things in mind. The insurance adjuster has, or appears to have, a lot of control over whom to hire. It is your right to select the contractor you want to do the work based on the bids you receive. Check out the company's references. Remember that the adjuster may not be familiar with the true costs to recover, dry, and clean the collection and the building. Have some cost ranges for recovery on hand to show the adjuster just what to expect in terms of a bill. If a contractor is predesignated in the response plan, this should work in your favor for permission from the insurance company to go ahead with recovery. When in doubt, ask for the water damage specialist in the insurance company and discuss your options and costs. Talking with and selecting a disaster response/drying company is an area where the disaster response or preservation consultant can help. You can also ask for consultation assistance from the Regional Alliance for Preservation.[3]

For the bid, especially if you don't have a predesignated contractor, you need to invite representatives from all the interested companies to see the damage. Walk them through the building and discuss what is damaged, the priorities for recovery, and the drying technique required. Listen to their descriptions of services and their interest in the successful cleaning of your collections. You should provide written specifications for the type of work to be done and the type of drying required. Hold the insurance adjuster and the contractor to these specifications. Discuss specifications for recovery of collections, furnishings, and the building with the adjuster. The institution has the right to specify a company in its plan and to specify particular treatments and drying techniques. Ask for an itemized bid from each company.

When evaluating the bid, watch for hidden costs, such as shipping, packing, and labor at the disaster response/drying company site. Also ask for clarification of any vague breakdown in price. Require a "Not to Exceed" bid.

Once the contractor is hired, the disaster response team member designated as the liaison starts to work harder. Assign another staff member to alternate with this disaster response team member. Get together with the contractor to

■ Review the priorities for recovery and the "to do" list

■ Walk through the damaged area again

■ Schedule frequent, at least daily, meetings with the contractor

■ Document all meetings, conversations, telephone calls, and e-mail messages

■ Provide written instructions for all changes to bid and get prices before approval of changes

■ Approve all changes in writing

Involve the director and the insurance adjuster if additional expenditures of funds are needed.

The disaster response team member should monitor the activities of the contractor and his or her staff; how they are handling the collection and how they are cleaning the building and collection. Provide feedback to the contractor. The liaison is there to answer questions and make some additional prioritization decisions.

Watch the costs incurred by the contractor and the institution. Remember that every change to what was asked for in the "Request for Bid" increases the cost of recovery. Do not sign off on the work until it is done to your specifications.

Working with contractors is one phase of response and recovery where an independent consultant will be useful. You can ask the consultant to write the specifications and recommendations for the bid and to perform quality-control checks. Consultants can be asked to meet with the administrators, to explain processes and specifications to insurance agents, and to discuss the disaster and secondary ramifications with the staff. In some cases, the consultant may be asked to work in tandem with the disaster response team leader or as an alternate.

Conservation centers typically provide two types of services in disaster response: a consultant and conservation of specific items that require specialized treatments. If you have an independent consultant already working with the institution who is capable of handling preservation and disaster response issues, use that consultant. This person is already familiar with the collections, mission statements, and staff. If the institution has not worked with an independent consultant, then contact a local or regional conservation center to ask either for their preservation consultant to help for a few days or for a referral to an independent consultant.[4]

As to individual items requiring specialized treatment, work with a local or regional conservation center to get a bid on stabilization and treatment. The items requiring this specialized treatment should be segregated from the mass-recovery effort early in the response phase. Such items should have been identified during the prioritization phase. Get the materials stabilized according to the conservator's instructions and placed in storage at the conservation center awaiting permission or funding to begin treatment. Money for conservation treatment may come from the insurance company or from a contingency fund, depending upon coverage and the type of work required. Be certain to ask when the center can begin treatment.

It is important to keep in mind that conservation centers traditionally treat specific items one by one and not en masse. They will not be able to handle the thousands or tens of thousands of items that are damaged during the disaster. Rely upon the conservation centers for specialized treatments, handling, and care.

## Recovery Decisions and Priorities

While you are assessing the damage to the building and the collections, keep in mind that some materials are more vulnerable to water than others. Some should stay wet, others dry, and most need attention within 48 hours of exposure to water or excess humidity. That means the disaster response team members need to make decisions about the packing and removal of materials as quickly as possible. During the planning phase, the disaster response team members in conjunction with the collection development librarians, archivists, or curators identified collections that should not get wet. Locate those items first. If they are wet, they probably require the services of a conservator. Contact the conservator for instructions as to removal and stabilization. These vulnerable collections are a first priority in terms of treatment and recovery. Once the process of stabilization and removal is under way, you can move onto the rest of the collection.

Below are some guidelines for how quickly various materials should be removed from water and stabilized or treated. These are just guidelines. You may need to adjust your priorities depending upon the size of your collection and the amount of damage. For more extensive discussion of stabilization and treatment of water-damaged materials see section 2, "Recovery."[5]

- Paper, plain—Attend to within 72 hours.
- Clay-coated (shiny) paper, including thermal-fax and self-carboned paper—Remove from water and treat within one to six hours of exposure to water.
- Microfilm/microfiche—Attend to within 72 hours. Hang to dry or keep wet and send for reprocessing.
- Motion picture film, post-1950 negatives, slides, and post-1950 photographs—Attend to within 72 hours. Hang to dry or keep wet. Do not freeze unless directed by a photograph conservator.
- Pre-1950 photographs and negatives—Contact photograph conservator before treating. Do not freeze.
- CD-ROMs, DVDs, and optical discs—Treat immediately. Dry and clean appropriately.
- Magnetic tape—Remove from water immediately. Dry and clean appropriately.
- Computer tapes without backup copies—Treat immediately. Identify format, computer type, and amount of space used on tapes. Send for drying, cleaning, and copying.
- Removable memory devices, including diskettes, Zip drives, and thumb (USB) drives without backup copies—Treat immediately. Dry, clean, and recopy.
- Hardware—Dry, clean, and recertify.
- Keyboards and mouse—Replace.
- Monitors—Clean or replace depending upon value and age.

■ Unique or obsolete hardware—Upgrade or clean depending upon insurance.

■ Office equipment: fax, copier, etc.—Dry, clean, and recertify.

Wet clay-coated paper will stick together and form a solid mass when allowed to dry without intervention. The substance that makes the paper shiny is called "clay," and it is essentially an adhesive that will stick to whatever it touches when wet. Clay-coated paper is found in many periodicals and books with reproductions of artworks and photographs. During the prioritization for recovery process (found in section 4, "Planning"), decide what will be done to water-damaged clay-coated paper.

Deep-freeze or blast freeze (that is, freeze quickly) soaked materials as soon as possible. This stabilizes the materials and prevents additional damage, inhibits mold, and prevents clay-coated papers from sticking together. Freeze-drying clay-coated paper can still result in a solid text block. There is an even chance that books with clay-coated paper cannot be saved. For all other books printed on paper, freezing is a delaying tactic until you have time to evaluate materials and determine whether to dry or discard the items.

Do not freeze books printed on or bound with vellum. Do not freeze leather-bound books. In both cases, the freezing process can damage the materials. Consult a conservator if leather- and vellum-bound books are wet.

Vacuum thermal-drying and vacuum freeze-drying were both invented in the 1960s and are the most common methods for drying water-damaged materials.

The vacuum thermal-drying process starts with materials in a frozen state. A vacuum is introduced, and the air is heated to between 50° and 100° Fahrenheit. As the vacuum is reduced, the ice melts and the water becomes a vapor. The freeze-and-thaw process may cockle or wrinkle the paper. The vacuum thermal-drying process can produce extreme warping due to the release of adhesives in the binding and under the cloth when exposed to heat; therefore, rebinding may be required. This process may be okay for loose papers and nonvaluable materials. However, water-soluble inks may run, and clay-coated papers may stick together due to the extreme heat and moisture. Vacuum thermal-drying is not suitable for leather or vellum.

Vacuum freeze-drying also starts with frozen materials. A vacuum is introduced, but no heat is added, so the contents are dried at temperatures below 32° Fahrenheit. Ice is sublimated into vapor by passing from the frozen to a gaseous state. Therefore, papers do not become wet a second time. As a result, less rebinding is required. This process is good for coated papers if they are frozen within six hours of exposure to water. Vacuum freeze-drying may be suitable for leather or vellum and water-soluble inks. Consult a conservator first.

Air drying and dehumidification are the best treatments for materials that are slightly wet and that can be handled within a working day. Clay-coated papers should be frozen if you are not able to attend to them within one to six hours of exposure to water.

Air drying uses fans in combination with a decrease in temperature in the building. Books may be distorted when dry and require rebinding. Dehumidification uses dehumidifiers in a controlled space to dry the books. But dehumidifiers heat the air, which can cause the paper to become brittle. The bindings may be distorted afterward, requiring rebinding. If air drying or dehumidifying, keep the temperature cool (below 65° Fahrenheit) and the relative humidity low (30–40 percent) for the best results.

Photographs and negatives (post-1950) are best suited to air drying without freezing if it is possible to treat them immediately. The same is true of microfilm and microfiche. Hang them on monofilament line using clothespins, and clean the surfaces carefully after the items are dry. If you have a small number of photographs, you can dry them face up on lintless blotter paper. Flatten the photographs after they are dry.

Otherwise, freeze the photographs and negatives if you are unable to treat them within three working days. Then either thaw and air dry or vacuum freeze-dry, if there is no monetary value attached to the images. Be aware that vacuum freeze-drying may result in loss of the emulsion layer. Consult with a photograph conservator if you have large quantities of photographs or your photographs were made with pre-1950 processes. Microfilm and microfiche can be stored wet in water and shipped to a microfilm processing plant for reprocessing and drying.

Microcards or micro-opaque cards should be stored in filing cabinets and drawers where they cannot get wet. Treat like clay-coated paper if they get wet. Consult a conservator if you need to dry them.

Remove video- and audiotapes, audio-, video-, and magnetic tape reels from water as quickly as possible. If these items were stored in plastic boxes, check to see if the contents are wet. If not, store in a dry, safe location. If wet, contact an AV conservator. Do not allow magnetic media to dry without treatment or you will end up with a paperweight.

Optical discs should be removed from water as quickly as possible. Rinse off and set in dish racks to dry. Clean the surface perpendicular to the central hole with a soft, lintless cloth.

Paper, books, and film-based materials can be vacuum freeze-dried with a minimum of distortion and loss. Magnetic tape can be vacuum freeze-dried but should not be frozen. Freezing makes magnetic tape brittle and can dry up the lubricants.

Remove soot, dirt, and mold after the drying process is complete.

# Computers and Disaster Recovery

When systems crash or data are garbled, the information systems department or librarian is usually responsible for restoring computer services and getting data loaded from backup tapes.

Computer systems that sustain damage from water, dust, soot, fire, or construction are not automatically lost or irreparably damaged. Hardware can sustain water damage without many problems. For water damage, turn off and unplug the equipment and peripherals, open the covers or cases, remove the standing water, and dry out the components. Clean the computer components, and check with your insurance company or computer maintenance contractor about recertification of the hardware. Do not plug in the computers or peripherals until they are dried and cleaned.

Fire and construction activities will introduce a fine layer of dust, soot, or debris on every surface of the library, archives, or historical society. If you are aware that construction is taking place in the building, cover all computer equipment and peripherals to prevent damage. If the equipment becomes contaminated with dust, soot, or debris, unplug the components and vacuum out the debris. Do not use water. When the equipment is clean, plug it in and check that everything works properly.

If data storage devices and hard drives appear to be damaged, do not lose hope. Remove the removable storage devices that are lying in water. If there is water inside the device, find out if there is a backup copy. If not, open them up and let the water drain out, copy the data to a new device, then clean the drive.

Check the new data storage device for completeness of data and make certain the data function properly before discarding the original. In some cases it is easier and more efficient to hire out the cleaning of computer equipment and peripherals and the copying of computer data.

There are a number of companies that provide this service in the aftermath of a disaster. When contracting for services with computer disaster recovery companies, be certain to differentiate between cleaning and recertifying the hardware and recovering lost data. The former entails cleaning the equipment, the latter reconstructing data or copying data from damaged, dirty drives to clean ones. Not all disaster response companies provide these services. During the planning process, ask the insurance company what aspects of data recovery the policy covers. Ask the disaster response companies you contact what services they can provide.

A separate disaster response plan for restoration of computer operations is imperative. The plan should stand alone. Be certain to indicate where the pieces of the disaster response plan for computers fit into the institution's disaster response plan. During a large-scale or wide-area disaster, integration of the priorities for restoring electronic and digital services, recovering data and computer equipment, resuming functions in accounts payable and receivable, payroll, and the use of contingency and emergency funds should be included. The assessment phase of the disaster response plan should include when and where to reassign staff in the case of a large-scale or wide-area disaster. Communication between the disaster response teams responsible for computer services and for collections during the response and recovery phases of the plan is essential. For basic plans for recovering the digital collections and online services of libraries, archives, historical societies, and museums, consult the publications listed in the computer section of the bibliography.

# Emotional Issues

During the response and recovery phases, emotions fueled by excess adrenaline run high. Together they create physical and mental stress. Sometimes the stress manifests itself in an inability to function, guilt complexes, and a decreased level of morale. In the aftermath of disasters, crises, and emergencies today, many institutions elect to bring in grief or crisis counselors. Provide opportunities for staff members to talk with counselors in groups and individually.

The emotions, adrenaline, and the event itself combine to create guilt. This shows itself in staff working very long hours without sufficient breaks and striving toward superhuman efforts to do more than possible in an eight-to-ten-hour day. The guilt can manifest itself in physical work that may result in accidents from doing too much and being overtired. Some staff members take disasters personally and think they are the only ones who can "set things straight."

In the case of a wide-area disaster, reactions may range from shock and disbelief to anger and guilt, from numbness and grief to depression. Some ways to deal with this guilt complex are to require and enforce breaks and to divide the staff into several shifts. Hold meetings to remind staff that the disaster is not their fault and to praise the staff members for their work and the results.

Mental stress will be most visible in the disaster response team and director of the library/archives. The mental stress comes from dealing with the overload of work to be done and the decisions to be made. Minimizing this stress is one of the main reasons for designing the plan and prioritizing recovery decisions ahead of time.

Physical stress, along with an inability to function, is the way some people deal with disasters. One way to deal with this problem is to put the staff person to work physically to try to release the tension and emotions that are bottled up inside. If this does not relieve the stress, either assign the staff member work unrelated to the recovery efforts or send the person home for a day or two.

Poor morale can be the result of a number of events, but it usually is present when the disaster is a repeat of the first or second disaster earlier in the year, or if the recovery efforts are going slowly and seem hopeless. Some ways to deal with decreased morale are to have the director of the library/archives or the head of the institution meet with the staff several times during the response and recovery phases of the disaster to provide updates on the situation. The director should praise the work and recognize the efforts made by all. If morale continues to decline or the recovery efforts continue for many days, schedule "off time" for the disaster response team and staff who are helping out, and arrange for food and drink during breaks. Don't forget that breaks are an opportunity to get away from the stress and the physical work and will assist with boosting morale.

During a wide-area disaster, emotional issues and stress are compounded when staff members worry about their families and homes. They will be torn between taking care of personal problems and the guilt associated with helping out at work. Many will feel that personal crises take precedence over work.

The following methods help deal with this conflict:

- Increase reliance on staff living outside the disaster zone. Put these staff members into the key positions and rotate them with the disaster response team members.

- Increase the use of contractors and consultants. Select the contractors from outside the disaster area if possible. Even though there may be more start-up difficulties with contractors unfamiliar with the area, they should be able to draw from less-depleted resources.

- Provide time off for staff dealing with family and home crises. This is especially important if all staff live within the damaged area.

- Allow for flexibility in the rules of reporting to work on time and unscheduled absences to permit staff to deal with home and family issues.

- Make counseling available to all staff members. This counseling serves two primary purposes: it allows staff to talk out the emotional issues and conflicts, and provides assistance with crises at home.

The disaster response team leader and members should be aware of the increase in emotions and try to channel them toward the desired end of the recovery operation.

We plan for disasters with the intention of responding to them quickly and efficiently. The end result is not always what we hoped for, that collections will be saved, intact, and the staff will take it all in stride. The larger and wider the disaster, the more everything and everyone within the institution are affected.

The response phase continues until the cleanup is well under way and administrators are beginning to think about resuming the full range of services and operations.

All too quickly, usually within hours, patrons and sometimes administrators expect the library, archives, historical society, or museum to resume reference services, provide electronic resources, and possibly circulate materials to patrons. In this age of instantaneous communication and connectivity, disaster response teams must consider how to recover collections at the same time staff members resume services. The next chapter discusses recovery, that is, resuming operations and services.

## NOTES

1. For basic guidelines for how long materials can remain wet and how to stabilize them, consult Betty Walsh, "Salvage at a Glance," http://cool.conservation-us.org/waac/wn/wn19/wn19-2/wn19-207.html; and "Salvage Operations for Water Damaged Archival Collections: A Second Glance," *WAAC Newsletter* 19, no. 2 (May 1997), http://cool.conservation-us.org/waac/wn/wn19/wn19-2/wn19-206.html.

2. Floors must be able to bear the load of full bookshelves, 75 to 100 pounds per square foot. Have the floors tested to confirm they can bear the weight.

3. The Regional Alliance for Preservation centers have a list of consultants who help with disaster response, preservation, and conservation of materials and objects in cultural institutions. These centers are located throughout the country: www.rap-arcc.org/index.php.

4. The Regional Alliance for Preservation, www.rap-arcc.org/index.php, has lists of consultants who can help with disaster response. The American Institute for Conservation of Historic and Artistic Works, www.conservation-us.org, has lists of conservators who can treat valuable materials damaged in the disaster.

5. Betty Walsh has a chart of time lines and stabilization for most materials found in cultural institutions. See "Salvage Operations for Water Damaged Archival Collections: A Second Glance," http://cool.conservation-us.org/waac/wn/wn19/wn19-2/wn19-206.html; and "Salvage at a Glance," http://cool.conservation-us.org/waac/wn/wn19/wn19-2/wn19-207.html. Judith Fortson has a chapter in *Disaster Planning and Recovery: A How-to-Do-It Manual for Librarians and Archivists* (New York: Neal-Schuman, 1992) outlining treatments for water-damaged materials. The guidelines above are based on suggestions from Walsh, Fortson, and numerous discussions with disaster response/drying company specialists.

# Recovering Collections and Restoring Operations

After all the adrenaline and the high-level energy evoked by the disaster have disappeared from your system, it is time to get down to the business of resuming operations and services. The standing water has been removed from the building, holes in the roof and the windows are covered over, and the undamaged collection is assembled to determine what is "still there." Damaged materials were sent to be dried and cleaned, or are frozen awaiting funding for cleaning. Other portions of the collection were destroyed in the disaster. Yet another portion is untouched and either in the building or in an alternative location to provide basic services to patrons, clients, and staff.

For some, this will be a time of great creativity and freedom, a time when "we have always done it this way" can be questioned, and innovations or changes introduced. This attitude is a natural extension of having to replace portions of the collection that were damaged or destroyed. Other aspects of this attitude arise from the need to provide services quickly and efficiently, allowing for shortcuts, and accessing alternative sources for information. In the long run, these "Band-Aid" methods may become the new routines.

The recovery phase is a three-pronged approach: resumption of services, restoration of cash flow, and recovery of collections. Within each approach, there are several activities to pursue while working toward normalcy. The recovery phase is followed by an evaluation, review, and revision of the disaster response plan.

## Making Decisions

If the building is intact, determine which areas of the building will be open to the public, if any. It is important not to open the building to the public until the response phase is complete. This avoids conflicts between "doing my job" and "helping with the disaster response team's job" of cleanup and recovery.

Bring up the most important and basic services first. These usually include circulation, basic reference services, and fiscal and administrative services. In the case of information systems, the circulation and online catalogs may be the first to be restored, and possibly the website if it is running on the same system. Cataloging operations can usually follow later.

Determine the order for restoring services and operations during the prioritization for recovery phase. The order for restoring the computer systems and operations is also decided during the planning phase. Remember that the information systems department is going to have its own plan for restoring operations, data, and services. Note the places where the two plans intersect and keep each other informed. At this point, don't rearrange the order of resumption of services; save this for the evaluation period.

Which services do you restore first? According to new studies, disaster response planning should be holistic.[1] This means all operations and departments need to be considered together so they act in concert with one another—better yet, so that each piece of the plan, each part of the institution, is not considered in isolation, but as a part of a whole. This is doubly true of recovery where time is a major factor in restoring the operations of the institution. This is critical in a large institution with multiple buildings or at a university where there are many players, locations, and departments all vying for time, funds, and reinstitution of services.

In today's age of dependence upon electronic resources, it seems logical to resume services as quickly as possible. Then focus on fiscal issues, and last, upon the collections. However, if you ignore the collections until all operations are working smoothly again, you risk additional damage to or destruction of the physical materials and a mold outbreak. Therefore, the recovery operations must be handled at the same time. It is impossible to write about resumption of services, restoring cash flow, and recovery of collections as intertwined functions. Consider each separately and indicate where the recovery plans intersect. Active and informative communications throughout the recovery phase are essential, especially as you coordinate the restoration of services and operations.

## Resuming Services

If your institution decides to resume public services (circulation and reference) from a remote location or alternative site, where will that be? This could be on another library on campus, in a storefront in the community, at another library or school in the community, or at a branch campus. One decision might be to provide reference services from remote locations or via chat or some other social media networking site. This option might be satisfactory for a short period of time, but in the long run operating remotely can reduce communication and collaboration and increase isolation.

Evaluate the staffing needs to operate from an alternative or remote site. How many staff members do you need to manage circulation, electronic services, and reference? How many supervisors do you need? Rotate staff between the disaster site and the alternative site. If you have more staff than you can keep busy, you might have to put some on leave or assign them to different branch libraries and campuses. You might even consider having staff work part-time for the duration of the disaster cleanup. In the aftermath of Hurricane Katrina libraries did all three. In the end, you must make decisions based on the size of your collections and patron base.

## Hardware and Software

Computers and data are often damaged during a disaster. The information systems or computer services department should have disaster response plans to deal with wet and damaged hardware and software. During the planning phase, find out where your department fits in their response plan. In many cases in a large institution, the library, archives, and museum are far down on the prioritization list. If so, you'll need to make your own decisions or depend upon your own staff.

Below is a basic recovery plan for computers. In this case, prevention and planning are the key. You should practice the reinstallation of software and data. It takes longer than you think, especially if you do not have all the software in one place. No matter what, store backups of operating systems, software, and data off-site in a safe location. Make certain all are up to date and at least two people in your institution know how to reinstall everything.

If computers are wet, all is not lost. Most hardware can be dried, cleaned, and recertified. However, it is best to keep equipment off the floor and away from overhead pipes.

Computer software, depending upon the medium, can also be dried and cleaned, and then copied. Don't delay, particularly as pertains to software on any type of magnetic tape. If it dries by itself, then you will not be able to operate the tape. If the data and software are stored on other media such as diskettes, optical discs, or removable drives, then you need to open the containers and dry and clean the surfaces carefully. This is best left to certified professionals.

Clean or replace the software. Reinstall the operating system, programs, and data. Information systems should make images for each department or function and keep copies off-site as well as in their offices and in the institution's main computer services department. Images speed the installation of operating system and software. They usually include the standard programs your computer systems department supports. So if you are running specialized programs, you'll want to keep copies or a list of them for installation later. These steps are just the same as those you would follow when purchasing a new computer for personal use. Think about how long it takes to install all your favorite programs and get them to function perfectly. Now multiply that time by the number of computers in your institution. Backing up your data and programs is particularly important if you keep lots of information on your personal drives and not the network drives. Remember that only network drives are backed up routinely by the computer systems department.

If the operating system or software is obsolete or proprietary, store the programs in remote locations, off-site. During the planning phase consider upgrading the software. Also discuss what would happen if you are forced to upgrade. How will that affect the data recovery time line?

If the hardware is obsolete, can the older operating system and software be mounted on new hardware? If not, how will you protect the old hardware from water and fire damage? During a disaster is not the time to learn the answers to these questions. (See "Backup Routines to Prevent Loss of Computer Data" in section 3.)

## Restoring Cash Flow and Operations

When an institution suffers a major loss, particularly if the building will be inaccessible for many months, this will affect cash flow, income, and your ability to bring in money. At this point, you need to activate your continuous operations plan, which considers how your institution will continue to operate without a steady flow of funds or income. Loss of cash flow and income should be covered under the "business interruption" or "business resumption" rider of your insurance plan. In many instances this conversation will trigger a risk management audit, which takes into account how much money your institution needs to operate in an emergency. Business interruption insurance covers accounts payable, payroll, and funds for paying unemployment insurance. It covers rent for temporary locations, furniture, and equipment, temporary employment fees, and more.

The operations side may include reassigning administrative and support staff, hiring human resources consultants to help place staff in temporary positions, and providing a variety of counseling services for staff. In addition, administrative and support staff may need to focus on new operational models and organizational reporting lines.

Some questions to consider during the planning phase are: What are the insurance deductibles? What types of emergency or contingency funds have you set aside for just such an event? How will you handle purchase orders for services contracted during a disaster?

## Recovering Collections

The order in which you recover collections depends upon the assessment made during the response phase. Depending upon the amount of damage to the structure, you need to move the undamaged collections to a dry, safe location. This could be at a remote location, a branch, or just to another part of the building. These decisions are based upon the amount of structural damage to the building, the estimated length of time for inspection and repairs, and whether the collections will remain in the building during building restoration. Your decisions about the locations of staff and collections will depend upon whether the building or institution will be closed for days, weeks, months, or longer.

The damaged collections should be packed and stored in freezer storage until they can be dried and cleaned. Decision making for drying and cleaning collections is covered in section 1 of this book.

If you choose to keep collections on-site but closed to the public, set up a method and schedule for retrieving books. Rotate staff members between public service functions and necessary recovery operations. Recovery operations include evaluating what is left of the collection and supervising any remaining physical cleanup. As the damaged areas are restored, open them to the public one at a time.

Part of this phase of recovery is surveying and evaluating what remains of the collection. Acquire new materials using your institution's mission statement and collection development policy. Replace lost items in the collection using established professional criteria. The insurance adjuster may emphasize replacing items. Before you do so, consider which lost and damaged items still fit within the mission statement and collection development policy. There is no sense replacing items that are outside the scope of the collection. During a disaster is not the time to rewrite your institution's mission statement and collection development policy. It is the time to strengthen the damaged collection by replacing out-of-date materials with new editions and publications and considering new formats and access methods.

In addition to recovering the collection, you need to make the building accessible to the public. Below are just some of the tasks you need to prioritize and schedule.

- Repairing the building and structural damage includes removing any damaged fixtures and furnishings, such as furniture, shelving, desks, carpets, and curtains.
- Dry, clean, disinfect, and stabilize the HVAC system.
- Dry, clean, and disinfect the fixtures and furnishings.
- Return the fixtures and furnishings.
- Return the collections, making certain all the surfaces are dry first to prevent mold infections.
- Confirm that the HVAC system is keeping the environment stable.
- Reopen the collections to the public.

## Stabilizing the Environment

It is important to keep an eye on the environmental conditions of the library or archives after water damage has been cleaned up. Make frequent and routine checks of the temperature and relative humidity. Keep a record of any fluctuations to document how the HVAC system is controlling the environment. This important documentation supports future insurance claims should the collections suffer a subsequent mold infection. Ask the facilities maintenance staff or the service contractor to examine the HVAC system and adjust it accordingly to keep the environment stable. It may require several adjustments to determine that

the HVAC system is working properly again. Filters, drains, and intake vents should be checked, cleaned, or replaced to remove any debris lodged within.

After water damage, the collections in the dried-out and the undamaged parts of the building should be checked regularly for mold. This is particularly important during the first year after the water damage as the building continues to dry and the trapped moisture escapes into the air.[2] A mold infection can occur even six months after the excess water is removed. Check for paint releasing itself from walls, or ceilings, watch for floor or carpet tiles coming loose, and moist or distorted acoustic ceiling tiles. These are all telltale signs that moisture is trapped and trying to get out into the building. If staff or patrons complain about unusual odors, don't ignore the reports. This is often a sign that moisture is trapped under paint or carpets and mold is growing there.

Simple, no-cost solutions for releasing trapped moisture are removing ceiling tiles, loose floor and carpet tiles, and scraping or removing the loose paint from the walls. When the building structure is completely dry, then repaint the walls and replace carpets and ceiling tiles.

# Revising Disaster Response Plans

## Evaluating the Plan

After services and operations are back to normal, it is time to evaluate the recovery plan. This is an opportunity to see if the planning worked, if the best decisions were made for dealing with the worst.

Look at the efficiency of the plan. Evaluate, review, and revise the disaster response plan. Here are a series of questions to ask during the review and evaluation phase.

- Were the instructions clear and easy to follow? Assess and adjust the prioritization for recovery decisions.
- Did the prioritization decisions provide the necessary guidance to recover and replace the collections? Discuss the effectiveness of predetermining collections for primary and secondary recovery. Assess your decisions in regard to the damaged items, particularly in terms of your collection

development policies. Were those items that were kept or recovered out of date? If yes, did they fit within the mission of the institution?

■ Were there disaster response team roles and responsibilities omitted from the plan?

■ Did guidelines for various disaster response activities work efficiently? Examine the effectiveness of the disaster response team members in the operation. Is it necessary to reassign duties? Did you discover a staff member who is incapable of working under stress? Did you discover strengths previously unknown among the staff and disaster response team, such as a great organizer or someone with lots of contacts within the building trades? Perhaps there are disaster response team members who are better suited to different tasks. In some cases you will find there are others who wish to participate more actively. Now that you have experienced a disaster, consider assigning staff to administrative or clerical jobs.

■ Did you need more assistance than originally planned? Evaluate the roles contractors and consultants played in the response plan. Consider asking for feedback from those contractors and consultants and use their suggestions to strengthen your response procedures.

■ Which relationships with other departments in the institution need strengthening? Who else do you need to get to know? Schedule a meeting with facilities maintenance staff and public safety and security officers. Discuss how your response plan fit with theirs and where you can avoid conflicts in the future. Repeat these discussions with emergency management and public safety liaisons from the community. The more you know about each response plan, the more efficient the decisions and actions during the next crisis.

■ How well did the disaster response plan integrate with the information systems department's disaster response plan? With the institution's plan? With the emergency management plan in the city or county? Revise your plan so it coordinates with their plans. Add the names and contact information for liaisons from these departments and organizations.

■ How effective was the communications plan for keeping in contact with staff, patrons, and the community? What additional steps could you take to make communications smoother and more efficient?

Consider which organizations you contacted to help in this disaster. Establish some informal or formal support networks to provide reference and other public services for your patron groups. Evaluate the procedures for contacting and informing staff about the disaster. Modify your emergency communications plan accordingly.

■ Did the order of restoring services make a difference? Did you discover that an operation was dependent upon some service listed as a lower priority? If so, rearrange the order of recovery of services.

■ What was missing from the plan? What could you skip next time? Think about what was missing from the response phase of the operation. Were the instructions too complicated? Were there local library/archives professionals who assisted who were not included on the contact list? If so, add them.

■ Were the prioritization decisions the best that could have been made? Were the response decisions useful and easy to understand? What was left out? Add the omitted procedures and decisions to the response plan.

During the bombing of the Murrah Federal Building in Oklahoma City in 1995, the windows of the Metropolitan Library shattered. The disaster response team members discovered their first aid kits were inadequate for dealing with anything more than a small cut or minor injury. Their first task upon evaluating the disaster response plan was to upgrade the first aid kit to include more supplies to deal with medical emergencies.

In another disaster, a library found that when the disaster response team arrived at the location of the disaster, none of the security, facility, or safety personnel could identify them. It made the response phase more complicated and confusing than it needed to be. Clearly identifying the disaster response team is essential. In the review session, the disaster response team decided they needed either vests or T-shirts to identify themselves.

Keeping in mind that the response plan should be simple and easy to understand, consider what you would like to add or omit, and revise the plan accordingly.

## Revising the Plan

Now that the plan, disaster response team members, and all assistance from staff and contractors have been evaluated for efficiency, it is time to revise your plan. Change the plan to reflect whatever deficiencies were noted during the evaluation. Amend the plan to incorporate the current situation and layout of the building. If you have moved collections to remote locations, include these new sites.

When you revise the plan, don't make it so specific that it only covers the previous disaster. Keep the disaster response team roles and responsibilities generic, while considering additional activities to make recovery faster and more efficient.

Revise and update the disaster response plan every year and most especially after a disaster. At least twice a year, the disaster response team should get together to review the response plan, update the disaster response team contact information, check the floor plans for accuracy, and perform a building survey.

Every year ask department heads to review and update the recovery prioritization list. The list should be revised based upon results of the disaster or, if there has never been one, based upon the same criteria as last time. Update prioritization for recovery to include any major additions to the collections, deaccessioning projects, and changes in the mission statement of the institution.

Revise the disaster response plan when departments and collections move due to a reorganization of responsibilities or physical space. Prepare for disasters when planning construction projects, large and small. Consider revising your plan to include new hires, new functions, new equipment, and most especially new locations.

Once each year hold a training session for the disaster response team and interested staff. Base the training upon any "new issues" that arose based upon experience with a disaster. Add new material to the training, focusing on areas where knowledge is lacking. Ask a consultant in security, safety, health, or emergency management to provide workshops and hands-on training in various aspects of disaster response.

Hold a yearly meeting with the security and facilities maintenance departments to focus on being better prepared the next time a disaster strikes. Evaluate conflicts in responsibility or territory that arose during the last disaster and how they were handled. Ask for input on how to make the next response effort more efficient. Discuss areas of conflicting responsibility so they are not ignored or efforts duplicated next time. Modifying responsibilities and dealing with labor union issues is essential. The goal is to minimize the number of union grievances during a disaster.

Schedule an annual building walk-through for the security and facilities maintenance departments and disaster response team members to discuss potential hazards. Familiarize contractors, consultants, and facilities maintenance staff with new configurations in departments and buildings. Include the fire and police department liaisons when you conduct tours and training sessions on disaster response. The more people who are familiar with your institution, the more successful the recovery will be. This cooperative effort and exchange will facilitate a smooth working relationship and open communications among all the parties.

## Following Up

It is essential to communicate with staff, administration, vendors/suppliers, and patrons after the disaster and cleanup operation is over. Write articles and memos about what happened. Describe the results of the disaster and changes to the disaster response plan. Highlight changes to the collection, services, and routines within the departments that were affected and to the institution as a whole. The articles and memos should come either from a single spokesperson within the institution, as when the disaster first occurred, from the disaster response team as a whole, or from the director.

Give presentations and papers about the disaster and your recovery efforts to professional organizations in the area and state as well as to community and civic organizations in your town. Talk about how your plan was effective and what you are changing. Acknowledge local support and funding from local organizations and foundations. Enlist continuing assistance through programs and presentations about the disaster, highlighting the recovery of collections and restoration of services to the community.

The disaster response team and the director of the institution should make recommendations to the administration and to facilities maintenance, aiming at the prevention of future (re)occurrences of disasters. The recommendations should include suggestions about how to prevent disasters in the future by repairing what went wrong in the first place. Solicit input from the outside consultants and contractors and from security and facilities maintenance departments.

When all is said and done, the library director should publicly recognize the efforts of all staff. This will boost morale and encourage the staff to participate wholeheartedly in the next disaster response operation. The director should also thank the facilities maintenance and security departments, and any others involved, for their assistance and participation in the response and cleanup operations.

## Marketing and Public Relations

Now that the disaster is over and the institution is open to the public, you need to market your success. Send press releases to the local and regional papers and news media. Sponsor a reception or a small conference highlighting the disaster and your recovery efforts.

Market the reopening of the building and collections. Do not downplay your efforts, success, or importance to the community. Invite donors to the reopening and ask for their continued support. Make the speeches short and acknowledge all your supporters, including your staff. The reopening should be a community celebration where you showcase the restoration of all services and any improvements made to the buildings and collections.

Some of your marketing and public relations can be low-key. Be certain to announce your reopening on various social media sites and on electronic discussion lists. Don't forget to put the information on your own website. You can even put together some passive marketing campaigns using bookmarks and flyers. Word of mouth is one of the effective marketing tools you have. Use it to promote your library and emphasize all the positive changes to your institution since the disaster.

Continue to ask for funding and donations to rebuild the collections. Do this as soon as possible, while the disaster is still fresh in your patrons' minds. Cultivate your strong supporters and ask them to help with fundraising and donations. Now is the time to ask for more funding, for emergency funds, and for appropriate donations of materials. Talk with the local civic organizations about continued support for your institution.

## Dealing with the Next Disaster—Physical and Psychological Issues

The more often disasters occur at an institution, especially if they are spaced closely together, the less willing the staff and even the disaster response team are to respond and contribute to the recovery of the collection and services. There will be a noticeable lack of motivation and a visible decrease in assistance from within the institution. The number of staff complaints will increase. These complaints may cite that the staff member is "being pulled away from her or his regular responsibilities" to deal with "someone else's" problem.

Health issues should be addressed. In some cases, mold outbreaks cause physical and allergic reactions, especially in staff members who have asthma, allergies, or immune deficiencies. Mold and excessive airborne particulate matter can exacerbate all these conditions and cause severe reactions. If a staff member is not able to work within a disaster situation, reassign his or her disaster response duties. Suitable disaster response assignments for staff members with allergies, asthma, and immune deficiencies are administrative and support operations in an alternative location for the duration of the cleanup operation.

For the "next" disaster, the disaster response team and the director of the institution might consider more seriously working with outside contractors and consultants. If the response and recovery operations placed unreasonable physical demands upon staff, consider contracting out the majority of the physical work, perhaps even the cleanup operations traditionally allocated to the facilities maintenance department.

With the increased frequency of disasters, allocate funds to correct and control potential hazards and chronic leaks. Institute a regular maintenance program to prevent future disasters. After the third or fourth disaster, even a small disaster is demoralizing.

In addition to morale issues, an increase in environmental problems may arise. The temperature and relative humidity may change more frequently and become more difficult to keep stable. Two environmental side effects that may arise are mold and the increased aging of collections. There is a definite chance mold will occur, and it will become more difficult to control its growth and spread, especially if there was water damage. Controlling the environment is the key to preventing mold growth.

The second side effect resulting from fluctuations in temperature and relative humidity is the increased aging of collections. As temperature and relative humidity change from day to day, or hour to hour, the collections are in danger of becoming brittle and fragile more quickly than before.[3] With every fluctuation of temperature and relative humidity, the chemical reactions within paper and photographs start and stop, contributing adversely to the deterioration of the collections.

Disasters where the causes were not eliminated through diligent maintenance and repair are demoralizing and dreaded. In fact, the frequency of occurrence, especially from the same cause, may color and skew thinking and decision making for future renovation and construction projects. For instance, if there is a history of water damage in the building, the tendency is to shy away from any product, such as sprinklers or heating systems, that contains water, no matter what its effectiveness. It is important to try to distance oneself from the past when making decisions about construction projects and future enhancements to buildings.

Reviewing, evaluating, and revising your existing disaster response plan will make the disaster response team's response to the next disaster faster and more efficient. Being prepared is the key to successfully weathering a disaster and swiftly restoring operations. A periodic review of the disaster response plan means keeping the disaster response team alert to changes in the environment and physical conditions in each building. Disaster response will become a part of your consciousness and your repertoire for handling crises and changes in routine.

## NOTES

1. "Taming the Data Demons: Leveraging Information in the Age of Risk," IBM Global Technology Services White Paper (September 2010), www.ibm.com/services/riskstudy. The IBM study emphasizes the importance of integrating business, event, and data-driven risk in your disaster response plan and in subsequent recovery operations.

2. It is common to have moisture trapped in plaster or concrete walls.

3. James M. Reilly, Douglas W. Nishimura, and Edward Zinn, *New Tools for Preservation: Assessing Long-Term Environmental Effects on Library and Archives Collections* (Washington, DC: Commission on Preservation and Access, 1995), see especially 10–14, or www.clir.org/pubs/abstract/pub59 .html.

# Prevention

As stated in the introduction, prevention can stand alone, but it also works in tandem with the planning phase of disaster response. Prevention includes looking for potential hazards in the building and either noting or correcting them. This phase is important because correcting chronic problems before they become serious can prevent them from becoming a disaster and costing the institution large sums of money and loss of time and efficient service. In an era of budget cuts, deferred maintenance, and postponed building projects, disaster prevention will identify where monies need to be spent to forestall a disaster. Some of these suggestions are straightforward and require little or no funds to correct. Other preventative measures are expensive and may never happen. Start with small changes while you justify the capital improvements. For small libraries, archives, historical societies, museums, and corporate libraries, prevention and planning for disasters mean the difference between existing and being defunct.

So where do you start? Because prevention and planning go together, a disaster response team should be selected ahead of time (see section 4, "Planning"); otherwise, select a small group of key personnel to perform these tasks.

Two types of surveys should take place during the prevention phase of disaster response planning: a building survey and a collections survey. For now let us focus upon a building survey. After surveying the building and its collections, get together with the disaster response team to work preventative actions and changes into the disaster response plan.

## The Building Survey—Inside the Building

Depending upon the size of the institution and the number of buildings covered by the plan, a building survey can be done by one member of the disaster response team or by groups of staff headed by a team member. In either case, the purpose and procedures are the same.

The purpose of a building survey is to look for evidence of past disasters (for example, old water damage, which should be easy to find) and areas of the library or archives that are potential disasters.

Draw a basic floor plan that locates fire exits and identifies rooms as to their purpose or contents during the survey. Ultimately, the floor plan will show where the first- and second-priority collections are located for removal or recovery. Remember that the library staff may not be able to enter the building and might have to show firefighters or a disaster response company where the most vulnerable and valuable items are that require removal and treatment.

Start the survey by looking at emergency exits to determine if they are accessible.

■ Emergency exits should be visible and clearly marked. Indicate which exits are handicapped-accessible from each floor. Note which exit doors open onto a staircase or step. These are not handicapped-accessible unless there is a ramp. If the emergency exit opens onto an internal staircase, indicate which direction (up or down) leads out.

■ Make certain the exit signs and doors are not blocked and that the alarms on the doors, if any, work.

■ It is important to ask where the alarms ring in the immediate vicinity and throughout the building.

■ Does the alarm ring or light up in a central security office, and if so, do the security people know whom to call in an emergency?

Stairwells in multistory buildings are particularly problematic. Emergency lighting must illuminate landings and steps. Many institutions have painted risers and baseboards with luminescent paint and have placed exit signs at ground level. Indicate with simple signs the direction of ground-level exit doors. Many of these changes were instituted in the aftermath of the destruction of the World Trade Center towers and damage to the Pentagon.

Other security and safety items to check are emergency lighting (do the batteries still work and how often are they replaced?); fire extinguishers (both location and type); fire alarm call boxes (where are they located?); and smoke and heat alarms (do they meet the appropriate needs of the collections in those areas, and where do the alarms ring?). All fire and evacuation alarms must ring and strobe or flash, to be in compliance with the Americans with Disabilities Act.

Many of these tasks fall under the domain of the facilities maintenance department. In other instances, the health and safety officer at large institutions oversees fire and safety policies. If you work in a small institution or a single-building library, then set up a regular maintenance check with the maintenance staff member.

The next step is to look for past and potential hazards such as water leaks; old and chronic leaks are sometimes identified by brown staining on ceiling tiles or leaching of minerals on walls. Water stains indicate that there was a problem and could occur again or that something is dripping on a regular basis, such as an air-conditioning duct that gets too much condensation and doesn't drain properly. A stain might indicate a small leak in the roof or flashing that allows water to get into the building when it rains. Routine inspections of the roof should be done by the facilities maintenance staff. Side effects of chronic water leaks include structural damage and weakening of walls and ceilings. Under the right conditions, fluctuations in the environment, in combination with a chronic leak, could create mold growth. When undetected, mold can spread through a sizable portion of the collection, infecting the air-handling system as well as causing staff discomfort.

Indicate chronic problem areas on the floor plan. Discuss the identification of the source of the water leak(s), and work with the facilities maintenance staff to correct the situation. For chronic water leaks on the floor, you might keep a small stock of storm water absorbing bags. These bags swell on contact with water and hold it back from collections. Depending upon how chronic the leaks are, you might keep them around drains, sump pumps, and basement doors. There are several different types of absorbent bags on the market. Ask the facilities maintenance staff members for suggestions.

Consider installing water alarms that ring in the facilities and security departments. Install water alarms near sump pumps, chronically leaking pipes and drains, in mechanical rooms, and near water heaters. Water alarms can be wired right into the security system. Review the location of various water alarms and procedures for alerting disaster response team members when activated.

Another potential hazard includes the use and storage of flammable chemicals in the library or building. These chemicals must be stored in fireproof cabinets when not in use. Handle them safely and appropriately. Keep a file of Material Safety Data Sheets (MSDS) for easy reference should an accident occur (see figure 3.1 for page 1 of the six-page form). Material Safety Data Sheets include handling and cleanup information as well as a list of ingredients. Supplies and collections should not be

**FIGURE 3.1** Page 1 of material safety data sheet. The form covers fire and explosion data, health effects data, spill and leak procedures, etc.

| Material Safety Data Sheet | U.S. Department of Labor |
|---|---|
| May be used to comply with OSHA's Hazard Communication Standard, 29 CFR 1910.1200. Standard must be consulted for specific requirements. | Occupational Safety and Health Administration (Non-Mandatory Form) Form Approved OMB No. 1218-0072 |

| IDENTITY (As Used on Label and List) GP# GBLN | Note: Blank spaces are not permitted. If any item is not applicable, or no information is available, the space must be marked to indicate that. |
|---|---|

**Section I**

| Manufacturer's Name GLUE-FAST EQUIPMENT CO., INC | Emergency Telephone Number (201) 939-7100 |
|---|---|
| Address (Number, Street, City, State, and ZIP Code) 727 COMMERCIAL AVE | Telephone Number for Information SAME |
| CARLSTADT, NJ 07072 | Date Prepared JUNE 1989 |
| | Signature of Preparer (optional) |

**Section II — Hazardous Ingredients/Identity Information**

| Hazardous Components (Specific Chemical Identity; Common Name(s)) | OSHA PEL | ACGIH TLV | Other Limits Recommended | % (optiona |
|---|---|---|---|---|
| | | | | |
| | | | | |
| | | | | |

NONE HAZARDOUS

--------------------------------------------------------------------

3. PHYSICAL DATA

--------------------------------------------------------------------

```
PURE MATERIAL OR MIXTURE.......... Mixture
PHYSICAL FORM..................... Liquid
APPEARANCE/PHYSICAL DESCRIPTION.. White liquid, typical slight sweet odor
PH AS IS.......................... 7-5    per JSullivan/Gluefast 3/31/92
BOILING-POINT..................... >212 F
MELTING/FREEZING POINT............ <40 F
SOLUBILITY IN WATER............... Miscible
SPECIFIC GRAVITY (WATER = 1)..... 1.100
BULK DENSITY...................... 9.2 lb/gal
VOLATILES......................... 49%/wt
EVAPORATION RATE.................. 1 ( Water )
VAPOR PRESSURE (mmHg)............. 17.5 at 20 c
VAPOR DENSITY (AIR = 1).......... 0.62
VOLATILE ORGANIC COMPOUNDS....... <5g/1
```

stored in stairwells and hallways. They are a fire hazard and may prevent firefighters and disaster response personnel from entering the building quickly and efficiently.

Walk through the building(s) with the regular facilities maintenance staff and ask them to point out where they see potential hazards or where they routinely fix problems. Ask them to show you where the sprinkler water control valve is located, and make certain that it is properly activated and maintained. Ask where the shut-off valves are located for the gas, electricity, and water. These should be listed in the checklist for the building. Discuss the reasons for disaster response planning with facilities maintenance staff. Ask where and how they see themselves participating in the response and recovery aspects of the plan.

Do the same with the security staff, looking for potential security problems, including identifying doors and windows that don't shut properly. Discuss the reasons for disaster response planning with the security staff. Ask where and how they see themselves participating in the response and recovery aspects of the plan.

Look for evidence of insects and rodent droppings. These are signs of food and drink that attract pests. Eliminate the water and food. Fumigate to prevent insects after consulting with a conservator. Trap rodents, birds, and bats and remove them from the building. Seal up holes and cracks to prevent their return. Do not poison animals as they may crawl into walls and die there, causing a new set of preservation and environmental problems.

To prevent water damage from below, shelve all materials 3–6 inches above the floor. Storing boxes and materials on the floor, in addition to being at risk of water damage, will attract insects and rodents. Both types of pests may nest in boxes and eat or chew contents. While shelving materials off the floor may not prevent insect and rodent damage, it will keep materials dry, until the water rises about the shelf height. Store boxed items on pallets or shelving to prevent their collapse into standing water.

## The Building Survey— Outside the Building

Next, the disaster response team and someone from facilities maintenance should walk around the outside of the building, looking for potential water and fire hazards. Notice where there are external stairs going below ground. The drains at the bottom of those stairs should be cleaned regularly to prevent water backing up into the foundation or the basement level. Locate the external fresh air intake shafts. They are large grates set into the ground or walls. They should be clear of debris such as leaves and bushes. Keeping the fresh air intakes clear will decrease indoor air quality problems. Talk with facilities maintenance staff about their regular external cleaning routines. Clean gutters and eaves regularly to prevent water backup under

the roof or into foundations. Pay particular attention to any mention of damage to the roof. Look for broken or cracked windows. Note windows that aren't shut completely. The same goes for external doors. Pay particular attention to emergency exit doors. They should never be propped open or obstructed. Follow up on any damage or potential problems that are scheduled to be fixed.

## Correcting and Preventing Fire and Safety Hazards

After the potential hazards have been identified, it is important to consider how to remedy the situations and prevent disasters from ever coming to fruition. Store flammable chemicals properly, house collections in appropriate areas of the building, and perform regular maintenance to prevent damage from external sources. Set up a routine for regularly walking through the building(s) and checking on these safety and maintenance points.

After looking at the building, review the fire prevention equipment, both type and location. This includes fire extinguishers, sprinklers, and smoke and heat detectors.

### Fire Extinguishers

The two types of fire extinguishers found in libraries and archives are ABC and A. The canister has a label on it that tells you the type of fire extinguisher. There should also be a tag attached to the metal ring at the top of the handle. This tag indicates when the fire extinguisher was checked last.

If you must use a fire extinguisher to put out a very small fire, make certain it is the proper type. Class A fires consist of ordinary combustible materials such as wood, paper, rubber, cloth, and some plastics. Class B fires come from flammable liquids, paints, flammable gases, and other types of liquids. Class C fires occur around energized electrical equipment, such as computers and office equipment; B and C canisters contain foam. The larger fire extinguisher canisters are usually type A, and they may contain water. Fire extinguishers have enough contents under pressure to work for 30 seconds to a few minutes. If the fire is too large or hot, leave the building and call the fire department.

## Sprinkler Systems and Smoke and Heat Detectors

Why is it important to have sprinklers in the library? Fire sprinklers, especially if they are zoned (that is, only those sprinklers in the immediate area of the fire activate), will cause less damage to the collection than fire hoses. Each fire sprinkler head puts out between 20 to 40 gallons of water per minute; a fire hose, wielded by firefighters, will put out more than 250 gallons of water per minute. Also, without fire sprinklers, the collection could be consumed by fire before the fire department can get to the building, even if the fire station is across the street or next door.

There are two main types of fire sprinkler systems: wet pipe and dry pipe. Wet pipe systems have water in them all the time, waiting for a fire to erupt so that they can release their load. Dry pipe systems come in a variety of types. Either there is compressed air in the pipes or nothing. When the sprinkler head is opened or activated by either the fire or the smoke detector, after about a two-minute delay, water flows into the pipe and then comes out of the head. Consider on/off sprinkler heads for both wet and dry pipe sprinkler systems in museums and archives. These heads are more expensive than the standard type. They turn on to emit water and put out the fire and then turn off. If the fire flares up again, the sprinkler head will reopen.

With the banning of new installations of Halon 1301, there has been an increase in the popularity of sprinkler systems called "Water Mist" or Micromist, which emit fine water droplets under high pressure of 100 to 1,000 psi or approximately two gallons of water per minute. Already in use on ships and in the oil drilling industry, this method of fire suppression is being considered for museums and other cultural institutions, where Halon was the norm.[1]

There are different types of smoke detectors. Some detect changes in temperature while others detect increased particulate matter in the air. It is imperative that libraries and archives install smoke detectors and alarms and that they work properly. The alarm should ring somewhere other than just inside the building. Who will hear it in the middle of the night if the smoke alarm just rings inside the building or in the basement? The smoke detectors and alarms should be tied into the general alarm system and should be able to trigger the fire sprinkler system to put out the fire.

Regardless of which system is installed in the library or archives, several features should be present:

- The smoke and heat alarms need to be tied to the activation of the sprinkler system.
- Smoke detectors and alarms must ring outside the building as well as inside.
- The sprinklers must be zoned, so that only the one or two sprinkler heads over the fire are activated.
- Sprinkler heads should shut off automatically when the fire is out and reactivate themselves if the fire flares up again.

Members of the disaster response team should know where the fire sprinkler shutoff valves are and should indicate their location on the basic floor plan.

If there are no sprinklers in the building because of its age, smoke detectors and alarms are even more important. Establish a routine to check regularly that they are in good working order and that the staff know who to call, and where to meet outside the building, when the fire alarms sound.

## Indoor Air Quality and Sick Building Syndrome

So far we have looked for visible potential hazards in the building. An invisible hazard is poor indoor air quality that can manifest itself in sick building syndrome.

Every time something is done in or to the library or the building that houses it, there is the potential to create an imbalance in the internal environment. These changes can cause the collection to deteriorate more quickly, can exacerbate allergies and make the staff sick, or can cause water damage to the building through carelessness or accident. Buildings that have windows that don't open, have chronic maintenance problems, or have experienced a water-related disaster are prime candidates for sick building syndrome.

The most common type of sick building syndrome and indoor air quality problem for cultural institutions is mold. It is present, all the time, in the air and on most surfaces, but mold does not cause a concern or problem until it becomes active. Mold growth comes from poor environmental conditions, increased levels of moisture, and high humidity. Mold likes warm, moist, dark places and will grow in carpets, under paint, in air ducts, and on collections. When mold growth is not controlled, it can cause a sick building. The Image Permanence Institute offers a host of monitoring tools and techniques for capturing and analyzing data about internal environmental conditions. They also collect data that can predict conditions under which mold grows and is controlled.

Two basic procedures can prevent and control mold growth, but it is important to realize that mold is never truly eradicated.

1. Keep the temperature and relative humidity stable:

   ■ Temperatures should be between 68° and 72° Fahrenheit and the relative humidity between 45 percent and 55 percent, but no higher than 65 percent.

   ■ In the winter it is sometimes difficult to keep the relative humidity above 35 percent. Discuss the dryness of the air with your conservation or preservation staff to determine the degree of damage this causes.

2. Act quickly if there is a leak or water damage:

   ■ Fix the leak or cause of water damage.

   ■ Remove the water as quickly as possible.

   ■ Use dehumidifiers to control excess moisture and to help stabilize the environment.

Once the standing water is removed, it is essential to stabilize the environment. It may be necessary to hire a dehumidification firm to provide temporary assistance or rental of equipment. While the building is drying, monitor the temperature stability and relative humidity with a recording hygrograph. If the relative humidity goes above 65 percent, watch for additional outbreaks of mold.

Additional steps should be taken to prevent the spread of mold throughout the building. If the mold is localized in one room or area, cover the air vents and ducts to prevent mold from spreading into the entire building. The next step in the recovery operation is to arrest mold growth by stabilizing the environment or freezing the infected portion of the collection.

Remove the mold to prevent serious problems for both the collections and the staff. After covering the air vents, begin the mold-removal process. Clean the infected collection, shelves, walls, carpets, and other affected furnishings. Be careful not to introduce

moisture or increase the relative humidity. If you do not control moisture, mold will grow again. These collections will be sensitive to mold forever and can become infected again if the relative humidity rises above 65 percent to 70 percent.

If the cause of the water damage is not eliminated, then mold will return again and again. Each time, it will be more pervasive, more difficult to remove, and more damaging to the collection. Constant disaster response for mold removal will create morale problems for staff who must repeat the process. Unfortunately, mold irritates allergies and exacerbates asthma. It can cause healthy staff to develop, first, a sensitivity to mold and then, allergies.

Reactions to mold may vary from a stuffy nose and flu-like symptoms to coughing, sneezing, and discomfort, the most common symptoms of an allergic reaction. It is important to keep track of these health complaints as they are signs of a potential sick building or a possible mold infection in the air-handling system. If there are a number of complaints, the air ducts and the HVAC system should be checked for mold. Clean and disinfect the air-handling system appropriately. The Environmental Protection Agency and Occupational Safety and Health Administration have guidelines and regulations for monitoring and treating indoor air quality problems.

After the mold is removed and the environment is under control, replace the filters in the air-handling system. It is essential to use the correct filters and to replace them on a regular basis.

Mold is not the only cause of sick building syndrome, nor the only factor that can affect indoor air quality. Paint fumes, cleaning fluids, air pollution, fumes from adhesives in carpets and furniture, and ozone from equipment are just some factors that contribute to create poor indoor air quality, but these issues are beyond the scope of this book.

## Remote Storage Facilities

When performing the building survey, it is important to check the collections stored outside the main building.

As available storage in the primary building decreases, there is a corresponding increase in the need for storage facilities away from the library/archives. Some institutions store little-used materials in another building on their campus; others use remote storage facilities. If any of your collections are stored away from the main, regularly staffed buildings, then they need to be treated as remote storage facilities.

There are two main types of remote storage: the first is a facility built especially for this purpose and owned by the institution itself or by a consortium of institutions in the same geographical area. The second is a rented building or designated space that may not have been built for this specific purpose. Some rented spaces were designed to be record storage facilities; others are just warehouses. The former is better for storage of library, archives, and museum collections as there should be built-in environmental controls and fire safety precautions.

What types of disasters are remote storage facilities vulnerable to? Fluctuations in environment, temperature, and relative humidity, if not monitored properly, will decrease the potential life span of all the materials. The contents are under risk of mold or increased physical deterioration due to pollution or particulate matter (which can cause scratches on surfaces, discoloration, or increased aging). Physical damage from improperly installed stacks and shelving is also a possibility. Bookcases properly secured to walls and floors are crucial if the stacks are high, mobile, or in earthquake zones. Stacks should be braced across the top shelves to prevent a domino effect if the ground shifts or something knocks into the shelving. Even if your institution is not in an earthquake zone, shelving should be braced to prevent shifting and skewing.

Earthquake tremors carry hundreds of miles depending upon the severity of the plate shift. In August 2011, an earthquake in Virginia, measuring 5.8, was felt as far away as Chicago, Maine, and Ontario. In the summer of 2010, a 5.0 earthquake in Ottawa, Canada, was felt as far away as Cincinnati and Chicago. In April 2008, a 5.2 earthquake in Louisville, Kentucky, awakened residents early in the morning and shook buildings as far away as Chicago. Buildings sway, objects fall, ground moves. No matter where your institution is located, all shelving should be braced across the top to prevent it from falling over. Fragile items should be stored securely on shelves and in drawers. Pictures should be securely mounted on walls so they do not shift or fall.

In remote storage facilities, the stacks are often two or three stories tall. These stacks consist of high, industrial shelving designed to hold little-used book collections or archival collections and are accessed from mechanized lifts. The shelf materials should be of appropriate strength, and the structure should be balanced for the appropriate height and weight. All shelving should be at least 3–6 inches above the floor. No items should be stored on the floor.

Flooding is always a possibility. If the remote storage facility is in a flood zone, keep drains clean and sump pumps working. If the storage facility is in a remote area, install a backup generator to run the sump pump, minimal lights, and HVAC systems. Service sump pumps and generators regularly, especially at change of season and where remote facilities are built below ground or below grade.

Note the following common characteristics of remote and off-site storage facilities:

- They are physically separate from the main collection, usually in a different building.
- If built for remote storage, the structure should not have regular water pipes running across the collections. Wet pipe sprinkler systems should not be a problem. Trouble comes more often from a faulty sprinkler head than from leaks in the pipes.
- The sprinkler system must be zoned.
- If the facility was built for remote storage, the utilities are usually concentrated in one area; therefore, water and fire hazards are minimal. Only HVAC ducts will run across the building. Watch for condensation in the summer.
- The environment should be stable and controllable, due to limited visitors and less random exchange of air.
- If the remote or off-site storage involves a rented space or a contracted service, then there is minimal control over the environment or the physical condition of the collection. Special environmental conditions should be discussed at the time of contracting the space, and regular visits should confirm that the environment and physical conditions are as requested.

Survey the remote storage facilities for the following:

- Physical layout
- Collection locations
- Utilities
- Potential hazards (should be minimal)

Establish prioritization during the planning phase:

■ Examine the types of collections stored there:

> Low-use collections
> Archives and paper records
> Data and magnetic media
> All of the above

■ Rank the value to the whole collection (where this collection fits into the scheme of things, and what its priority level is).

■ Indicate if the collections stored there are from the institution or if it is a shared or regional facility.

The remote storage facility should be treated the same as the main building(s) during the planning phase:

■ Survey the building for potential hazards.

■ Prioritize the collection for recovery. Create floor plans identifying and locating the utilities; collections, with their associated priorities for recovery; and emergency exits.

■ Identify personnel who are familiar with the remote storage facility collections and the building layout. These persons (usually the head of the remote storage facility and the second in command) should be able to gain access to the building after hours.

■ Create a basic disaster response plan using the remote storage facility personnel as key disaster response team members.

■ If the remote storage facility is a rented or contracted service, then include the emergency contact personnel names and 24-hour emergency numbers in the disaster response plan, along with the names and numbers of the institution's liaisons.

■ Include a map and directions of how to locate the remote storage facility, together with identification of main and auxiliary entrances, in the disaster response plan.

■ Establish a schedule for inspection of the facility and the collections. This inspection should be more frequent than for the main collections, as "out of sight, out of mind" definitely holds true in this case.

## Backup Routines to Prevent Loss of Computer Data

The more computer- and data-dependent the institution, the more important it is to make copies of data and software on a regular basis. A number of methods can be used. The backup method depends upon the size of the institution, library, or archives; the amount of computer activity; and the types of services provided to your staff and your patrons.

If the only data on the computer are letters and payroll records, then back up the data on removable storage devices (other than the one that holds the data) whenever the data are altered, and store the removable storage devices (tapes and discs, drive or servers) off-site or in another location in the building.

If the library, archives, or information center uses data heavily and has large databases, then a regular backup routine is required. A tape backup is the most effective and economical. Back up new data at the end of each day. If the data are critical or sensitive, back up the data more often. This incremental backup routine is important for inventory or cataloging operations, database design and input, and websites. Keep in mind that it takes a day to reconstruct each hour of lost data. Backup is the guaranteed method of data recovery. If you do not back up data, they will not be there to restore.

If the library stores its data on a mainframe, a local area network (LAN), institutional servers, or with a third-party remote backup service, determine how often the system is backed up and confirm that the library is included on a regular basis. Some institutions back up data to remote servers, remote locations, or even virtual machines and clouds. Regardless of the location of the backed-up data, it is imperative that there is a backup created on a regular basis, at least once a day. Consult with your IT department and set up an appropriate routine.

The most important question to ask your staff is "how much data can we afford to lose if there is a power outage or loss of access to data and databases?" The less you can afford to lose, the more important it is to back up more frequently. Discuss the various backup options with your IT staff and the institution's computer services specialists. You may choose to back up time-critical data synchronously, while you perform asynchronous backups daily on less critical data. No matter which method you choose, confirm that the system is indeed backing up data and that IT can restore the data to the database using current software.

Remind staff members to back up their data after altering their files. It is best to store files on shared drives and institutional network servers. Back up all data that are stored on local drives onto removable data storage devices, or onto shared drives. In many institutions, individuals are responsible for backing up their own data and personal files.

For smaller institutions, the most common method of routine backup is the "Grandfather" rotation. It consists of daily incremental backup routines, that is, copying the data or files accessed or changed that day. Copy the data onto tape or a removable data storage device daily. On Friday, copy the entire file set, keep that tape, and store it off-site. This routine is repeated on the used tape every day for a month, keeping the Friday and full backup tapes separate. Perform a full backup on the last day of the month and store it as a "month end." The tapes can be kept as monthly or quarterly compilations, depending upon space and data constraints.

Ideally, only the day's data will be lost, or less if you back up more often, if the disaster occurs during working hours. No data are lost if the disaster occurs at night after the backup is performed. Backup tapes should be stored in a fireproof location, either at an off-site data center or data vault. Fireproof cabinets do not necessarily protect tapes, as they can melt at 125° Fahrenheit. The full backup tapes should be checked to make certain that the data can be read and imported should the need arise. Faulty tapes are just as bad as no backup at all.

Don't forget to make a copy of the operating and program software, both commercial and custom, and store it off-site with the data. These copies will be important if the entire system is lost or inaccessible.

Establish a testing routine to practice uploading or importing data to the software. Test the routine at least once a year, if not more often. Write out these routines in simple language in case the expert in the department is not available on the day of the disaster.

Remember that business interruption insurance and extra expense insurance riders usually do not include funds for reconstructing lost data. The insurance company assumes that data are backed up on a regular basis and are accessible, readable, and importable, should it become necessary. The insurance company also assumes that an institution with extensive computer needs has contracted with a hot or cold site—a location designed for operating a computer system off-site on a temporary basis. A business interruption insurance rider should cover the costs of computer rental. Check the policy to confirm that it covers your computing needs.

## Survey to Identify Vulnerable Collections

While surveying the building(s), you identified where there is a potential for damage. This survey is designed to identify collections that are vulnerable to water or heat. Materials that fit this description include early photographic processes, especially nitrate film; phonograph records and other forms of early audio recordings; all magnetic tapes, whether audio, video, or computer; and, most prevalent, clay-coated paper. These collections are in the most danger of total destruction when there is a disaster involving fire or water.

Early photographic processes are very water-sensitive. If the photographs sit in water, it is possible for the adhesive that binds the image to the base to release and allow the image to slide off. Wet collodion negatives are very sensitive to water and are difficult to recover. This process includes ambrotypes and tintypes. Daguerreotypes are also sensitive to water.

Nitrate film should be stored separately from all other collections and protected from water at all times. When decomposing, nitrate film is flammable. Contact the fire department before disposing of nitrate film. Let the fire department know if the area where nitrate film is stored is involved in the disaster. Mark the boxes with early photographic processes to indicate two things: water-sensitive and heavy. Nitrate film should be labeled clearly. Make certain all boxes containing photographs are stored in areas that have the least potential for water damage.

Early phonograph cylinders are made of water-sensitive materials, including wax, acrylic plastics, and acetate. Pre-1950 phonograph records have a base of anything from cardboard and acetate to glass and metal. Some of the materials are sensitive to water, others to heat. Most phonograph records will withstand some water, but they should be removed from it and dried as quickly as possible. Acrylic phonograph records are sensitive to heat and may melt. Mark containers of metal and glass phonograph records to indicate they are heavy.

Magnetic tape is sensitive to extremes of heat. At about 125° Fahrenheit, most forms of magnetic tape will start to melt. It is important to realize that computer backup tapes will be damaged irreparably if stored in a room that has no fire-protection system. Fireproof cabinets and safes may be sufficient to keep tapes from melting if the temperature stays below the heat rating for the safe; however, they are not airtight and may permit the entrance of dust and soot. Magnetic tapes can be dried and cleaned if embedded with soot, dirt, or dust. However, it is not possible to ensure that data are not damaged if the surface is abraded or scratched.

Textile collections are also sensitive to water damage. If your institution has a collection of textiles including rugs, quilts, costumes, and other fiber-based materials, ask a conservator for advice concerning proper storage, handling, and disaster prevention routines. If textile collections do get wet, contact a textile conservator for assistance in stabilizing and drying these special collections.

Other types of hazardous materials can be found in collections of medical, pharmaceutical, and scientific samples. These collections may contain anything from radioactive materials, poisons, and pesticides to bacteria and diseases. Consult with institutional or community health, safety, and emergency management officers if your library, archives, or museum collects these biologically and chemically hazardous materials. Indicate the location of these hazardous materials on your floor plan and coordinate this section of your disaster response plan with the appropriate offices at your institution and in the community.[2]

After you identify water- and heat-sensitive collections, indicate where they are on the floor plan. Prioritize recovery and drying decisions. List specialized consultants who can assist with disaster response and stabilization of collections. Once prioritized, the disaster response team will know where the most vulnerable collections are and which need to be removed first.

## Outside Contacts

Whether there is a preservation librarian on staff or not, that person is not always an expert in conservation nor proficient in dealing with the recovery of all formats in the collection. There are plenty of experts in the field of conservation who deal with special or nonprint formats such as photographs, paintings, textiles, and furniture. Keep in mind when you read professional literature or attend seminars that the authors and speakers may be experts in their fields. Put their names and contact information on a list. When the disaster occurs, preferably beforehand, contact them and ask if they perform conservation work. If the specialists don't do disaster response consulting or deal with water-damaged materials, ask for a referral.

If there is a special or rare collection at your institution, find out the names of several conservators who could help you recover the collection from water or fire damage.

Identify conservation centers in the area or the country that specialize in the formats that are most difficult to deal with. Ask them what their "disaster response" policy is and how they can help your institution. Ask for references and check them out for reliability and performance. Ask consultants and conservators about their services and associated fees as well as emergency contact information. Confirm their contact information regularly when you update the disaster response plan.

If your institution has an unusual collection, consider asking the consultant or conservator to visit and review the collection and any associated preservation issues. Discuss potential water and fire damage, best practices for avoiding damage, and costs associated with recovery treatments. Ask for training in basic disaster response treatment or stabilization of nonpaper, nonprint materials should they be damaged by water. The conservator might suggest a different storage area or off-site location when not in use.

Create a list of consultants and conservators who can deal with different damaged formats in your collection. Place this list in the back of your disaster response plan and consult it when a disaster occurs.

Other professional contacts to add to your disaster response plan are consultants who specialize in assisting institutions in recovering from disasters, writing disaster response plans, and training in recovery of water- and fire-damaged items. Just as you have alternative disaster response team members, keep a list of alternative disaster response consultants and conservators.

## Construction and Renovation Projects

Construction and renovation projects should raise a flag indicating that a disaster response plan needs to be created or the current one revised. This is the time when your institution's collections and structure are most vulnerable to damage. Plan for fires from electrical and mechanical equipment; water damage from open roofs and walls; and increased threat of mold and mildew. There will be increased levels of dust, dirt, and pollution created by the act of construction itself. Lack of control of the environment (temperature and relative humidity) means an increased risk of mold infections that may not be able to be controlled until the building is sealed again. And let us not forget power and telecommunications outages.

When planning a renovation or construction project, consider the vulnerability of the collection, what parts of the collection are closest to the construction, and how they might be adversely affected. If you choose to move a vulnerable part of the collection, determine the following:

- Where will you store it?
- How will you access it?
- When will it be returned to its original or new location?
- How many areas of the collection will be moved, and how many times?
- Can the collection withstand the move and the change in environmental conditions?
- What about the costs, inconvenience, staffing issues, and the environment of the temporary location?

If you decide to leave the collection in place during construction or renovation in the building, take precautions to protect the collection:

- Cover the collection with plastic sheeting to protect from dust and debris and maintain air flow to prevent mold growth.
- Some libraries and archives shrink-wrap their collections if they are in remote storage facilities or if the area is under construction. The shrink-wrap film is very thin and is gas impermeable. It also protects against water and dust particles.[3]
- Make certain that the dust and debris generated by the construction do not enter the air-handling system. Check and see where the intake air goes into the ceiling or into ductwork. If the latter is the case, then the ducts should be closed off in the construction areas. If the air goes into the ceiling (also known as an open plenum system), then seal off the space between the "false" ceiling and the "true" ceiling to prevent moving the debris through the building.
- Separate the construction area from the rest of the building. If possible, use a fireproof material to separate the two areas.
- Confirm that the building will stay warm enough during construction so that the pipes do not freeze and crack, causing water damage.
- Seal openings in walls and roofs at the end of each day to prevent water damage from rain or snow.

Tarps must be anchored securely and have drainage so that they don't fill with water and then collapse into the building, causing water damage.

Consider possible hazards from changes in the environment. When there is construction or renovation in a building, the building envelope is often broken. The building envelope allows for control of the temperature, relative humidity, and pollution. There will be an increased amount of dust, dirt, and debris in the building and entering the air-handling, or HVAC, system. Is the system designed to handle the increase? Can it or will it be modified for the duration of the construction? No matter what, the filters will need to be changed more often; change them once again when the building is resealed and the construction cleanup is completed.

Discuss with the facilities maintenance staff and the construction supervisor how they will control or minimize fluctuations in temperature and relative humidity. Will the building be open or relatively open to the outside for a long period of time? If so, temperature- and mold-sensitive collections need to be moved to a different part of the building or a different location. When the construction and the cleanup are completed, recalibrate the HVAC system to ensure minimal fluctuations in temperature and relative humidity.

During a renovation or construction project, security should be increased, especially if the construction is going on when the building is closed or regular staff members are not present. Security staff should be alert for theft of collections and equipment and should know who has access to the main building and its collections, especially after hours. The security staff should watch for water, fire, or other types of damage and should have contact information for the disaster response team leader.

Steps to be taken during construction should include the following:

- Policies and procedures necessary to control the potential damage
- An increased number and regularity of inspections of the collections to make certain they are not being adversely affected by the changes in environment and physical conditions
- An increased awareness on the part of the staff, the disaster response team, the facilities maintenance staff, and the construction workers that fire and water damage are risks that must be avoided

- Restrict smoking, eating, and drinking to one area, if not outside the building
- Regular removal of debris, garbage, and food

Take the time to discuss vulnerability of the collections and the building with the head of the construction crew or the senior supervisor. Ask what types of precautions they take to prevent fire and water damage. Provide them with disaster response team emergency contact information in the event of a disaster. Assign a disaster response team or staff member to be the liaison between the construction crews and the library, thereby allowing open communications.

Prevention is the best way to head off a disaster. Disasters are not always caused by fire and water. Carelessness, lack of forethought, and lack of control, especially during construction projects, can wreak havoc on carefully stabilized environmental conditions in both general and special collections.

## NOTES

1. Nick Artim, "An Introduction to Fire Detection, Alarm, and Automatic Fire Sprinklers," Technical Leaflet—Emergency Management—Section 3 Leaflet 2, Northeast Document Conservation Center, 1999, www.nedcc.org/resources/leaflets/3Emergency_Management/02IntroToFireDetection.php.

2. See Judith A. Weiner, "The Element of Surprise," *Journal of Archival Organization* 5, no. 4 (2007): 33–49, for detailed information about hazardous materials in archives.

3. Janice Stagnitto, "The Shrink Wrap Project at Rutgers University Special Collections and Archives," *AIC Book and Paper Group Annual* 12 (1993), 56–60. Reprinted in *Abbey Newsletter* 18, no. 4–5 (August–September 1994); also available at http://cool.conservation-us.org/byorg/abbey/an/an18/an18-4/an18-418.html.

# Section 4

## Planning

The planning phase is where everything comes together on paper as well as in the minds of the disaster response team. The more forethought and preparation for disasters and interruption of services, the more effective the response. Now is the time to assign responsibilities for activating and implementing the disaster response plan and to designate priorities for recovery of collections. Take the time to review the insurance policy and evaluate available financial resources for recovery of damaged materials and structures. Very small or one-person libraries, archives, and historical societies should enlist the assistance of others in their community to help create and activate a plan to recover the operations and collections of the institution. Consider this a community plan and consider response procedures that can be applied to all the local libraries, archives, record centers, and museums.

During this phase, the disaster response team performs a building survey to identify chronic leaks and drips so they can be repaired and locate vulnerable collections to protect them from potential leaks. Draw floor plans and allocate responsibilities for handling the various aspects of disaster cleanup. There is more on this in the chapter on prevention.

It can take a year or more to hammer out the details of a disaster response plan. During this time, consider how your institution's staff members will handle a crisis, who will be in charge, and how that authority is allocated or acknowledged by the administrators. All disaster response team members should be familiar with institutional policies and procedures. This is particularly important during a wide-area disaster where the infrastructure of the institution and the community is affected.

When it comes to dealing with the disaster, no matter what shape the disaster response plan is in, no matter whether it has been approved by all the administrators and lawyers in your institution, the disaster response team should follow the plan. It was conceived and discussed while all was calm and normal. Stick with your plan. After the disaster is over, revise the plan to take into account issues encountered during the crisis.

# Elements of a Disaster Response Plan

The following list outlines the four phases of a disaster response plan: response, recovery, prevention, and planning. Use it to make certain all the components are accounted for. You want to consider how your plan coordinates with the institution-wide disaster response, emergency management plans, and continuous operations policies and procedures already in place.

For a quick response plan, use the following three response phases in conjunction with the seven steps in the introduction's subsection "What If the Disaster Happens before You Have a Plan?"

## Response (Three Phases)

1. Respond to notification of the disaster.
   - Gather the team.
   - Alert outside professionals of the disaster.
   - Determine if the building should be closed and for how long.
2. Assess the situation and damage.
   - Call in outside assistance.
   - Coordinate with other disaster response/emergency response teams—institution-wide, IT/IS plan, continuous operations, facilities, and security.
   - Organize recovery operations based upon prioritization (developed or assigned in the planning phase).
   - Set up communications—internal and external.
3. Begin to rescue and recover collections.
   - Reassign/reallocate staff as needed.
   - Deal with emotional issues.

## Recovery

- Restore primary services (skeleton staff).
- Restore primary functions (skeleton functions with available staff).
- Return to normal (most staff back to regular duties).
- Evaluate response procedures and revise the disaster response plan.

## Prevention

- Survey the building and collection for potential damage and hazards. Check fire, smoke, and door alarms and exit signs to confirm they function.
- Mark collections that are water- or heat-sensitive. Make certain they are stored in areas that have the least potential for destruction.
- Monitor indoor air quality.
- Examine remote storage facilities.
- Plan for construction and renovation projects.
- Create a list of consultants and conservators who can deal with damage to valuable objects, paintings, and non-book and -paper formats. You want at least two people to call upon for each format, or a regional conservation facility that handles all types of media.

## Planning

- Select the disaster response team and alternative staff members.
- Assign responsibilities for each of the response phases and activities.
- Set priorities for recovery of each of the collections (by format, type, department, floor, or building).
- Plan for large, small, and wide-area disasters.
- Coordinate disaster response plan with continuous operations plan at your institution and the emergency management response plan in your community.
- Plan for damage to computers and other equipment. Coordinate your plan with that of IS and computer services.
- Review insurance coverage and update as needed. Determine what is not covered under the policy. Determine the various deductibles and limits. Review and update the insurance annually.
- Establish a communications policy that includes social networking and Internet communication methods.
- Contact disaster response companies and consultants for a walk-through and discussion of their roles in potential disasters. Enroll in priority response programs for your institution.

■ Work with facilities and security staff to discuss their roles during a potential disaster. Ask about their policies and procedures during an institution-wide disaster. Discuss the types of supplies and services needed to protect and recover your collections.

■ Train the disaster response team and explain responsibilities to the rest of the staff.

■ Practice response phases, evaluate plan, and revise.

Add to the list above or modify it to reflect the needs of your institution and your specific disaster response plan. Use it as the table of contents for your plan. Just add page numbers to each section or category.

Make a basic response plan with contact information (phone numbers and e-mail addresses) on the first page of your disaster response manual for easy reference and contact. Post the daytime contact information for the disaster response team by phones and computers for a swift response (see figure 4.1).

Now that you have reviewed the basic aspects of a disaster response plan, let's begin to put the pieces of the plan into place. Remember, the planning phase may take many months to discuss, write, revise, rewrite, and modify to fit your institution. If positions, collections, or responsibilities change while writing the plan, you need to update what is written. The disaster response plan is always a work in progress and a series of guidelines. Do not design the disaster response plan so rigidly that you cannot adapt to unforeseen circumstances and crises.

## Disaster Response Team

A disaster response team is essential for the smooth execution of the disaster response operation. Members of the team should be capable of executing the plan and performing the tasks. As members of the disaster response team, individuals should have the authority to make decisions that result in the swift recovery of materials and resumption of services. Together with administrators and boards, the disaster response team sets parameters of responsibility and authority. The disaster response team should be trained in techniques to recover water-damaged materials and be familiar with recovery priorities.

Most disaster response teams consist of four to six people, with several backup persons to call in an emergency. Ideally, the team should be headed by the person in charge of preservation or data management. In some institutions, the head of facilities is the disaster response team leader. Some disaster response team members should live in the community, others far away. This diversity in distance from the institution is important, especially in the aftermath of a wide-area disaster. Those nearby can assess damage without traveling far under adverse conditions, lack of infrastructure, or in inclement weather, but may be affected personally during hurricane or flooding. After a wide-area disaster, team members who live farther away should be less affected emotionally, as in theory their personal lives will not be affected by the natural disaster. Once they arrive at the scene they should be able to direct their attention and emotions toward assessing the damage to the institution and efficient assessment and response.

Leadership depends upon the bureaucracy of your institution, its size, and personalities. In some instances, all members of the preservation and information technology (IT) departments are the team. Select other members of the team from the professional and paraprofessional staff. If there are several departments or locations, designate a team, or point person, for each. In the case of a smaller library, a representative from the building's facilities maintenance department should be on the team.

The disaster response team is the first to be called to the disaster site. They will assess the scope of the disaster, determine the tasks to be accomplished, and the number of personnel necessary to complete the recovery operation. Once the assessment is made, response and recovery operations begin.

During the planning phase, create identification cards that show you are members of the disaster response team. Consider obtaining vests or T-shirts with "Library/Archives DRT" to identify team members to the other people in the area. It is very possible that this is the first time you will come in contact with the facilities maintenance staff and with safety and security personnel. Depending upon the type of disaster, safety personnel may be in charge of the site. You need to introduce your team members and inform them of the needs of the collections. If you are told to wait, get your disaster response team organized and put your consultants and contractors on standby.

**FIGURE 4.1** Disaster response team
contact information

| Name | Phone |
|------|-------|
|  |  |
|  |  |
|  |  |
|  |  |
|  |  |

**Emergency Meeting Place** is located at

_____

Alternative operating location: _____

Street address: _____

Contact name and phone number: _____

Directions (or append map): _____

## Roles and Responsibilities

For a disaster response plan to be effective and to avoid several people dealing with the same problem at once, assign responsibilities to the members of the disaster response team, the library director, and other staff and personnel. It is important to have a second person as a backup for each of the responsibilities in case a team member is out of town or unavailable. Some responsibilities fall naturally into the domains of team members and staff, such as assigning the IT librarian (the one in charge of the computer systems) the responsibility of dealing with computer problems and issues and ordering cleaning and replacement of damaged equipment and software.

Disaster response team members should be able to deal with the responsibilities assigned them and be capable of making decisions concerning how to carry out the associated duties. In some cases, the responsibility will require the team member to contact consultants and contractors or purchase supplies and minor pieces of equipment. The person assigned that responsibility must have the designated fiscal authority to do so. If necessary, the disaster response team should set up criteria to follow before exercising this type of emergency fiscal authority.

The responsibilities and roles for disaster response team members may be assigned in phases to correspond with the different aspects of disaster response: immediate response, assessment, and recovery. Preassigning responsibilities is important so that the disaster response team knows what to expect of their energies and time from the minute they are informed of the disaster until the situation has returned to "normal." Below are just some of the many responsibilities of the disaster response team. The smaller your institution, the more you need to work cooperatively with community members and consolidate tasks.

## Director

The library director and the deputy director, if the library is large enough, deal with the administration or board of trustees or governing board. Except for one-person libraries, the director should not head the disaster response team because, in addition to the duties of running the library, the director's job and responsibility are to be the chief administrator of the institution. Once the disaster is declared, the director must make informed major decisions and allocate funds and extra staff to assist with the response and recovery phases of disaster response. In most cases, the library will be insured for some of the loss or will have funds set aside for such an emergency.

The director may deal directly with the insurance agent and adjuster or designate that responsibility. Make certain that the designee is familiar with the insurance policy and has the authority to contact the insurance company.

In addition, the director may wish to work with consultants and disaster response/drying companies directly or assign those responsibilities to the disaster response team leader. In either case, it is helpful if the consultants and disaster response companies are familiar with the workings of the institution, the staff, and the recovery priorities. The director's involvement in the disaster response plan is crucial to boost morale both during and after the disaster. The director might provide food, drink, and rest periods or may assign that responsibility to the disaster response team leader.

Regardless of how involved the library director is in the disaster response and recovery phases, there should be regular meetings of the disaster response team and the director and regular updates for other staff about the overall recovery of the institution.

## Chief Financial Officer

If the institution is large enough it will have a fiscal officer who is responsible for allocating funds. In public libraries, this position is often held by the clerk-treasurer. During a disaster the director may need to go to the financial officer or clerk-treasurer to request emergency allocation of financial resources. This officer may handle the insurance policy, or it might be under the domain of the risk management office. During the planning phase, identify who to go to for emergency funding and for initiating insurance claims. If the disaster is small, it may merely require the director to allocate emergency funds from the budget to cover the disaster recovery expenses.

## Team Leader

The team leader coordinates response and recovery operations; works with team members; communicates with the director, team members, and the public information officer; coordinates volunteer efforts; and arranges for multiple shifts. The director may ask the team leader to assign rest breaks and provide frequent updates about the overall situation to the team and the staff. The team leader either arranges for a temporary work location or assigns a team member to do so, and assists team members with their designated responsibilities (see a list of jobs to assign in the subsection "Lists to Create and Update during the Planning Phase"). The team leader lets staff know where to report and for which shift.

## Team Members

The disaster response team members lead efforts in designated tasks from the team leader and wherever else needed, such as supervising the move to a temporary location and arranging for phone connections, equipment, and temporary staff. They train staff and volunteers, locate additional supplies, and communicate with the team leader on a regular basis.

## Public Information Officer/ Communications Officer

As the institution's official spokesperson, the public information officer (PIO) communicates with the media by writing and sending press releases to television and radio stations and the newspapers as to the situation, temporary hours, and services. The PIO also releases contact information to vendors, suppliers, and patrons. This person should also provide information to keep the institution's website up to date with press releases about the disaster. Consider placing abbreviated press releases on social networking sites where the institution maintains a presence.

## Information Technology Librarian

The IT librarian gets data and computers up and running and oversees remote access to electronic resources and databases. This may include stand-alone PCs, CD-ROM towers, servers, wireless access, LANs, and other networked computer systems and their associated peripherals. The online public access catalog may or may not fall under the domain of the IT librarian; the same is true of the website and digital resources. If the IT librarian is not responsible for the library's computer systems, then the main computing staff or IT department should be involved in getting the public access terminals and their associated programs and data up and running. Don't forget to involve the IT department in the library's disaster response plan process so that they know when they might be called upon and the disaster response team knows what the IT department can do for them.

## Administration

The administrator, possibly the director, allocates emergency and contingency funds, approves hiring of disaster recovery firms, meets with insurance adjusters, and works with the overall plan. The administrator should arrange one or two meetings with department heads about the disaster response actions and progress. If your institution has a complex administration hierarchy, identify who oversees your operations and will assist during a disaster.

## Security

In the event of a disaster, triggered alarm, water leaks, or broken pipes, security staff should notify the disaster response team. Security should help prevent theft and notify the library/archives about broken windows and doors. If there is no security department, or it is small, hire temporary security staff for the duration of the disaster response and recovery phases. Institutional security officers should have keys to all the rooms in the building. Invite security staff to your planning sessions and ask for advice about securing the facility and protecting collections. Ask about their roles and responsibilities during a disaster and how they can assist your disaster response team.

## Facilities Maintenance

The facilities maintenance staff should clean up water, fire damage, and debris; board up broken windows and doors; and help with miscellaneous cleanup efforts. It may fall under their domain to hire a disaster response/drying company based upon the library/archives' recommendation. They should know the location of all utility shutoff valves and how to shut them off. Invite facilities maintenance staff to your planning and training sessions. Ask about their roles and responsibilities during a disaster and how they can assist your disaster response team. Getting to know facilities maintenance staff before a disaster will make response and cleanup operations smoother.

## Consultants

A consultant should be able to recommend treatment options and write specifications for drying the collection and the building. He or she should help coordinate response efforts and locate necessary resources, supplies, and services. Consultants should help train staff and volunteers; explain options for recovery; and serve as liaison with the director, administration, team leader, and the insurance company, if requested. Consultants can direct facilities maintenance staff if no drying company is hired. A good consultant can identify and locate additional contractors who are trained and certified to work under "hazardous" conditions and should know conservators and specialists who can work with your collections. In some cases, consultants may be asked to direct or lead response and recovery efforts. Invite the disaster response consultant to planning meetings and ask for suggestions to streamline your response and recovery operations. Disaster response consultants can provide assistance even if they have never been to your institution, but their advice is best when familiar with your institution, its mission, and needs.

## Disaster Response/Drying Companies

These companies dry and "recover" wet materials, furnishings, and the building. They should provide the best possible treatment based on specifications for recovery called a "scope of service." A disaster response/drying company should return all treated items in the best possible condition after drying the materials and removing mold, dirt, and mud from them. A disaster response/drying company may be called in by the consultant, the insurance adjuster, or the institution. On the other hand, some disaster response/drying companies regularly contract with preservation consultants for work with cultural institutions. If your institution is insured, the drying and recovery of the collection is usually covered by the insurance policy. During the planning phase, contact local representatives of the disaster response companies to learn about their services and availability. Ask about registering for their first response or priority service. Familiarize the disaster response company with your needs, specific issues, and idiosyncrasies of your building layout. The more familiar the disaster response companies are with your needs, the more efficient their response is when you need them.

## Risk Managers

These professionals evaluate the level of insurance needed and should be able to identify potential risks and hazards to collections. The risk manager is usually associated with your institution and knowledgeable about the specifics of various insurance policies. For a small institution, the director and the board will have to make determinations as to risk and liability. In some cases the clerk-treasurer will be involved in purchasing insurance, approving emergency purchase orders, and allocating emergency or contingency funds to pay for disaster recovery services.

## Insurance Agents and Appraisers

The insurance agent is the representative who works in the area or region and handles coverage for businesses and cultural institutions. When the disaster occurs, the assigned disaster response team member or director must contact the insurance company. The insurance company will send out an adjuster; ask for the adjuster who handles water damage claims or specializes in cultural institutions. You want an experienced adjuster who can answer your questions, provide contacts in the disaster response industry, and approve your expenses.

Now that we have discussed what each of the various roles entails, let's look at the tasks necessary to quickly and efficiently respond to a disaster and deal with the damage. All or some of these jobs will need to be done during the response phase. Designate the appropriate disaster response team members to perform these tasks or make these decisions during a disaster or ahead of time.

- Contact the director.
- Assess the damage.
- Determine if the building needs to be closed and for how long.
- Contact outside assistance, including a consultant and a disaster response/drying company.
- Arrange for security and maintenance to secure the premises. This needs to be accomplished immediately to prevent theft, especially if the disaster occurs at night, on the weekend, or during a holiday.
- Contact an insurance agent and assess the status of contingency funds.
- Organize the staff to perform "duties as assigned."
- Determine if the work needs to be done in shifts.
- Decide if volunteers are needed and where to use them.
- Have standing water removed and humidity decreased.
- Check equipment (computers and peripherals, photocopiers, etc.) for damage and arrange for drying, cleaning, and recertification. Don't forget to check removable data storage devices and tapes for damage and arrange for cleaning. When computer equipment is ready for use, check the functionality of the operating system, software, and data. Restore data and operations as required. This is primarily the job of the IT or computer services department.
- Order supplies for packing boxes of water-damaged books and other media.
- Arrange for shipping and freezing of water-damaged items, as appropriate.
- Supervise packing of boxes whether done by staff, volunteers, or disaster response/drying company personnel.
- Arrange for an alternative location from which to operate.
- Send press releases to the media. Inform patrons, suppliers, and vendors about hours, address, and phone number. The public relations or communications

officer should be the official spokesperson for the institution. Designate a disaster response team member to provide current information to this department on a regular basis, at least once a day.

■ Monitor the building for mold, increased relative humidity and temperatures, and other environmental problems such as excess dust, debris, and soot. The building should be checked after the HVAC system is stabilized, then at least once a week for the first six months after the disaster. Make this part of the regular disaster prevention routine.

■ Arrange for breaks, food, and drink during the response and cleanup phase.

## Lists to Create and Update during the Planning Phase

As part of the planning phase, designate the following jobs to specific disaster response team members:

■ Identify suppliers of packing and shipping products and services, including a lumber supply store and a freezer- or cold-storage facility.

■ Identify and contact preservation consultants who specialize in and have actual experience with disaster response. Include local and regional conservation facilities. Put them on the contact list.

■ Contact local and regional disaster response/drying companies. Put them on the contact list.

■ Designate a place to meet if the building is damaged or inaccessible. Select one location on the grounds of your institution and one in the community.

■ Identify temporary office space for administration and non–public services work. If there is a lot of office space in your community, then note where to find it and how to contact the rental agencies. Also identify empty storefronts and shopping centers in a nearby community. These locations are perfect for temporary library and archives sites, and off-site storage.

■ Make a note of the local cellular phone and office equipment rental companies in your community and a nearby community.

■ Identify local security companies.

■ Designate a team member to review the insurance policy yearly.

■ Designate one or two team members to be responsible for updating the building survey and prioritization for recovery decisions yearly.

■ Put together or purchase a basic disaster response kit (see a list of contents for a basic disaster response kit in the subsection "Basic Supplies" at the end of appendix B).

■ Find out who is responsible for stocking and maintaining the first aid kits. Check them regularly.

Place this information and the contact lists in the back of the plan. Disaster response services lists are often found in the back of disaster response books. Customize the list to include local companies and consultants you contacted during the planning phase. Make certain that the companies and consultants provide the services you desire. There are lists of companies and organizations that can assist you in planning, response, and recovery in appendix B. Select a few, contact them, and put them in your emergency contact list. Also check the yellow pages in your town or county under "fire and water damage restoration" for local companies that can remove standing water and provide emergency dehumidification, fans, pack-out, and assistance.

Ensure that the disaster response team leader distributes the plan, in draft and final forms, to the disaster response team members and facilities maintenance and security departments. All versions should be distributed to every department. The disaster response team members should keep a copy of the most up-to-date plan at home, on a removable data device, or in their cars in case the building is inaccessible, the power is out, or the disaster happens at night. Keep new versions of the disaster response plan on computers and remote servers and removable data storage devices. Update them regularly.

Now that responsibilities during the planning and response phases have been assigned, the disaster response team begins planning for response and recovery of collections.

## Prioritization for Recovery

One of the most difficult phases of the planning process is prioritizing the collection for recovery in the event of a disaster. The disaster response team has already identified vulnerable collections. Now each department and institution must make decisions that are specific for their collections, mission statements, and services to patrons and clients.

Prioritization requires looking at subject areas of the collection as a whole in an attempt to determine in what order items should be rescued and recovered should they be damaged in a disaster. It is the difficult matter of trying to save the most important items in the collection. This process looks at the core collection for unique, irreplaceable items. Are they shelved together? Are the items most vulnerable to water stored away from overhead water pipes, safe from vicarious disasters? Or is everything shelved together? In the second phase of the prioritization process, examine how each department's collection fits into the mission of the institution as a whole. In the case of a large-scale disaster, where the entire building is affected, the disaster response team will have to know which departments are more crucial to the mission of the institution in order to rescue what they can.

Determining the priorities of recovery also provides an opportunity to consider future collection development projects. For example, if the periodical indexes are damaged, would the institution replace them with electronic formats or electronic databases? Or if paper issues of periodicals are affected, do you know the overlap of the microfilm collection and electronic resources with print periodicals? Would the institution replace paper copies with new paper copies or rely upon digital resources and interlibrary loan? Few institutions have the financial resources to purchase new paper copies. Most will opt for document delivery tapping into the resources of the local consortia or interlibrary loan. If the periodicals are available on the Internet, either for free or with a subscription, most institutions will decide to discard water-damaged journals rather than freeze-dry them. If that is your institution's decision, then label the journals as the lowest priority, with the collection development decision to discard and update with the newest format. It is important to remember that if there is no damage, then there is nothing to discard. Disasters are not the time to weed a collection, no matter what the format.

During the prioritization phase, departments might initiate overdue weeding projects. Recovering damaged items and rescuing the undamaged are the primary concerns of the disaster response team. In the same vein, a disaster does not mean the institution will get a completely new collection. Not only is this impractical, but very few, if any, institutions have the insurance to cover the cost of purchasing an entire collection. The only time an institution may have the opportunity to purchase a new collection is if the building burned to the ground. Keep in mind that insurance may not be sufficient to replace every lost volume.

After the collection has been surveyed and prioritization for recovery decisions made, the areas of each department or floor should be clearly marked to identify the different levels of prioritization. Remember that this cannot be an item-by-item prioritization, but one by area or type of collection.

Indicate the levels of prioritization for recovery on the floor plan for each department or floor. This step is important, for during a disaster, it can be very chaotic, with collections in disarray. Also, the collection may be packed out for recovery or storage by disaster response company personnel who cannot and should not make these decisions for your institution.

All the prioritization for recovery decisions should be made during the planning phase, while staff is in a rational state of mind and emotions are stable. At this time (before the disaster), staff who are emotionally connected to the collections can make informed choices about the future of the collections and the institution.

If prioritization decisions are not made ahead of time, they will have to be made "on the fly," under the following situations:

■ While awaiting permission to enter the building

■ While looking at water-damaged areas during the assessment phase

■ By an outside consultant who works with the library, the insurance company, or the disaster response company. Although a consultant may be familiar with the workings and basic needs of cultural institutions, he or she may not know the collection development policy or mission statement of your institution. If the outside consultant is a librarian, then ask for solid, unemotional suggestions for the staff to work from. An overview of the institution's mission statement and collection development policies is in order. If you intend to use an outside consultant, it is best to meet during the planning phase, describe policies and missions ahead of time, and acquaint the consultant with the building and collection layout. In fact, if an outside consultant is prearranged, then write the consultant into the plan and place contact information in the primary response phase.

■ By the disaster response firm while packing out the collection. Remember that the disaster response firm may have no experience with libraries, archives, or museums. Suggestions from the disaster response firm for recovery and removal of collections may be random and uninformed, especially if there has been no prior contact between the firm and the institution or the disaster response team. During one disaster, a company worker once asked if the books on the bottom shelf were the least valuable. When asked why he thought this, the worker replied, "well, they are the ones that always get wet." After a horrified silence, the disaster response consultant said "no, it was just unlucky those books were on the bottom shelves." The company worker went on to remark that he hadn't been to a library since he was a child. Don't assume that the disaster response company laborers know anything about libraries, archives, or museums. While disaster response companies train their supervisors, lead workers, and full-time laborers to a high level, in a large-scale or area-wide disaster, most hire temporary workers to pack and move boxes, nothing more.

During the planning phase, prioritize your recovery decisions. Making the decisions without forethought, while emotions are high, is not in the best interest of the collection or institution's mission as a whole.

Review prioritization decisions regularly:

■ At least once a year

■ Whenever a new collection is added

■ When the mission statement is reviewed or changed

■ When new services are offered, especially those key to servicing patrons

■ When a department is added or consolidated or if a floor, wing, or building is added or consolidated

When a major shift in the shelving or reorganization affects the floor plan, revise

■ The floor plan

■ The prioritization for recovery list

The disaster response team should work with de--partment heads and building administrators to prioritize the paper-based collections; nonprint and nonpaper collections, including photographs and audiovisual materials; computers and their associated magnetic media.

Prioritize office, administrative, and institutional records according to the records-retention schedule at your institution. When it comes to disaster response planning, most people forget to prioritize their own offices and computers. Prioritize what you need most to do your day-to-day job and either back up or store those items where they are most accessible during a disaster.

## Prioritization Categories

Prioritization decisions fit into five basic categories:

1. Irreparably damaged or irreplaceable due to format or value

2. Essential to the mission of the institution or to provide basic services to patrons

3. Important to round out the basic collections or services

4. Nice to have but not essential to the primary mission of the institution

5. Can be discarded because they are replaced on a regular basis (usually standing orders and serials)

Office and business records fall within the third category. Computers, peripheral equipment, software, and data may fall in category 2 or 3 depending upon the type of institution and its dependence upon computerized services.

Category 1 includes all those items that are irreparably damaged by water or excess temperatures and those items that are irreplaceable such as "rare books" and reference tools that are crucial to the mission of the institution and are also out of print. These items include photographs on glass plates, nitrate film, and the various processes that react poorly to water, thereby destroying the image. In the case of glass plate negatives and some other nineteenth-century formats, the adhesive in the bonding layer releases from the base and the image slides off the support. Nitrate film reacts violently with water and so should be stored away from any chance of water damage. It should be disposed of appropriately as it is considered a "hazardous material."

In the case of water-sensitive photographs, mark their containers in such a way as to identify them at a glance. Mark them with a special color or label, so they can be removed quickly and boxed again if necessary. Mark heavy boxed collections for handling with caution as they may be damaged if dropped. This is very important when using temporary or hired labor.

Magnetic tape can be irreparably damaged by excessive temperatures. Tape begins to melt at 125° Fahrenheit. Magnetic media can withstand the ravages of water for a short period of time, but they should be removed from water as quickly as possible and sent to an appropriate vendor for drying and copying. Do not freeze magnetic media.

Electronic resources that were created by your institution should be backed up on a remote server with duplicates stored off-site. Discuss remote access of these resources with your IT or computer services staff. These resources should be part of the IT disaster response plan.

Category 2 includes those items that are essential to the mission of the institution. The staff of the institution cannot provide basic, key services to patrons or clients without these items. Category 2 recovery decisions can be based upon collection development policy and overall mission statements or upon the mission and focus of each department or building. For example, if the institution has a special architecture reference department where the focus is on the history of architecture, it might contain various formats and media but also unusual reference materials to answer specialized questions. If so, the entire department might be designated for removal and recovery as quickly as possible. Other types of collections that fall within this category are special ready-reference items that are not part of the standing order system.

Category 3 items are important to round out the basic core collections or services. These materials flesh out the different departments and services, creating the identity of the institution as a whole. These also include the rest of the special collections materials, less-rare "rare books," and the archives. Within this category are the records created by offices and the business and financial records of the institution. Priorities for recovery, discard, and destruction of business records should be based upon the records-retention schedule established by the records manager of the institution. If there is no records-retention manager, then consult a specialist and place the core retention schedule in the disaster response plan.

Note that business, office, and financial records that are held within the archives and special collections department are not the same as an archives collection, which is a unique collection of documents. Although the office and business records may fall under the jurisdiction of the institution's archivist, they should not be treated the same.

The following are some basic rules of thumb for the archives:

- Papers that comprise the legal history of the institution are considered permanent records and must be retained for the life of the institution. These are a top priority for recovery.

- Business and financial records may be considered permanent depending upon their content; otherwise, follow the records-retention schedule.

- Office files are usually not considered permanent records and should follow the records-retention schedule. Consider digitizing and microfilming the most important records. Store the originals off-site and access the surrogates as needed.

Category 4 includes all materials that are nice to have but are not essential to the primary mission of the institution. These items may prompt the question, "Why do we have these in the first place?"

Category 5 is materials that can be discarded because they are regularly replaced via the following mechanisms: standing orders (directories, basic reference tools); annual or regular replacements (almanacs, encyclopedias). Electronic resources, microfilm, and journals were discussed above. Identify vendors for electronic journals and books, note the methods of access, and discuss methods of remote access with the IT and computer services department. The last category may be supplemented by document delivery services, especially if the damaged collection included an extensive number of periodicals.

## Prioritization for Recovery of Computers

Prioritization for recovery of computers, peripherals, software, and data varies depending upon the mission and services of the institution or the department.

*Computers and peripherals:* These can be dried, cleaned, and recertified if they are not damaged by excessive temperatures. If they are damaged, the prioritization statement may be the same as for periodicals: consider the age and replace if old or recover if new after checking on the scope of insurance coverage.

**Software:** If it is unique, obsolete, or proprietary, the software must be recovered. This type of software should be backed up on a regular basis and stored in an off-site location. Any changes to the program should be backed up immediately and should replace the tape or data files in the off-site storage area. Check to see if this falls within the domain of the computer services department of the institution and how their disaster response plan fits with the library/archives. Some recent studies show that software programs won't read versions more than three generations old. This has changed over the past few years with companies providing compatibility programs so that data on newer versions can be read by older software. This is particularly true of PDF. However, to prevent loss of data when your institution does upgrade, you should upgrade software within three generations or five years.[1]

**Data and information:** Data should be backed up regularly if created on-site. If it comes to the institution from external vendors or databases, then discuss the vendor's disaster response plan. Ask what services they provide when a client's data are lost. How quickly can they install and ship a comprehensive database and what will it cost? If your vendor does not keep servers and hard drives on hand, find out which companies stock what you need and how to ship it to your vendor. If all is lost, you'll need to have this step well thought out. The local IT department should coordinate these activities and queries with the institution's computer services staff.

**Internal data and projects:** Keep data files on the network or shared server so that it is part of the regular, institution-wide nightly backup. The same holds true for locally created electronic resources and data. Individuals should save their data and files to the shared drives. If departments and individuals store data on local drives, they must back the files up regularly onto removable data storage devices, network servers, or remote (cloud) servers. If the files are not backed up, then they could be lost completely in the aftermath of a disaster.

**OPAC (online public access catalog):** Back up the local catalog regularly. The local OPAC usually contains item-level cataloging records as well as circulation records. In this day of integrated catalogs, it is essential to maintain current versions. If you don't do this in-house, then contact the service provider or vendor to determine if backup is done on a regular basis and who is responsible for reloading the data should the system crash or the hardware fail. Ask who provides temporary hardware. Find out how long it takes to get a new server installed with current data. Discuss this aspect of disaster response with the IT department to determine under whose domain catalog backup falls and who will contact the service provider. Make certain to write the appropriate contact information in the primary/secondary phase of the response plan. If you are part of a consortium with a shared catalog, talk with their computer services personnel.

**Website:** Back up the layout and data on your website regularly and keep a backup copy accessible should you need to reload it onto the web server. If the library's servers host the website, then care should be taken to back up regularly. If the website is located on a remote server, find out what their backup and disaster response plans are and back up accordingly. If the remote server crashes and your site is destroyed, you will have to reinstall or remount from your most recent backup.

**Personal files and data:** Recovery of personal office files depends upon the needs of the individual. Items the individual might wish to rescue include a personal and professional contact file, personal data, unique projects, and research materials. Critical data and files should be stored on removable data storage devices, remote backup services, or shared network drives. Personal office files are not usually part of category 1 prioritization for recovery of materials or in the first wave of pack-out and removal. Provide time for staff members to clean out their personal areas after the primary affected areas are dealt with.

**Journals and periodicals:** As discussed above in prioritization categories 4 and 5, cultural institutions house journals in paper and micro-formats. Increasingly they provide access to journals through electronic databases, freely accessible full-text on the Internet, and on-site licensing agreements. Unfortunately, not all journal databases provide complete access to entire runs, so it is important to note which are incomplete before designating journals as priority 5. As discussed above, if periodicals are printed on clay-coated paper, it may be difficult or impossible to rescue the items before they are irreparably damaged. Many institutions have decided to use document delivery and interlibrary loan for lost issues.

It is important to remember when acting on the prioritization for recovery decisions that if the items and equipment are not damaged or in danger of damage, then keep the materials safe. Prioritization for recovery only pertains to collections and departments that are damaged.

## Planning for Small, Large, and Wide-Area Disasters

As discussed in section 1, there are three sizes of disaster to consider when designing the disaster response phase of the plan: small, or localized; large; and wide-area. Every size of disaster involves the same basic procedures, so start with a small-scale or localized plan. If you have a large-scale or wide-area disaster, then adjust your plan to accommodate the loss of building, infrastructure, and external support. You may also have to look outside your community for assistance or a temporary location.

Small-scale disasters affect a department, floor, or collection. This type of disaster could be caused by a water pipe break, leaking roof, isolated flooding from below, an isolated fire, or a mold infection. It may require closing the building or department until the situation is under control or merely suspending local services. If you decide to close the building for the duration of the cleanup, then consider directing services to another library at your institution or another branch. You can also consider relocating basic services and core collections to a storefront in the community. Relocation will require assistance from and coordination with facilities maintenance departments, security, and IT. If your community is small or your institution isolated, consider cooperating with the other cultural institutions in the township or county and provide mutual assistance to one another in the event of a disaster. Create a simple, informal letter of agreement or mutual assistance between your institution and the others in the vicinity. See a sample letter in figure 4.2.

Large-scale disasters affect the building or institution as a whole but are "defined" disasters, with community resources available. This type of disaster is usually caused by fire or a large water main break, and even construction accidents. Large-scale disasters often require closing the building or interrupting services for one to two days. Even for this short period of time, consider providing services at an alternative location either in another building at your institution or in the community. You can even provide reference services through e-mail, chat, instant messaging, and social networking sites.

Wide-area disasters are usually caused by natural disasters (earthquakes, tornados, hurricanes, or huge forest fires) that affect the infrastructure of the city or a large geographical area. In the wake of the destruction of the World Trade Center and damage to the Pentagon, we learned many lessons about the impact of wide-area disasters on the infrastructure of cities and businesses. These lessons were reinforced in the aftermath of Hurricanes Katrina, Rita, and Wilma, as well as other disasters that affect cultural institutions, cities, and lives across the world. Wide-area disasters affect the personal lives of staff members. Community resources and those of the surrounding area are stretched to provide for all affected businesses. The building or institution will be closed until at least the infrastructure is restored. Seek assistance and services from beyond the affected area.

Many institutions plan for large-scale and wide-area disasters. These types of disasters may happen in the life of an institution, maybe even more than once, as in the case of the World Trade Center on September 11, 2001 or the earthquake in Haiti in January 2010.

Start your response plan by considering the occurrence of small-scale disasters. They are fairly common and are encountered on a routine basis, maybe even once or twice a year, depending upon the condition and maintenance of the building. If the scope of damage is small enough, response may require only the disaster response team and the members of the affected department.

Because small disasters are more common, response and recovery decisions are easier to define and decide upon. Lack of preparedness for small disasters can create larger disasters and ultimately affect the entire building or department. Sometimes small disasters occur as closely spaced events. In this case, willing and enthusiastic participation in response and recovery activities will decrease as the disasters increase in frequency.

Large-scale disasters affect large portions of the building or the entire building. This scale of disaster will

# Library Disaster Mutual Support Agreement

The following libraries agree to support each other during and after a disaster:

_____

_____

_____

Support may include:

- Assistance during the immediate recovery, if possible
- Support for the continuity of library services after the initial recovery

Libraries not affected by the disaster should be prepared to offer the following support for continuity of services:

- Work space for disaster-affected staff
- Reference assistance for disaster-affected patrons
- Pick-up location services for disaster-affected patrons
- Technical support, if possible
- Space for air drying library materials, if possible

The administrators of each of the libraries will keep contact information for the other library administrators and agree to contact them as soon as possible in the event of a disaster in order to put disaster response plans into action.

Library: _____

Administrator: _____

Signature: _____

Phone (home): _____

Phone (cell): _____

E-mail: _____

Alternate e-mail: _____

require the disaster response team and additional staff to deal with containment and recovery. The best way to deal with this type of disaster is to close the building until everything is under control. If possible, provide reference services from remote locations and alternative sites. Service will definitely be affected and may require relocating the most severely damaged departments. The disaster response team needs to consider emotional issues because whole portions of the collection may be damaged or destroyed. In this case, it might be useful to ask for outside assistance, such as a consultant, for one or two days to help assess the damage, make decisions about recovery and vendor selection, and act with the disaster response team leader as liaison between staff, administration, and the outside vendors. The consultant can provide additional or specialized training and education to the rest of the staff if necessary.

In a wide-area disaster, the infrastructure of the institution or the city is affected. Ask for outside assistance immediately, preferably from outside the affected area. Contact vendors of services from outside the affected area. Outside assistance is imperative in this case because their employees are not emotionally tied to the collection or institution; their families and homes were not damaged; and they should be able to draw supplies and services from far outside the affected area.

A wide-area disaster may require waiting to activate the response plan until the basic infrastructure is in place. However, evidence of a written response plan could hasten permission to enter the building to begin recovery of affected and damaged collections, especially if no water or power is needed. At the very least you want to secure the site from looters and board up the windows, doors, and roofs. Remove standing water and try to stabilize the environment if possible, if you have electricity or generators. Consider two goals: protecting the integrity of the collection from theft and damage and stabilizing the environment to prevent excessive water damage and mold growth. As we learned after Hurricane Katrina in 2005, flooding rivers in Iowa in 2009, and the earthquake in Haiti in 2010, it can be months before the area is safe to enter and major cleanup can occur. Operate from remote locations and restore services as quickly as possible while your buildings are inaccessible. In a wide-area disaster, your institution will activate its continuous operations plan to provide service and income. Find out where your library, archives, or museum fits within the priorities of the institution's continuous operations plan.

Coordination of recovery during a wide-area disaster is more difficult than during the other types of disasters because work must be done within the constraints of a compromised infrastructure and a heavy demand upon resources in the immediate and surrounding communities. There may be a shortage of trucks, storage space, supplies, temporary help, and temporary working space. Select at least one of each type of contractual service from outside the immediate geographical area of the institution. Remember that cellular phones will be heavily relied upon during wide-area disasters, causing delays in communication. Initial reports of the earthquake in Haiti were placed on Facebook and Twitter. Some institutions even created a wiki to keep staff informed of progress during a disaster. Consider how your institution will communicate during a disaster when bandwidth and communications and radio wavelengths are reserved for emergency management and public safety officers. Ask the institution's emergency management/public safety officers for advice concerning a method of communication during a disaster. Remember that most of the time, even during a disaster, land phone lines work if they aren't overloaded.

A large-scale disaster could be long-term and just as devastating as a wide-area disaster if caused by an outage of power or phones. If the institution is small or provides time-critical services, this type of outage could destroy your financial base. This is doubly true if your service providers are local businesses with few resources. Consider the option of working from a remote location. Disasters caused by power and telecommunications outages can be devastating because libraries, archives, and museums are even more dependent upon technology to provide even the most basic of services. A backup power and telecommunications system is especially important for access to computer and automated services.

The aftermath of Hurricane Katrina is a great lesson for all cultural institutions. It took more than a year for some libraries, archives, historical societies, and museums to resume normal operations. We have to plan for help from the outside and to work from alternative locations for an extended period of time. The previous editions of this book included lessons learned after the bombing in Oklahoma City. Those lessons applied to cultural institutions and businesses after the attacks on New York City and the Pentagon on September 11, 2001. The devastation of cultural institutions in communities in Mississippi, Alabama, and Louisiana after

Hurricanes Katrina and Rita, to Florida after Hurricane Wilma, and the loss of buildings and collections after the earthquakes in Chile and Haiti in 2010 and Japan in 2011 are all lessons to learn from, particularly as they pertain to loss of infrastructure and community support in a wide-area disaster. Cultural institutions must plan to work from remote locations and alternative sites in the community. To be included in emergency management plans, we have to be part of the community and be considered integral to the recovery of social and communal services.

## Planning for Damage to Computers and Data

The focus of this publication is planning for disasters caused by water and fire, not computer crashes. However, with the prevalence of computers in almost every facet of library and archival services, for public use and behind-the-scenes operations, it is necessary to plan for the loss of computer access.

There are usually two or three types of computer services in libraries, historical societies, and archives:

■ Public catalogs and circulation systems, and Internet resources

■ LANs and networked public access to locally owned and maintained databases, and access to digital collections through local and regional consortia

■ Internal resources, electronic files and databases both networked and stand-alone, including computers used in administrative and fiscal departments

Most large institutions have both an information technology department for computers institution-wide and a staff member in the library/archives responsible for the computers in the building. The internal staff member usually deals with computers running the OPAC, circulation system, cataloging functions, and other data services. This includes computers and peripherals for patrons and staff members. Departmental IT staff members also provide support and basic training for staff and administrators. Institution-wide computer services departments traditionally provide support for all personnel and manage and maintain servers and networks. They are usually responsible for institution-wide backup of servers, systems, and other computer

operations including e-mail, remote access, and restoration of service after any type of outage. During a large-scale or wide-area disaster, the institution's computer services staff members may be directed toward restoring service for everyone. It is essential that departmental IT staff have the skills to restore local computer operations and be aware of priorities and schedules in the institution's disaster response or contingency/continuous operations plan. Knowing where the library, archives, or museum fits into the institution's plan will help you design your own policies and priorities.

In the planning phase, just as you established priorities for recovery of print and nonpaper collections, it is important to decide which computer services and systems to restore first. Use mission statements and collection development policies to guide decisions. In the case of computers, three types of disasters could occur: fire and water damage, power outages, and telecommunications (including Internet and network) outages. Work on this part of your plan with a liaison from the local IT department and design your responses and priorities accordingly.

Look at the services the library/archives provides via computers and the Internet. Discuss how the institution will function without these services and for how long. Is the institution so dependent upon computer services that operation from an alternative location or remote access is essential? This is true of corporate and special libraries. As bricks-and-mortar libraries, archives, and museums are increasingly dependent upon computers and electronic resources, alternative operation locations are key to quick resumption of service.

*Primary recovery:* public catalogs and circulation systems, and Internet resources, including the local website. Determine how long the library/archives can function before lack of an automated circulation system will cripple public services. How far behind can your institution be? Is there a portable, battery-operated, or smaller backup system that can be utilized in the meantime? And for how long?

■ In terms of the public catalog, is there another way to access the institution's holdings, such as a printed subject-access catalog with associated call numbers? Is the staff able to use that method of access effectively enough to have the building open when the computers are down for a long period of time? If the answer to the last question is indefinitely and the circulation functions are separate from the catalog, the OPAC does not belong in the primary recovery category but in the second or third category. The OPAC should then come up at the same time as cataloging.

■ Determine what lack of access to the website and its associated services means to the library and its patrons. Can the students and faculty access the digital collections of texts and journals through another computer system or are the OPAC and website interdependent? If the website is integrated into the OPAC or the circulation system, then it needs to come up at the same time. If catalog and circulation systems are not integrated with the website, then the website can wait and be categorized as a secondary priority. Of course, if the website is housed on a separate system, which may be preferable, then the plan should be modified accordingly.

*Secondary recovery:* LANs and networked public access to locally owned and maintained databases, and access to digital collections through local and regional consortia. Discuss how the library/archives can provide reference and research services without local electronic and digital resources. What about remote access? Is the library/archives willing to offer remote access or remote authentication to patrons? If electronic and digital services provide full-text access to journals not held by the institution, are there provisions to offer document delivery? At what cost, and who pays the cost? Is this an alternative if the periodical collection is damaged? Some of these questions about periodicals should be answered when prioritizing their physical recovery.

*Tertiary recovery:* internal resources, electronic files and databases both networked and stand-alone. Include computers used in administrative and fiscal departments. Where do you rank fiscal and payroll services in the prioritization for recovery of computer operations? If payroll and fiscal services are contracted out, does that company have a backup or disaster response plan? If payroll is internal, how will the institution pay staff while the fiscal computer system is down? Where are the backup files and how often do you back them up? Update the business inter-ruption or extra expense rider of your insurance policy regularly with input from payroll. Don't forget about administrative services and human resources. Their computers and data files may contain personnel records, policies, and other documents not available through the institution's intranet. If you don't back up the data and files locally, then place password-protected files on a secure server. Of course personal files and reports should be stored on networked servers. If the information or data are proprietary, then use secure passwords. As a rule, if data are stored on local drives, then back up the files regularly onto remote or removable data storage devices. If the local drives are damaged, then it may be impossible to recover the data.

What other services are available online or via computers? How long can the institution do without them? What are your options? Determine which of these services fits into what recovery category. Can your patrons access local databases and resources using remote authentication? If there is an outage, are these resources maintained locally or on a remote server? Does a power outage affect all digital and electronic resources or just those housed in your building?

During a disaster is not the time to find out that all your electronic and digital resources are inaccessible from a remote location. Nor is it the time to build a new system. Work together with the IT and computer services department to test your databases from remote locations and using remote authentication. Write down the procedures in simple, easy-to-follow steps.

After determining the order to restore computer-based services, the next step is to create a list of the types and locations of hardware and software in the building. This will make it easier to identify the damaged and lost items for recovery or replacement.

Inventory each department, system, or floor, depending upon how the equipment and software is distributed. Note if the software is on a LAN. What is the serial number? Is there a licensing agreement? Which version or update are you using? Do the same thing for hardware, noting the configuration of the peripherals. Put together simple instructions for rebooting the system and loading data from backup tapes. This information will be necessary for replacing the lost and damaged computer equipment and software. The insurance company will want a list of the damaged items.

In terms of software, unlike publishers and book jobbers who may have a plan to lower prices or lease books in the event of a disaster, software companies may require the purchase of new software and licenses. If this is the case, will your data run on updated versions of the software? The rule of thumb is that after three software generations, you may not be able to convert forward. You can almost never read backward; that is, if you have data in version 4 and you are using version 6 or 7 it is readable. But if you save the data with version 7, you will probably not be able to read it with version 4. Backward compatibility has improved over the years, but not every program can do this.[2] It is very important that you continue to update the software that is in storage and used for backups so all data can be read.

Remember that both the hardware and software can be recovered if water-damaged. It is lack of access to the information that compounds the crisis.

## Prioritizing Restoration of Computer Services

The increased dependence of libraries and archives on computers, data, databases, telecommunications, websites, e-mail, data-sharing services, and other technological advances requires increased diligence in disaster response and contingency plans. This part of the plan should both stand alone and be integrated into the plan for the library/archives.

During the planning and prevention stage, determine where in the list of priorities computer and information technology functions fall. The most important functions need to be back up and running right away. Statistics show that for every hour of lost data it will take a day to re-input it; and for every day lost, a week, during the course of a normal workweek.

For most libraries, the most important computer function to restore first is the circulation system. This way books can be checked out and returned. Just think about how many books come back in the course of a normal workday. How much time will it take for you to check them all in? You will also need to decide what your policy will be for circulating materials without the computers. Do you write down all the bar code numbers by hand? How long will that take to input when power is restored? Will you use the same manual system to inventory remaining collections after a disaster? Consider some type of handheld bar code or inventory device that runs on batteries. Determine how you will load those data into the circulation system to update the inventory when power is restored or you are operating from a remote location.

The second priority for getting computers up is probably the catalog so that reference and research functions can be restored. It will be important to determine how the website for the library and its online catalog are integrated with the catalog used by staff. If they are one and the same, how long can the website be down before you lose patrons?

During the planning phase, another important question is who hosts the website and electronic resources for your library. Is it in the same physical location as the main library or is it someplace separate? If the first, then how will IT maintain the website and its functions when access to the building is restricted? If the website is hosted on another computer or in another location, then determine what type of disaster response/contingency plan they have.

Next, a solid review and test of the daily backup procedures is very important. More than one person should know how to back up the information, databases, and websites. All backup data must be stored off-site, whether in the trunk of your car, your house, or a data vault, or all three. Clear, simple instructions should be posted so that anyone could back up and take down the system in an emergency. Make certain that the UPS (universal power supply) is rated to last as long as the shutdown procedure takes.

Part of planning is testing to make certain that people know what to do in an emergency. Thus it is important to test the backup tapes or data files to make certain they work. It is also important to test how long various restoration and remounting procedures take, and that more than one person knows how to perform partial and full restoration of software and hardware. Make certain the instructions for this procedure are clear and simple.

Test the full restoration of your system, which should include the operating system, the software, and the data. Know the hardware configurations and requirements as well as the software systems necessary to rebuild the system. This is incredibly important if your library is using obsolete or proprietary software and hardware. Make certain you have current copies of all changes to software and hardware configurations stored with the backup data.

It is essential that two or more people be familiar with your hardware and software needs. Undoubtedly one of them will be on vacation when the crisis occurs.

When planning and practicing your plan for restoration of computer functions in the library, review the frequency of backups, where they are stored, how long it takes to get the backup tapes to whatever location you are at, and how many hours a full restoration of systems will take. (Reloading all your software on a personal computer can take more than four hours.) Be certain to document all this in the appendix of your plan. Some IT departments keep images or copies of software that are standardized for an institution or division. In this case, it may be simple to place the institution's supported software on new and recertified computers. Individuals who use specialized or proprietary software programs still need to back up their files and data onto networked servers. While designing this part of the plan, ask all staff members to create a list of any software they downloaded or own themselves and use regularly. Individuals should store these lists on their server space or in a remote location. Emphasize that they are responsible for backing up any software not supported by the institution.

During the response and recovery phase of your disaster, you will be assessing damage to hardware and software. Therefore maintain lists of hardware, software, and peripherals for each department, floor, and building. During the assessment phase, document which pieces of hardware are scheduled for cleaning and recertification. Burned and melted hardware need to be replaced. A careful review of the computer rider in your insurance policy during the planning phase will provide monetary guidelines for operating servers at a temporary or remote location. Depending upon how badly the building that houses the computer systems is damaged, you may need to find an alternative location to operate all IT services. This is the location where hardware and software will be set up. Don't forget to tell the company that stores your backup tapes and files where you are located and how to access the building. At the same time, you may need to arrange for telecommunications and Internet access from the computers to the library or your remote server.

The IT department will need to retrieve the backup tapes or data and determine where they will be operating from. It may be easiest to operate from a remote location temporarily, to be out of the way of the disaster response companies that are cleaning, deodorizing, and restoring the library.

There are computer disaster response companies that provide technical support and temporary locations for restoring software and data. These locations are called hot sites and require an annual contract. Usually large computer services operations contract with hot sites, which also provide computers configured to your needs and space to work. Computer riders usually pay for two to three months in a hot site, but check with your insurance company before assuming that's what the rider covers. Computer disaster response companies also offer cold sites and remote sites. The former are spaces in their facilities that are wired for electricity, telecommunications, and Internet access but have no equipment so you have to supply your own. The latter are usually trailers, again wired with electricity, telecommunications, and Internet access that can be brought to your location. You need to provide the computer equipment with this option. Backup sites for computers are costly and require multiyear contracts and regular testing. Before you decide to purchase a contract, discuss these options with the institution's computer services department and your insurance company representative.

Testing and preparation are the key to successful recovery of data and restoration of computer systems. The recovery phase is not the time to purchase new software and install it only to find out that it doesn't work with the data. Planning ahead makes all the difference, especially as your plan pertains to computers, hardware, software, and electronic resources.

As the library comes back to some sense of normalcy, the IT department will reintegrate the computer functions. After the crisis is over, evaluate what changes need to be made in terms of procedures, hardware and software, and priorities.

## Insurance

Reviewing the insurance policy enables the institution to respond quickly, thereby limiting the damage to the collections. There are some important things to keep in mind about insurance policies. When a disaster occurs and there is enough damage to warrant calling the insurance company, let them know what happened. You do not have to wait for an adjuster to arrive to either activate the plan or begin to recover the collections. Talk with the adjuster or claims representative, provide information about the type and scope of the disaster, and ask what documentation they require as you begin response and recovery. Document the damage with photographs or video. Create a checklist of problems that reflects your assessment of the damage before starting any recovery efforts. After reviewing the insurance policy, you will know how much your deductible is (that is, how much the institution pays out of contingency funds before the insurance kicks in). Insurance is complicated and convoluted. Be certain to read all the small print and ask questions about valuation, replacement, inventory, and any other term you do not understand. Make certain your collections are adequately insured.

Today, library, archives, museum, and historical society collections are often covered by institutional or even state-wide insurance policies. These blanket policies need to adequately cover the collections, resources, and special equipment. The director or administrative designee should be part of the overall discussion with the risk manager about insurance policies and coverage. Make certain the director and the disaster response team members understand the aspects of the insurance policy that cover library, archives, museum, and historical society collections.

Libraries, archives, and historical societies purchase many different types of insurance coverage and have internal funding constraints. Many institutions are insured, but it is not uncommon for the policies to have a large deductible. The smaller the institution, the more likely it is to have insurance with a manageable deductible. Individual items may be underinsured and undervalued, so you want to make certain you have an idea what it would cost to replace items and insure for that amount. Insurance for the structure may be adequate or not, depending upon the age of the building and the financial status of the institution. Insurance riders for "recovery services" and business interruption may be present; if so, there is a ceiling on the recovery amount after the deductible. The library should create a contingency fund that covers the deductible. Find out if the signature of the financial officer for the entire institution is needed before expenditures are permitted. If the job needs to go out for bid, hope that there is an emergency provision at your institution for fast bids and preliminary allocation of funds. It is even more important to ask about purchasing protocols when continuous operations plans are activated. Contact the facilities maintenance department and find out what is covered under their contingency funds for repairs, outside services, and general consulting.

It is not unusual for public institutions, those funded by state, city, county, and federal agencies, to be self-insured. This means that the institution must pay from its own funds. Some public institutions may be covered under the county or city insurance policy. If the institution is self-insured, funds may need to be legislated to be able to afford recovery from a large-scale or wide-area disaster. That means a bill would have to be drawn up and voted upon for allocation of state, county, or city funds unless there is an emergency executive order for release of funds or an official emergency is declared. If the latter is the case, the Federal Emergency Management Agency (FEMA) comes into play (state or federal). The institution usually has to lay out the funds, or at least contract the work, and then be reimbursed by FEMA. Corporate libraries and information and records centers are usually insured under the corporation's insurance policy.

## Aspects of an Insurance Policy

### Building or Structure

It is essential to have insurance that covers the loss of a building or structure so that the building can be reconstructed after a fire or total disaster. If the building is not a total loss, the insurance should pay for the drying and reconstruction of walls, floors, ceilings, and the mechanical equipment in the building.

If the business, library, or information center is located in rented space, the insurance policy should cover recovery, cleaning, and reconstruction of the area. Do not assume that the building owner's insurance will cover the damage within rented space. In fact, if the damage is the result of negligence on the part of the renter, such as broken water pipes from turning the heat too low, the renter may be responsible for all the damage.

If the property is jointly owned or owned by a government agency, determine ahead of time which organization's insurance policy pays for damage and loss.

Make certain that the insurance is adequate to cover potential hazards. If the building is in an active earthquake or flood zone, determine if the insurance will cover these potential hazards. If not, arrange for adequate coverage. This is particularly important if the building is located in a 100-year flood zone. In the past few years, there have even been floods in 500-year flood zones. Ask your insurance agent about the availability of flood insurance. If it exists for your location, then make certain your building, contents, and collections are adequately insured for flooding from natural causes, and water from below.

With the increase in the number of claims for mold damage and removal or remediation, insurance companies rarely cover this loss. Thus it is essential to (1) make certain that the causes of mold, that is, water and high humidity, are removed to prevent mold growth in the first place, and (2) that you review the amendments to your insurance policies and understand what is covered and what is not. If mold damage has been excluded from your policy, discuss this issue with your insurance agent, facilities maintenance department, and the disaster response team to forestall mold growth during and after a disaster.

## Contents

Insurance policies consider contents to be everything in a building or space that is not records, files, papers, and documents. The policy usually covers equipment, furniture, shelving, carpets, curtains, and everything else of this nature. As the institution or each department adds staff and uses more space, make certain the insurance policy keeps pace.

The insurance policy should cover the replacement value of the contents. In this way, the items could be replaced if irreparably damaged or dried and cleaned if they sustain minimal damage.

## Valuable Papers

Every business, library, archives, museum, historical society, and information center should have a rider for valuable papers. This rider covers the damage or loss of documents, archives, books, art, paper records, journals, microfilm and microfiche, books, optical discs, and so forth. In short, it covers all the items that make up a library. At some point in the past, an inventory with item values was taken, and insurance was based upon that replacement cost. If the inventory is outdated, the institution is underinsured for such a loss, so make certain your inventory is up to date and replacement costs are adjusted accordingly. It is important to look at the different caps in the insurance policy annually to make certain the library collection is adequately covered. Evaluate the policy at least every three years to adjust for inflation and the increase in size of the collection. The insurance policy should cover the replacement cost of your collection no matter what the format.

If the library or archives contains a rare book room or special collections, you might consider a separate valuable papers rider for these items. Determine the average price for replaceable books in the rare book or special collections room. That should be the replacement cost, or "agreed amount," such as $400 to $500 per volume. For a unique or valuable rare book collection, discuss how the valuable papers rider covers conservation costs, including drying, rebinding, and other conservation work. Any item appraised over $10,000 should be listed separately on your insurance rider. You might need to have this collection appraised. Contact local rare book dealers and conservators for recommendations and referrals to qualified appraisers. Make certain that blanket insurance policies cover rare and expensive items individually or on appropriate riders.

An inventory of the titles may be requested to satisfy the insurance adjuster of the loss. Provide the titles or a count of the number of books and a range of costs for replacing the collection. Always include the cost of processing and cataloging materials in the replacement cost.

On the business side of the library, valuable papers include articles of incorporation, stocks and certificates, minutes, leases, and other legal papers that are essential to continue in business. To prevent loss, originals should be stored off-site in a safe-deposit box.

If you have a total loss, then you want to be able to rebuild your library and its collections to modern standards. Discuss with the insurance agent and adjuster what "replacement cost" means to them. When you replace your collections, you want to replace with "like kind," not items as they existed before the disaster. In other words, if you have a huge LP or video collection, you want to replace with the newest formats to take advantage of the newest technology. Continuing this scenario, unless your institution collects LPs of pre-1990 sound recordings and is known for this, you probably want to replace your collection with CDs or digital recordings if the original items cannot be dried and cleaned. In addition, you should be able to replace books with new editions and similar titles, not be locked into replacing your collection with specific items on the inventory. Just remember, if the items are water-damaged but recoverable, you want the insurance to pay for recovering collections in their original formats. You don't get to purchase a new collection just because it is wet. In fact, if a part of the collection is not damaged, you don't get to replace it just because there was a fire or flood.

### Computers

The computer rider covers the cost of replacing any item that involves computers and data. It usually covers renting space in a hot or cold site. Computer riders assume that you back up data appropriately and often and that you can get the data operational at the alternative site. The insurance policy usually will not cover reconstructing lost data. The policy could cover the "recovery" of the physical objects, such as disk drives and removable data storage devices.

Computer riders cover drying, cleaning, and reconditioning or recertifying the computer equipment. Insurance companies usually insist on recovery and recertification of more expensive computer equipment. Just because hardware is wet doesn't mean it is destroyed.

This rider of the insurance policy should include "functional replacement." This is the type of replacement policy you want for computer equipment and peripherals. It provides funds to purchase newer equipment that performs the same functions as older, outdated models.

Update the computer rider regularly to include new equipment and configurations so the insurance policy adequately covers replacement.[3] Note the monetary and time limitations for recovering full computer operations in the insurance policy. Computer riders usually cover expenses and rental for two to three months.

### Business Interruption or Extra Expense Insurance Rider

This rider covers renting equipment, space, furnishings, and phones; hiring temporary employees; and paying unemployment insurance, if needed. Business interruption or extra expense insurance should cover relocation and technology needs while in an alternative location. It includes covering payroll and accounts receivable/payable, up to a point. Business interruption insurance usually covers the reconstruction of paper documents and files but not computer files. There are many limits to business interruption insurance, including the duration of displacement and the amount of expenses that will be covered per month. The maximum duration is usually twelve months, but this varies depending upon the policy and projected needs.

Insurance for computer operations and for business interruption is often predicated upon a risk analysis. Risk managers evaluate existing and projected fiscal needs and types of risks to data and operations, among other things. Insurance companies will require a risk analysis prior to writing a rider for business interruption.

If your institution has a continuous operations plan in place, they analyzed risk to the organization as a whole. Ask what types of risks were identified that could affect the restoration of library and archival services. Address those issues during the planning and prevention phase.

### Short-Term Insurance Policies

In addition to insurance and riders for your permanent collections, you may need coverage for exhibits, transportation, and special events. Discuss these events and costs with your insurance provider, risk manager, and financial officer. Make certain that the insurance adequately covers damage or loss of items whether they are at your institution, on the road, at a conservator's facility, or on exhibition somewhere else. In the same vein, you'll want to note how the insurance policy covers items from other institutions when on exhibit at your library, archives, historical society, or museum. Assign monetary values to these items so that if they are damaged, the same or similar items could be purchased to replace them, or they can be sent to a conservator for repairs.

## *Insurance Terminology*

- Replacement cost—with like kind at current cost
- Actual cash value—the value of the item today. The amount is usually less than what it costs to replace an item or the fair market price.
- Functional replacement cost—with like kind to perform same functions
- Business interruption or extra expense insurance rider—pays costs to temporarily relocate, pays for lost income, has monetary limits and time constraints
- Average replacement cost—across-the-board average purchase price for each category of materials
- Coinsurance—(protects the insurance carrier) limits the reimbursement after a disaster. It is a cap on expenditures by the insurance company. Note that an insurance underwriter may cover some of the deductible, and this policy has an upper limit where the major insurance carrier picks up coverage.

## *Contingency Funds*

In addition to insurance, every library and information center should have a contingency fund to cover unexpected, uncovered expenses and the insurance deductible.

The amount of money each institution sets aside to deal with a disaster depends upon available capital, projected risk, and the ability of the institution, library, archives, or historical society to raise funds in a short period of time. Money might be put aside to cover initial expenses until the insurance kicks in.

In the case of a national, state, or countywide "declared disaster," FEMA will probably require that you pay first and get reimbursed second. Try to submit the claim as a group, agency, government, or area. This will speed the reimbursement process. Based on experiences during Hurricane Katrina in 2005 and flooding in Iowa and North Dakota, you could wait months for reimbursement. Don't get caught waiting for someone else to bail you out. Put the funds aside for that rainy day, because sooner or later it will arrive.

### Replacement Costs

Work with your acquisitions and cataloging department to determine ahead of time replacement costs with processing. Everything goes up in price so adjust prices as needed. Don't forget to include costs for conducting an inventory of damaged and remaining items, evaluating the remaining materials based upon the collection development policy, acquiring new materials, cataloging and processing replacement items, and, of course, shelving.

Approximate costs, including processing, follow:

- Books: replacing books costs $30–$40 per volume of fiction; $70–$175 for nonfiction; and $300 and up for reference tools.
- Audiobook CDs: abridged $25–$30 each, unabridged $50–$150 each.
- Videos and DVDs: $35–$45 for popular fiction, $90 and up for nonfiction and educational series.
- Microfilm and microfiche: commercially produced film costs $100–$150 per roll; independently produced microfilm is not expensive to duplicate ($10–$25 per roll) if the master print positives or negatives are stored in a safe, off-site location.
- Software: stand-alone products vary in price from $100 to thousands of dollars, while products for LANs and networked systems depend upon site licensing fees.
- For special collections, rare books, and archives, determining the replacement costs is a time-consuming task. You could have the collection appraised for total value. Then take a price to replace some of the replaceable items, say $400–$500 each. Some books will cost less, some more to replace. But the sum total, if the entire collection were destroyed, will provide enough funds to begin building the collection again.

Modify these costs to match those of your institution.

Average costs to dry a book using dehumidification or vacuum freeze-drying are $65 per cubic foot or $5–$10 per volume. Treatment is cost-effective even if the materials need to be bound afterward because of loss of structural integrity.[4] If you are having the dried volumes bound, discuss this with your binder and ask about special prices to keep the costs under control.

## Communications

Communications is one of the aspects of disaster response that is often forgotten in the planning phase. Three types of communications activities are essential for an effective response and recovery. They include communications

1. With employees, and in a large institution, with other staff and departments
2. With suppliers and customers, patrons, or clients
3. With the media and general public.

Before the crisis arises, discuss with the public information or communications officer how the library/archives will inform nonstaff of the disaster. Decide who will handle the different aspects of communication. The ideal situation is to have the communications officer handle it all, or at least the outside communications, but part of the responsibility will undoubtedly fall upon the disaster response team leader or the director of the library, archives, museum, or historical society.

Create a basic press release for the public and a script for informing staff of where to go and who will be needed when (see figure 4.3).

Send this basic press release along with contact information to local and regional radio and TV stations and newspapers. Forward the same information to local libraries and archives, the regional library consortium, and state library. Next, send updated contact and shipping information to suppliers and vendors, insurance carriers, the post office, and creditors. Update your website and any other web presences, such as Facebook and

**FIGURE 4.3**  Sample press release
for the public and media

The _____ Library is temporarily closed due to _____

_____ damage. Materials can be returned to the _____

_____ branch.

[or]

Please hold all materials from the library/archives. Fines will be suspended during the period the institution
is closed.

[or]

The _____ Library is operating out of a temporary location

due to fire and water damage to the building. Our temporay location is _____

_____.

The new phone number is _____.

Our hours are _____.

Twitter, even a wiki or blog, with information about the library/archives. It is important to share this information with as many people and organizations as possible to keep them aware of the status of your institution. In the case of disasters, out of sight means out of mind and can mean a dramatic loss of income.

## Communication with the Staff

Several decisions must be made, usually during the initial response phase, concerning staff communication. If it is a large disaster, are all the staff needed to deal with the disaster or just the disaster response team members? Do you want the staff there in shifts? Where should they report when they arrive at the "office" and to whom? You cannot always make these decisions ahead of time, because every disaster varies. You can create basic guidelines to follow.

When the disaster occurs, the disaster response team along with the director must make these decisions during the assessment phase of disaster response. At the same time, you need to inform security and facilities about decisions to open or close buildings and the type of assistance needed from their staff members. Provide the security and safety office with a list of authorized library staff members, including the disaster response team, who will be working in the damaged and closed areas of the building. Security and safety personnel should check on the safety of staff members working in empty buildings. For their own personal safety, no staff member should ever be in a building alone.

The external meeting location and command center should be designated or identified ahead of time and everyone in the library or archives must know how to get there. In the case of a small library or an information center within a corporation, consider a secondary location where some staff members can report. In the plan, list the phone number of the person to call who will tell staff where to report.

Employees of the institution should be notified how to contact the library or archives. Will the institution or certain departments be closed or immediately reopen at the secondary location? Where are they located? What are the temporary hours? What are the new phone and fax numbers and e-mail address? Where do staff go for information when the library is closed?

In many instances, the information sent to staff in the immediate aftermath of a disaster can follow the same guidelines as those for inclement weather. Send out information via your institution's emergency communications system, through a public service announcement over the radio and television, or through e-mail. Department heads or their designees should call all department members to alert them as to closure of the library, alternative places to report, or notice to remain at home until further notice.

It is important to maintain good communications within the organization and keep the administration apprised of all unusual expenses, circumstances, and problems that arise. Designate a liaison from the disaster response team or the administrative professionals to communicate with the institution's administrative staff, preferably the director of the library or archives.

## Communication with Suppliers and Customers

Maintaining contact with those who supply services, products, and equipment is crucial. They must know where to send products, how to communicate with you, and who is authorized to make emergency purchases and issue purchase orders.

For online and information services, new account numbers may be necessary. Supply temporary phone numbers and an address for billing and sending materials. Set up new passwords and security codes. You may need temporary IP addresses or remote authentication software. Discuss these issues with your IT or computer services department. In some cases, you may need to lease computer and office equipment for your temporary location if the building is inaccessible. Contact that vendor as soon as you decide to use your temporary location.

Customers need to be reassured that you will open and when. If there is a temporary location, let customers know where it is and what the hours are. Again, you need to post this information on your website, on the building, and in other institutions that would refer patrons to your library. Update hours, locations, and phone numbers as soon as you decide to activate the temporary location.

## Communication with the Media and the General Public

In a crisis, communications is key for a successful recovery. To that end, it is important to have only one spokesperson for the institution. With the approval of the administration, this person should discuss what occurred. Indicate when the operation will be back up and running; what services are available; where the library, archives, or historical society is temporarily located; and what hours it is open. Keep the message simple, positive, and supportive.

Provide information about the disaster to the media through your spokesperson. This will enable the institution to get publicity about the disaster, the collections, and services and to solicit assistance and donations.

Now is the time to ask for donations of money to assist in the recovery of the building and its collections. As soon as the next disaster hits the news, yours will languish and be forgotten. It is essential for nonprofit and cultural institutions to ask for assistance and funds from community members, local organizations, and your patrons immediately. Fund-raising campaigns are the most effective during the first six months after the disaster. If you need to rebuild the collection or the building, start the fund-raising and development campaign immediately.

## Communications When the Disaster Is Over

When the disaster is over, write articles and give interviews to let the institution, libraries, and archives, as well as the general community, know what happened during your crisis. If you wish donations of services and materials, specify what you want and in what format. For instance, if the library lost a large number of books and reference materials to a fire or flood, don't just ask for books. Request the titles or topics needed. Specify if you wish them to be cataloged and how.

If you are part of a consortium, enlist the organization's assistance with coordinating the acceptance of donations of services and materials. They can be a channel for communications and information. The consortium may have emergency response policies and services that your organization can take advantage of. If you are not a member of the local or regional consortium, ask the state library, archives, or historical society for assistance.

Don't be shy. Ask for help from friends, colleagues, and professionals in the area. The more people who know about the disaster, the more support you will receive, be it moral, emotional, physical, or financial.

## Phone and Internet Access

Just as communication with customers, suppliers, vendors, and staff is important, telecommunications is an integral part of the services provided by your institution. Without phones, fax machines, Internet access, and e-mail, outreach services and access to information deteriorate quickly. It is essential to be prepared for part or all of the telecommunications services to fail for some period of time during a disaster. In a disaster you will need phones that work without electricity. If your institution still has telephone landlines, you'll also need phones that don't run on electricity. Keep a few phones that can plug directly into the wall in the main disaster response kit.

■ Determine how long phone and Internet service will be out before declaring a disaster and activating the plan.

■ Make use of cellular phones and handheld radios. Set up a contingency contract with the local service. You might consider some prepaid calling cards for emergency long-distance calls.

■ Telephone service provided by Internet companies runs over cable lines and is considered VOIP or voice over Internet protocol. Unfortunately these services do not work when there is no electricity. If the electricity is out, then wireless and all Internet-dependent services will not work. Make certain you have an alternative method of communication. Place a phone that does not require electricity in your disaster response kit.

## Contacting Disaster Response Companies and Consultants

One of the aspects of disaster planning is to ask for assistance from knowledgeable consultants and outside contractors. Using the services of outsiders will relieve some of the stress from the disaster response team members. But you cannot just list contractors, consultants, and disaster response/drying companies in your plan; you should talk with them to find suitable contractors. Invite the ones you are interested in to visit the institution for a walk-through and discussion of their roles in potential disasters. In this way, they will become acquainted with the needs of your library/archives, know what they need to bring, and understand how to assist the disaster response team in responding to and recovering from the disaster.

Why use outsiders? After all, that is the job of the disaster response team, right? Well, if the disaster is small, then the disaster response team may be able to handle everything with the assistance of staff members and facilities maintenance personnel. However, if the disaster area covers a large portion of the building or has created secondary damage, it is essential to call in outside contractors to assist with recovery of collections and restoration of services. Use their labor and expertise for advice and recommendations in recovery and cleanup. Be certain to include the facilities maintenance department in these meetings so that (1) they will know what type of assistance is required during a disaster, and (2) they will be able to provide input in terms of selecting a contractor and assisting during the cleanup operation.

The following are some of the issues to discuss when you select and meet with outside contractors:

■ What types of services they can actually provide for your institution

■ How much of the work they do themselves and what types of work they contract out

■ How much experience they have with libraries and archives disasters. Ask for references and check them out.

■ How they ship, handle, and dry water-damaged materials

■ What techniques they use to remove soot, dirt, and mold from items

■ Costs for services and labor

■ Emergency contact numbers for after-hours disasters

■ Whether they have a "first-come, first served" policy or, if preapproved by the institution, you are the "first priority" during a wide-area disaster

■ What types of information they keep on hand about institutions that have listed them in disaster response plans

■ Whether they have specialists they can call in to treat unique and fragile items in the collection

Once you decide upon the contractor(s), write them into the response and recovery portions of the plan. Have an emergency purchase order issued or standing by, so that the initial amount of expenses is known and allocated. Preapproving the contractor as a vendor may save time. For insurance purposes and for dealing with the insurance adjuster, decide if you wish the vendor designated as a primary contractor(s).

Preselecting outside contractors decreases stress, worry, and physical labor. It eliminates the need for the disaster response team to find suitable and qualified vendors while dealing with all the other issues and crises in the preliminary response phase.

Provide the contractor with a copy of your disaster response plan so he or she can be ready to perform the required services with minimal lead time. Having a copy of your plan will allow the contractor to make a list of necessary equipment and arrange for staff and temporary help to get the job done quickly and correctly.

A side benefit of preapproving vendors is decreased stress on the facilities maintenance personnel. The facilities maintenance staff should know how to contact the vendor, what services are provided in-house, and what the contractor will provide. Assign a disaster response team or staff member as liaison to the contractor(s) and facilities maintenance department. This is particularly important if more than one building is involved in the disaster or if the disaster is widespread.

Two types of services can be contracted from the vendors of disaster response/drying services: cleanup and recovery.

Cleanup could be done by the facilities maintenance department itself or with the disaster response company as a subcontractor. These types of services fall under cleanup:

■ Removing water
■ Basic cleaning of the building, shelving, and furnishings
■ Removing debris, soot, dirt, and mold from surfaces

Recovery may be contracted out, especially if a large portion of the collection was damaged or if there is limited staff available. This is important if the library or archives has only a few staff members. These types of services fall under recovery:

■ Drying and cleaning contents
■ Drying and cleaning collections
■ Removing dry and undamaged collections to an environmentally controlled facility if necessary
■ Drying and cleaning (and recertifying) equipment, including office equipment and computers

Some disaster recovery companies provide building reconstruction services, replacing drywall, ceilings, flooring, and other structural components. If your institution is small, you might consider contracting these services also.

During the planning and prevention phase, review lease and maintenance agreements for office and computer equipment. Determine the scope of "recovery" the maintenance contract includes, acceptable dealers or vendors to perform this work, and a list of where to lease or rent the needed equipment while damaged or wet equipment is cleaned and recertified.

Other services might be contracted out:

■ Maintaining, cleaning, and calibrating the HVAC to balance the environment to where it was before the disaster
■ Restoring computer services, including OPAC, LAN, and internal (nonpublic) computers
■ Loading the backup databases, including the online catalog and such internal systems as payroll and financial information

## Training

The primary purpose of training is to know what to do and how to channel energies and adrenaline when the disaster strikes. The secondary purpose is to have a basic idea of what actions to accomplish first. Sometimes training is a matter of teaching how to pack wet books and files, handle wet materials, and prioritize which wet materials get packed first. It is important to emphasize during the training session that while recovering materials and packing them out for storage or freezing is not the time for weeding the collection. This is a time to rescue and stabilize as much of the collection as possible. Once materials are safely in storage or frozen, the staff in charge of collection development can make weeding decisions.

There are two views on training. The first is to teach just the disaster response team members who lead all the operations and train the others when the disaster strikes. Assign each disaster response team member a specific set of tasks or responsibilities. The need to train for specific tasks will definitely occur when the disaster response team works with volunteers. It is essential to review procedures and proper handling when temporary laborers are brought in by the institution or the disaster response company to perform much of the manual labor necessary to move books, pack boxes, and clean surfaces.

The second training method is to make the entire staff aware of the plan and basic response actions and then provide additional training for the disaster response team and interested staff members. The second method, although preferred by preservation librarians and consultants, is not always accomplished before a disaster strikes. One of the best reasons to teach staff members about the disaster response plan and basic response methods is so that minor leaks, isolated water damage, mold, and other "small" emergencies can be handled locally by department members, especially if the disaster response team is not available. Teaching all the staff, or key members in each department, is very important if collections are spread throughout a large building or many buildings.

Invite members of the facilities and building maintenance, security, and health and safety staff to participate in the disaster response training. These training exercises are opportunities to share expertise, build communication lines, and coordinate response efforts across department and administrative lines. Most important, they provide opportunities to share best practices and precautions when dealing with water-damaged and potentially contaminated materials.

When disaster strikes, no matter whether you train the entire staff or just the team, you still need to provide training and guidance. Don't just jump in and start packing. Take the time to assess the scope of the damage, determine what needs to be removed first, and then assign staff and workers specific tasks. Diagrams for simple procedures will ease the way to safe handling of water-damaged materials.

## Necessary Training

- Dangers from primary and secondary damage caused by water-borne bacteria, mold, and ozone
- Reaction to disasters. Never assume that the next person will deal with the problem or that it is "not your job."

- Contact information for the disaster response team, administrators, and director when the disaster occurs
- Emergency contact numbers in case a disaster occurs after regular working hours
- Locations for the basic disaster response supplies and their appropriate use
- Decisions and rationale for immediate response procedures, including evacuation of the building
- Prioritization decisions for damaged collections. Emphasize that changing the criteria during the response phase is not necessarily in the institution's best interest.

## Additional Training

- Handling and moving water-damaged materials
- Packing boxes for freezing and vacuum freeze-drying
- Labeling boxes so materials are returned to the appropriate institution and department
- Dealing with special collections and handling non-print formats such as photographs, audiovisual materials, and manuscripts. Discuss where the list is for specialists who can be called in to assist with their recovery.

Some hands-on disaster response training seminars involve teaching the use of fire extinguishers and fire hoses. This should be taught by professionals, either the fire department or a fire extinguisher or fire protection company. If your institution has a security department that handles small fires, ask them to provide a training session for the disaster response team members and other interested staff.

Fire extinguishers are not hard to use. Just set the canister upright on the floor, pull the pin or metal ring at the top of the handle, point the nozzle away from you, and squeeze the trigger handle. Make certain you do not touch the nozzle; the contents may be extremely cold and could freeze on contact! Fire extinguishers can be heavy to lift and operate. When in doubt, pull the fire alarm.

When should you use a fire extinguisher? On a small, self-contained fire only. Fire extinguishers have about 30 to 60 seconds worth of liquid. If the fire is larger than that or is spreading rapidly, walk quickly away from it and pull the fire alarm. Then leave the area and assemble staff in the designated location outside the building.

Disaster response team members should know where the fire extinguishers and hoses are, where the heat and smoke detectors ring, and what type of sprinkler system is in the building.

The more training, education, and awareness the staff and disaster response team members have, the more quickly and efficiently you will be able to respond to disasters and get them contained or at least organized for the recovery of the collection and services.

## How and Where to Get Training in Disaster Response

■ Read the multitude of books and articles available in libraries, archives, and computer and business literature.[5]

■ Attend seminars sponsored by local and regional consortia and at conferences.

■ Attend classes through the preservation departments in some universities or library science programs. Programs in continuing education in preservation are offered at Johns Hopkins, Pittsburgh University, University of Texas at Austin, Kent State University, and the University of Wisconsin at Madison and Milwaukee, to name a few.[6] Some universities, organizations, and government agencies offer courses and certification in emergency management and business continuity.[7]

■ Attend hands-on recovery classes that teach how to pack and handle water-damaged materials.

■ Ask preservation, disaster response, and security consultants. They often teach seminars in disaster response and planning for cultural institutions.

■ Conservation centers often sponsor specialized disaster response classes, especially about photographs, textiles, furniture, or works of art on canvas. If your institution has a large collection of any of these items, it would be worthwhile to either attend a seminar or have the names of specialized consultants who deal with these water-damaged items.

■ Government agencies and various library consortia offer training. A new series of training seminars offered through the American Institute for Conservation is FAIC Collections Emergency Response Training (AIC-CERT) program. This program is funded by a grant from the Institute of Museum and Library Services. These are workshops in emergency response for conservators, preservation administrators, and allied professionals.

Follow up the planning and training phases by practicing the response plan. Evaluate the plan based on problems that arise in procedures when you practice, and revise accordingly. Don't forget to distribute the revisions to all the disaster response team members and insert the revisions in all the printed plans.

Establish a regular revision and evaluation schedule and stick to it. Keep the printed plans updated.

While designing the response plan, it is important to consider who will help during the disaster with management, with contractors, and with the overall physical work of recovering from the damage and restoring operations. Larger institutions can and do reallocate staff, professional and paraprofessional, clerical and administrative, to assist with the physical cleanup and resumption of services. The reallocation of staff is contingent upon the size of the disaster and the areas or buildings affected. If there are unions at your institution, now is the time to talk with labor union representatives about disaster response and reallocation of personnel. These discussions may prevent grievances and complaints during a disaster and subsequent cleanup.

An integral part of planning is to determine where staff will work if their departments or buildings are damaged by a disaster. Do you send them to another building or branch or city? Do you move them to temporary quarters in another department? You can make general decisions during the planning phase that will guide both temporary decisions while in response mode, and semi-permanent decisions while in recovery mode.

What if you are a small institution with fewer than four staff members? How do you cope with coordinating response and performing standard reference and circulation services? These questions are even more important to ask if all your staff live outside the community where your library is located. Who will be your "first responders" making on-the-spot assessments, calling the team, and providing knowledgeable information to the public safety personnel?

At the beginning of the chapter, we discussed the creation of a disaster response team and their responsibilities within the plan. One of the criteria was to select team members who live within walking distance or within the community, and others who live far away. The reason was to have local team members who could walk to the institution in bad weather and assess damage, whereas other staff members who live far away might be less affected and distracted by a wide-area disaster because they live in a different community. Again this philosophy works well when there is a large staff. What about an institution where everyone lives more than twenty miles away? Who will be your first responders?

Here's where your networking and community relations come into play because no institution can do this alone. To respond and recover efficiently and effectively, everyone has to work as a team and trust the judgment of others to make informed decisions under tremendous stress. This is the rationale behind planning; otherwise you make decisions on the fly that may not be in the best interest of the collections and patrons.

Talk with librarians, archivists, historians, museum curators, and other professionals in the community about your disaster response plan. Ask them about their institution's disaster response plan. What are the resources and expertise in your community? Now is the time to discuss providing mutual support to one another during a disaster. This mutual support includes physical assistance with cleanup in the aftermath of the disaster, supervision of temporary workers who box and load books for freezing or relocation, a drop-off location for materials that are stored until the building is usable, and professional advice.

In a small community, this network is your lifeline for the survival of your institution. Think of other ways you can support one another during the response and recovery phase. Here are some other services you can extend to one another. Be a command center for the other institution, provide desks and working space for their staff members, and let their reference staff answer their patrons' questions. This is a fairly simple solution today, especially with the wide array of electronic resources available and remote authentication for access to proprietary networks and subscriptions.

Provide staff to assist with the response phase, supporting the first responders with local contacts and your professional network. If no one on your staff lives in the community, ask the local institutions for a local liaison who can go to the disaster site and provide professional guidance while the disaster response team travels from home. That local liaison should be familiar with the layout of your building and have a list of disaster response team members to contact.

Sounds radical? This is the basis for your community's emergency management team. They come together from broad backgrounds and with varied experience to work together to respond to emergencies. Why can't we? Gone are the days of responding to disasters in isolation. More important, gone are the days of planning for disasters alone.

Do we formalize these offers and agreements for mutual support and assistance during a disaster? It depends upon your institution and relationships with your colleagues and board of directors. In the end, some type of informal agreement is important and should be reviewed and discussed each time your revise and update your disaster response plan.

## NOTES

1. Reagan Moore et al., "Collection-Based Persistent Archives," available at www.dlib.org/dlib/march00/moore/03moore-pt1.html and www.dlib.org/dlib/april00/moore/04moore-pt2.html. See also Gregory Hunter, *Preserving Digital Information* (New York: Neal-Schuman, 2000).

2. Google Docs can read some older data files, but not all. If you think that the data will be stored for many years, create files in .txt or ASCII for long-term accessibility. Further discussion on this topic falls under data curation or long-term preservation of digital objects and is beyond the scope of this publication.

3. Use the checklists for hardware and software in appendix A to keep track of what each department has.

4. George Cunha, "Disaster Planning and a Guide to Recovery Resources," *Library Technology Reports* (September/October 1992): 542–43.

5. See the bibliography at the end of this book.

6. CoOL (Conservation OnLine) contains information about seminars, conferences, and classes in preservation and is available at http://cool.conservation-us.org. Information for subscribing to the Conservation Discussion List (ConsDist .Lst) and links to other preservation and conservation sites are available at CoOL.

7. Disaster Recovery Journal, www.drj.com, is a good place to look for disaster response classes and training, especially as it pertains to the business side of cultural institutions.

# Response and Recovery Procedures

## Basic Response Procedures

### *Fire*

- Pull the fire alarm.
- Call fire and police departments.
- Evacuate the building.
- Meet at the prearranged location.
- Activate the disaster response plan.
- Notify the insurance company.

### *Flood/Water*

- Get the water turned off.
- If flooding, evacuate the building.
- Activate the disaster response plan.
- Notify the insurance company.
- Call a disaster response/drying company to have the water removed.

### *Power Outage*

- Initiate controlled shutdown of the computer system.
- Notify the power company of the power outage.
- Initiate paper-based procedures.
- Assemble the disaster response team and decide whether to relocate reference services to an alternative location while the power is out.

■ Send a press release to the media with information about temporary location, hours, and emergency phone numbers, update website and any other social media sites where institution has a presence.

■ Send emergency closing information to staff members via e-mail, text, or blog.

## Telecommunications Outage

■ Locate or rent cellular phones.

■ Notify the phone company of the outage.

■ Send a press release to the media with information about temporary location, hours, and emergency phone numbers, update website and any other social media sites where institution has a presence.

■ Send emergency closing information to staff members via e-mail, text, or blog.

## Computer Crash

■ Contact the computer systems operator or information technology librarian or staff member.

■ Identify the cause of failure.

■ Notify the insurance company.

■ Arrange to replace damaged equipment.

■ Reload software and data.

## Computer Theft/Damage

■ Contact the computer systems operator or information technology specialist.

■ Contact the insurance company.

■ Locate hardware and software checklists.

■ Contact a computer rental company to deliver necessary equipment.

■ Load software and data.

## Building or Institution Inaccessible

■ Notify staff of alternative location.

■ Arrange for phone service and Internet access.

■ Contact a computer rental company to deliver necessary hardware and software.

■ Send a press release to the media with information about temporary location, hours, and emergency phone numbers; update website and any other social media sites where institution has a presence.

■ Send emergency closing information to staff members via e-mail, text, or blog.

# Packing Procedures for Books, Documents, Archives, and Office Files

## Removing Water-Damaged Books, Documents, Archives, and Office Files

■ Remove items lying on the floor first.

■ Remove items from shelves in order, starting at the top shelf, unless the bottom shelves are submerged or soaking wet.

■ Move materials to a packing area, and try to maintain the order of the items.

■ Pack items in ordinary boxes no larger than one cubic foot or in document storage boxes. Pack the boxes on a table or book truck. Do not jam materials into the boxes.

■ Pack books flat in boxes.

■ Count the number of items in the box as you work.

■ Label each box with the number of items, format or type, location, and box number (for example: 27 Books, Science Library, OSU, Box 36; or 125 Microfilms, Government Documents, U Mich., Box 105).

■ List each box on the inventory sheet.

■ Seal the boxes with tape and move them to a loading area.

■ Send one copy of the inventory with the boxes; keep one copy for the disaster response team and one for the insurance company.

## Wet Document Storage Boxes

■ Remove files.

■ Place dry materials only in new dry boxes.

- Pack wet materials vertically in dry document storage boxes or plastic crates.
- Label the boxes with contents information before shipping.

### *Wet Loose Documents or Manuscripts in Filing Cabinets*

If contents are filed vertically:

- Remove contents from drawers.
- If materials are soaked or in colored folders, wrap them in precut freezer paper, shiny side toward documents.
- If materials are wet in the filing cabinet drawers but not yet swollen, you could send files to freeze in the filing cabinet drawers. It is better to box to control loss.
- Place contents vertically in boxes or milk crates for transport.
- Label the boxes with contents information before shipping.
- List each box on the inventory sheet.
- Seal the boxes with tape and move them to a loading area.

Note: If filing cabinet drawers are stuck shut from the force of wet files and papers, use a crowbar to open them.

If contents are stored in flat file drawers:

- Use Mylar to remove (see the directions for handling large-format materials later in this section).
- Place wet documents on the shiny side of precut freezer paper.
- Pack documents flat in bread trays or on cardboard. Tape Mylar or cardboard on top of trays to prevent damage or loss.
- Label the trays with contents information before shipping.
- List each tray on the inventory sheet.
- Move them to a loading area.

Note: Materials will not look "pristine" when returned. They may be wrinkled and distorted if they were wrinkled before being frozen.

## Selecting a Drying Method— Dehumidification vs. Vacuum Freeze-Drying

Each drying job is slightly different. The following factors must be considered before selecting a drying method:

1. How long the items have been wet
2. How many items are wet
3. If they have monetary or legal value
4. If there is sensitive or confidential information on documents
5. Where you want the materials dried
6. Consider reformatting when dried

### *Factors and First Decisions*

#### How Long the Materials Have Been Wet and What Type They Are

If paper is wet for several days and begins to dry without any control, it can form a block of cellulose or the pages may stick together. Clay-coated, or shiny, paper is notorious for sticking together solidly within hours of getting wet. Plain paper can handle a few days of being submerged in water. Soaked paper that dries on its own can either dry in sheets and come apart, or it will form a solid block of cellulose and be useless.

If paper is slightly wet or the moisture content of the paper is just above 8 percent and there is not a lot of paper (less than 10 cubic feet), then dehumidification is the easiest but most time-consuming method for drying.

If paper is soaked, vacuum freeze-drying is most appropriate.

For clay-coated paper, vacuum freeze-drying is the best method to use, provided the paper is stabilized and frozen within six hours of exposure to water. There is only a 50 percent success rate in drying clay-coated paper, no matter what drying method is used or how quickly you freeze the items.

#### Estimate the Number of Items That Are Wet

If there are only several cartons or cubic feet of wet items, the method may not matter as much as if there are many rooms or thousands of cubic feet to dry. Most paper, whether bound into books and journals or loose, can be frozen. Do not freeze leather- or vellum-bound materials without consulting the preservation officer or a conservator.

Consider the following rules of thumb:

■ If there are more than ten cubic feet or document storage cartons, contract out the drying.

■ If there are more than 300 volumes, contract out the drying.

■ If there are fewer than these quantities and you have the space, you can dehumidify the room and provide air movement, or have the items freeze-dried. Remember, wet paper may wrinkle or cockle and distort bindings, if air dried.

Some institutions choose to replace small quantities of wet books. Again it depends upon your institution, what and how much is wet, and what your budgets are like. Make decisions after consulting your collection development policy.

When in doubt, freeze items as quickly as possible. This accomplishes two things: it buys time to make decisions and raise money and permits treatment in manageable batches. Freezing will forestall a mold infection in the books, on paper, and in the building. Unless the collection is contaminated with a hazardous waste, such as sewage, the frozen items do not pose a health threat. Ask the freezer/cold storage company to cold shrink-wrap the cartons onto skids, after labeling for easy identification. (Cold shrink-wrap is plastic that sticks together without heat. Skids are wooden pallets.)

Freezing quickly provides another benefit. The ice crystals that form are smaller and less likely to harm or deform the surface of items. The slower the freezing, the larger the ice crystals and the greater the chance for damage.

### Items with Monetary or Legal Value

For collections with monetary value, contact a conservator or conservation center and ask how the materials should be shipped to them.[1] Some conservation centers want the materials shipped wet if they can be treated immediately; other items may be frozen to permit time to treat. Inquire about leather and vellum before freezing these items.

Collections with legal value are often the permanent records of the organization or institution and may include the articles of incorporation (see appendix A.17). If these items are the originals, they will need to be dried and cleaned. Original versions of permanent, vital, and legal records should be stored off-site, with copies and microfilm on-site. If the duplicates were damaged, they should be destroyed and discarded. Contact your legal counsel to discuss legal surrogates.

### Where You Want Materials Dried

If you must keep items on-site (for security reasons, etc.), then dehumidification and air drying are your only options. If materials can be removed from the building, then dehumidification and vacuum freeze-drying are your drying options. Note that the vacuum freeze-drying process is the only process that does not require removing items from their boxes. Dehumidification and air drying require removal of items from boxes to make certain all surfaces are dry.

Vacuum freeze-drying and dehumidification off-site take at least three or four weeks, depending upon how wet the materials are and how soon the disaster response/drying company can get the materials into the drying chambers. Assume your materials will be at the drying facility for at least two months from the time they receive the items until their return.

The only manner of drying available for collections that must remain on-site is dehumidification, or air drying by spreading out books and papers onto flat surfaces, while providing air movement with fans to make the paper dry. Air drying in-house (with fans) with the institution's staff is very labor-intensive, requires security, and has the potential side effects of distortion of paper and swollen bindings. Keep the temperatures low, dehumidifiers running 24 hours a day, and air moving to prevent mold growth.

If you are considering digitization or reformatting the materials after they are dried, then the dry method doesn't really matter. Contact the drying company to find out if they can provide a reformatting service for you.

## Preliminary Treatment

### Clay-Coated Paper

This is the most difficult paper to handle. This paper is coated with clay or an adhesive to give it that shiny surface. When the paper is exposed to moisture, the adhesive reactivates and sticks to whatever it touches. To try to recover, interleave clay-coated, or shiny, paper with precut freezer paper or double-sided wax paper, shiny side toward text, if labor and time permit. Soaked clay-coated paper will stick together permanently within six hours. Clay-coated paper can be stored in water for a short while until there is time to treat it. Be aware that the printing is often embedded in the clay and can dissolve and wash away from the surface of the paper. If there is not sufficient time to interleave clay-coated paper, then freeze it and vacuum freeze-dry. Vacuum freeze-drying provides better end results than dehumidification or air drying. The success rate is about 50 percent regardless of the drying method used. Many libraries and archives choose to discard clay-coated materials if they are easily replaceable, duplicated on microfilm, or in electronic collections. Decide during the prioritization phase if you will keep water-damaged clay-coated paper.

Only treat or discard clay-coated paper if it is damaged. Otherwise, store it in a dry location.

### Photographs, Negatives, and Film

Separate photographic materials into different processes, if possible, and remove from paper envelopes before drying. Do not let photographic materials dry by themselves in boxes, folders, or sleeves. Quickly freeze photographs if unable to treat them immediately and if this method is approved by the preservation or conservation officer. There is a chance that freezing will damage the surface of photographs. Ask a conservator before freezing photographic materials with monetary or artistic value.

### Magnetic Tape

Remove magnetic tape from the water as soon as possible. Do not freeze it. If the magnetic tape is unique or the backup tape has been destroyed, send it to be dried, cleaned, and copied onto a new tape. Some of the disaster response/drying companies can provide this service for you. If the magnetic tape is not unique and has been water damaged, discard and replace it.

## When Paper Dries

Paper changes in character and form as soon as it gets wet. Paper also changes shape when exposed to high humidity or when it is stored under extremely dry conditions. Wrinkling or cockling is an indication that moisture was present and the paper dried slowly.

What causes this? Paper fibers expand when exposed to water or humidity. When the paper dries, the fibers shrink but at different rates. The more control of the paper's shape during the drying process, the less visible the cockling when the fibers shrink back to "normal."

Wetting and then drying cellulose or paper fibers has an adverse effect on the strength and mechanical properties of paper. Drying paper without restraint or control will result in cockling.

Choice of drying method can influence the amount of distortion. How much paper becomes distorted depends upon how wet the papers were when they were removed from the water or area of high humidity. Paper dries from the outside in, that is, from the fore edge to the binding. If dehumidification is the drying method used, carefully monitor the condition of the paper and the moisture content of the paper at the spine of the book or the center of the folder. Watch for deterioration of paper and mold growth.

Vacuum freeze-drying can reduce the amount of cockling, but there is no guarantee how materials will look when they are dry. If materials go into a dehumidifying or vacuum freeze-drying chamber wrinkled, they will come out that way. Dehumidification and vacuum thermal-drying, in and of themselves, can cause wrinkling or cockling because the items stay wet until all the excess moisture is removed. Those methods are okay for damp and slightly wet materials. Vacuum freeze-drying does not permit the item to get wet again, reducing the chance of wrinkling. Paper looks no worse than when it went into the drying chamber. This process is most suitable for soaked and clay-coated materials.

## Drying Processes

In all drying processes, the moisture content of paper is usually too low after the drying treatment is completed. Use a meter to read moisture level in the paper. The moisture content must be increased to 6 percent to 8 percent. Paper will stabilize to the moisture content of the surrounding air on its own. Adjust the temperature and relative humidity slowly until it is the same as in the location the materials are shelved to prevent mold outbreaks.

Keep in mind these other factors when selecting a drying method:

■ If the items are needed on-site or close by, then dehumidification may be the only choice.

- Vacuum freeze- and thermal-drying chambers are not usually mobile.

- Soaked materials and clay-coated paper should be vacuum freeze-dried.

- Photographs, film-based materials, and leather and vellum may be dehumidified or vacuum freeze-dried if acceptable to your conservator.

- Vacuum freeze-drying chambers are safe and secure because materials are dried in the boxes they were shipped in. Contents may be removed when dried using dehumidification.

- Prices for all types of drying treatments are similar, ranging from $65 to $75 per cubic foot (10 to 25 books) or about $5 to $10 per book. Labor for packing and cleaning and shipping charges are extra.

## Desiccant Dehumidification

A desiccant dehumidifier traps and absorbs moisture in the air while still in a gaseous state as it moves across the desiccant's surface. Dry air is pumped out the other side of the machine. Desiccant dehumidifiers can dry the air to less than 30 percent rH (relative humidity). With careful monitoring, the environment can be controlled precisely. The equipment doesn't need to be physically in the building; ducts can pump moist air out of the building while fans move the air around. Desiccant dehumidification will make the air very hot. Require that the drying company maintain temperatures below 72° Fahrenheit. Higher temperatures can damage and prematurely age paper- and film-based materials. Desiccant dehumidification works well at cold temperatures and is efficient in large or small spaces, depending upon the size of the equipment. This method is excellent for drying photographs, film, negatives, X-rays, and microfilm/microfiche. Remember, however, adhesives may release from covers and spines of bound materials after prolonged exposure to moisture requiring rebinding of books. Desiccant dehumidification is great for drying out buildings after water damage has occurred.

## Refrigerant Dehumidification

This technique condenses moisture from the air onto coils and then into a drip pan. Then the water must be flushed into a drainage system or emptied regularly. If the water is not removed from the refrigerant dehumidifier, the air will rehumidify, especially if the air is warm. The process of condensing moisture onto coils makes refrigerant dehumidification less effective at cooler temperatures. Refrigerant dehumidification can dry the air to 30 percent rH. This drying method also warms the air but not as much as desiccant. Refrigerant dehumidification equipment is portable and available in small units that condense and collect water within the unit. It is excellent for small drying jobs.

## Vacuum Thermal-Drying

With vacuum thermal-drying, materials often enter the chamber in a frozen state. A vacuum is introduced, and the air is heated to between 50° and 100° Fahrenheit. The ice thaws and melts; then the water is turned into a gas, which is pumped out of the chambers. Contents become wet again and may cockle or wrinkle the paper during the drying process. The vacuum thermal-drying process may produce extreme warping of cellulose fibers due to the release of adhesives in bindings and under cloth covers when they are exposed to heat or prolonged moisture. Rebinding of books may be required.

Note: Water-soluble inks may run. Coated papers may stick together as a result of heat and the reintroduction of water. Vacuum thermal-drying is not suitable for leather or vellum materials.

## Vacuum Freeze-Drying

With vacuum freeze-drying, items can go into the chamber frozen or wet. First, a vacuum is introduced, but no heat is added. Contents are dried at or below 32° Fahrenheit in the vacuum chamber. As the vacuum is reduced, ice is sublimated into vapor, meaning the ice is changed directly into a gas and pumped out of the chamber immediately. Therefore, materials stay frozen until they dry. This is the best method for drying clay-coated papers if they were frozen within six hours of exposure to water. Vacuum freeze-drying may be suitable for water-soluble inks; check with a paper conservator first. When vacuum freeze-drying is used, less rebinding of previously wet materials is required. Check with a conservator before vacuum freeze-drying leather, vellum, or pre-1950 photographic processes.

## Air Drying

This process involves using the institution's air-handling, or HVAC, system in conjunction with fans and portable dehumidifiers. This method can be used in very small areas and with small collections that are water damaged. Air drying presents the greatest chance for paper distortion, structural damage to paper and bindings, and mold growth.

Air drying is perceived to be the least expensive drying method for libraries and archives, but it is extremely time- and labor-intensive for the staff involved. It also poses the most risk of a mold infection.

Film, photographs, negatives, X-rays, microfilm and microfiche, and Mylar maps and drawings can all be air dried quickly, using dehumidification and air movement from fans. Just hang the items up on a clothesline made of plastic fishing line or monofilament with plastic clips. Environmental conditions should be 65°–70° Fahrenheit with 30–55 percent rH and active air movement.

After materials have dried, remove soot, dirt, and mold carefully to avoid scratching the surface. Removing such particulate matter before paper or photographs are dry may create permanent staining and will be nearly impossible to accomplish. Contact a conservator for training.

## Documents and Files—In-House Handling and Drying Methods

Dry materials with dehumidifiers in-house until the paper's moisture content is between 6 percent and 8 percent. Then slowly adjust the relative humidity in the drying room to that of the area where they will be returned. This is done to prevent a mold infection.

The wet area must be completely dry. Stabilize environmental conditions so that relative humidity is 45 percent to 55 percent and temperature is 65° to 72° Fahrenheit. When the environment in the building is stabilized, adjust the drying room to the same environment. Watch for mold. When the moisture content of the paper is 6 percent to 8 percent in the drying room, you can move the materials back.

### Drying Room

- Isolate an area so that humidity and air movement can be controlled.
- Segregate dry materials from wet. Store dry materials in a controlled environment away from high humidity.
- Set relative humidity as low as possible (35 percent to 45 percent) and no higher than 55 percent.

Temperature should be as low as possible (65° to 72° Fahrenheit). Keep temperature and relative humidity stable. There should be no dead air pockets in the room.

- Set up shelves, racks, or tables for the files and books.

### Procedures

- Remove files, documents, and bound materials from one box at a time. Try to maintain the shelf or filing order.
- Put files into milk crates, standing up. Do not jam documents into crates. Provide support to prevent sagging and distortion. Put books on tables upside down or on their spines while providing support. Bound materials should be rotated every six to eight hours to prevent irreparable damage to binding structure.
- Separate self-carboned and thermal-fax paper; they become sticky when wet. Place these papers shiny side up on blotter paper or drying racks.
- Separate out photographs, negatives, and Mylar. Dry them according to directions below.
- Decrease temperature and relative humidity and increase air movement, preventing mold growth. Do not blow air on items directly.
- When the moisture content of paper is 6 percent to 8 percent, paper is dry.
- Replace materials in the proper folders and label folders with contents.
- Return items to the shelves.

## Books and Paper Files— In-House Handling and Drying Methods

### Temperature

- As cold as possible
- No temperatures above 72° Fahrenheit

Note: High temperatures will decrease the life of paper and photographic materials, causing irreparable aging and such secondary damage as release of adhesives and distortion of bindings.

## *Humidity*

- As low as possible, but not below 30 percent. Very dry air can cause paper and film to become brittle.
- Moisture content of paper should be 6 percent to 8 percent when dry.

For very hygroscopic materials such as leather, vellum, textiles, furniture, and framed works of art on canvas:

- Very slowly reduce humidity to prevent additional distortion and to prevent structural damage
- Contact conservators who specialize in these formats before treating or stabilizing

Before accepting dried materials back from the disaster response/drying company:

- Stabilize temperatures in the institution to prevent absorption of excess moisture and to prevent a mold infection
- Clean the area and get it ready for shelving materials

# Large-Format Materials— Handling and Drying Methods

Large-format, or oversize, materials are difficult to handle when wet. Large-format materials include, but are not limited to, maps, posters, broadsides, blueprints and architectural drawings, and works of art on paper. These materials are usually larger than 11 by 17 inches. They are printed on a variety of materials, including paper, Mylar, cloth, and coated stock. The combination of size and material creates difficulties carrying, separating, and physically handling them. Drying jobs that involve these materials must be performed by at least two people working together. If you have a large collection of oversize materials, contact a conservator for training in handling and drying.

Large-format materials can be found in map rooms, government document depositories, and science departments. Archives and historical societies that contain historical records and blueprints; art, art history, and popular cultural collections; and records centers often house large-format materials. Some rare book and special collections may contain large-format materials. Of course, large-format materials are stored in architectural and engineering departments and building maintenance offices.

These materials can be stored in a variety of ways:

- Flat in drawers or cabinets
- Rolled, stored on end, or on their sides
- Rolled on a pole and stored vertically or horizontally
- Folded in filing cabinets
- Hung in vertical cabinets

Large-format materials may be in poor condition because of the type of paper or cloth, the age of the item, or excessive handling by the public and staff.

If there is a lack of storage space in the institution, large-format materials may be relegated to basements, storage closets, or attics. These collections should have been identified during the prioritization phase and ranked for recovery.

## *Removing Large-Format Materials from the Building or Water-Damaged Area*

Wet large-format materials should be handled by teams of two.

- Remove water from any drawers or cabinets before moving the materials.
- Place a sheet of Mylar, Remay (a polyester spun cloth), or plastic over the top of materials before moving them. Covering these materials protects them from dirt and soot as well as preventing loss of items and accidental damage during transport.
- If necessary, move and freeze items in the drawers. Cover the drawer with Remay or Mylar to prevent loss or damage.
- Covered material may remain in place in the vacuum freeze-drying chamber.
- If air drying, remove items from the drawers (use procedures listed below) and dry flat under white blotter paper and weights.
- Check with a conservator before handling or drying works of art on paper.

## *Removing Large-Format Materials from Drawers*

All these procedures require at least two people working together.

### File Folders in Drawers

- Remove by folder first. The folder may be so wet it requires additional support.
- Slip a sheet of Mylar larger than the folder under the folder and lift up.
- Place it flat on a table or a bread tray or any large, flat movable surface. Be careful not to tear wet items.
- Transport items to a vacuum freeze-drying chamber or a freezer to await drying.

### Loose in Drawers

- Slip a sheet of Mylar larger than the materials into the drawer and under the materials.
- Lift up and place items flat on a table or bread tray.
- Transport items to a vacuum freeze-drying chamber or a freezer to await drying.

## Separating Wet Large-Format Materials

To separate wet large-format materials, use sheets of Mylar larger than the materials. Mylar is better than plastic sheeting because it provides additional support. If Mylar is unavailable, plastic sheeting or Remay can be used.

### Paper Items

- Place the Mylar on top of the item and lift up slowly. The static electricity in the Mylar makes the paper stick to it and allows you to lift it up. Do not attempt to separate paper using your hands. The paper will tear.
- Place the item flat on blotter paper or Remay.
- Items should be dried face up.

  Note: Some large-format materials, such as art and posters, may have water-soluble inks, which will run when wet. Do not touch these materials with your hands. Place them face up on blotter paper or Remay. Contact a conservator to treat.

### Mylar Items

- Mylar should separate if pulled apart slowly. Be careful, because Mylar can rip.
- Blot items dry, then hang on monofilament with plastic clothespins. These materials dry quickly when exposed to air movement and low relative humidity.

- Do not allow Mylar to dry touching another surface. It may fuse permanently.
- Clean carefully after the Mylar is dry.

### Linen or Cloth Items

- Use Mylar to separate.
- Cloth becomes very heavy and fragile when wet.
- The older the materials, the more fragile. Many colors will run when wet.
- Dry face up on white blotter paper or Remay. Contact a conservator to treat.

### Encapsulated Items

- Open each item along the seam or tape.
- Place the item face down.
- Remove the Mylar carefully; turn the item over onto blotter paper, so it is face up; and remove the other sheet of Mylar.

## Supplies for Drying Large-Format Materials

- White blotter paper or Remay
- Mylar sheets (40 by 60 inches) or plastic cut to size
- Monofilament
- Plastic clothespins
- Bread trays or flat drying racks that support each item
- Lots of flat surfaces for drying

## Potential Problems

Large-format materials, when wet, may be problems to dry. The following types of problems may exist.

### Maps 11 by 17 Inches or Larger

- Maps are fragile when wet.
- They will shred if not supported.
- Use Mylar or Remay to lift and move or separate wet sheets.
- Dry maps flat under blotters or weights. Watch for colored inks—they may bleed when wet.
- If the maps are encapsulated in Mylar, remove the top sheet of encapsulation and dry; then,

encapsulate between new sheets of Mylar with new buffered sheets of paper or card stock for support.

■ Contact a conservator if there is a large quantity of wet maps.

### Posters

■ Posters are often backed or mounted.

■ If the posters are encapsulated in Mylar, remove the top sheet of encapsulation and dry.

■ Encapsulate between new sheets of Mylar with new buffered sheets of paper or card stock for support.

■ If the posters are colored, contact a conservator for advice about drying processes.

### Blueprints, Architectural Drawings, and Engineering Prints

■ Blueprints, usually printed on paper that is acidic by nature, are created using a diazo process.

■ They become brittle with age.

■ Blueprints are usually rolled and wrinkled.

■ Poor storage conditions are not unusual.

■ They shred when wet and are extremely fragile, so handle with care.

■ Dry flat on white blotter paper or Remay.

■ Treat only if there are no "exact" copies and they have monetary or artifactual value.

### Linen Tracings

■ Linen tracings become sticky when wet.

■ They may separate, if you are lucky. Treat immediately.

■ They lose their finish when exposed to water.

■ Dry flat face up on white blotter paper or Remay.

### Mylar Tracings

■ Mylar tracings will stick together on contact when wet.

■ They will stay wet for months if untreated.

■ If left wet and under pressure for long enough, approximately six months, Mylar tracings will stick together permanently.

■ Separating stuck sheets may lift off printing.

■ Dry flat or hang on monofilament with plastic clothespins.

■ Do not fold. They will "learn" this position permanently.

If blueprints, architectural drawings, and engineering prints are available on microfilm, microfiche, aperture card, or in a digital format, then only small reproductions of originals remain. Microfilm readers/printers cannot enlarge to scale or original size. Many new large-format printers can print out microfilm and digital files to original size or scale. If patrons need to use blueprints, architectural drawings, or engineering prints in their original size, make the extra effort to treat the large-format items. Set priority levels for these items during the planning phase.

## Textiles in All Formats— Handling and Drying Methods

This is a job for at least two people, maybe more depending upon the size and weight of materials.

■ If textiles are dry, then move to a safe, dry location or segregate from the rest of the building while maintaining stable temperature and relative humidity levels.

■ Remove wet textiles carefully from water as they can tear and may be very heavy. The older the textiles, the more sensitive to water they may be. Colors may run and fabrics may shrink. Decorative materials such as beads and sequins are very heavy when wet, the colors may run, and the edges may tear the fabric. Pearls and gemstones are also heavy and may damage wet fabric.

■ Contact a conservator immediately for specific handling and stabilizing procedures before moving or drying.

## Modern Film-Based Materials 1950–Present—Handling and Drying Methods

Film-based materials from 1950 to the present include

■ Photographic prints

■ Motion picture film

■ Microfilm and microfiche

■ Slides and negatives

This information applies to film-based and photographic prints that were created after 1950. Items older than 1950 may be constructed of different elements and require very special handling and treatment, as the elements are unstable and extremely susceptible to moisture and exposure to water. Some will deteriorate or separate upon exposure to water. If you have a large photography collection that contains pre-1950 processes, contact a photograph conservator about procedures for stabilization and treatment if they are water damaged. These items should be identified during the prioritization phase and ranked for recovery. Detailed information for dealing with water-damaged pre-1950s photographs can be found in *Care and Identification of Nineteenth-Century Photographic Prints* by James M. Reilly and in *Disaster Recovery: Salvaging Photograph Collections* by Debra Hess Norris.

Photographs of all ages should be stored properly in sleeves of Mylar or paper and in appropriate storage containers such as file cabinets and boxes. Early photographs and those susceptible to water should not be stored near or under water pipes. All photographs and film should be stored at least a foot off the floor.

Photographic prints that were developed and processed after 1950 are constructed out of paper and an emulsion surface, which contains the photograph. Prints are able to withstand water for several days. However, as the surface of the film starts to dry, it will stick to whatever is touching it. Therefore, photographs should be kept wet until you are able to treat them and then hung up to dry on monofilament with plastic clothespins. If you are unable to treat the photographs within three days of getting wet and they do not have monetary value, freeze them (they can be vacuum freeze-dried at a later time). The photographs curl while drying. A conservator or professional photographer can assist you in flattening the prints once they are dry.

The inks on photographic prints from digital files or printed on laser and inkjet printers may run when wet. Store these items away from overhead water pipes. Treat like pre-1950 photographs or discard if the original digital files are safe and dry. Set priority levels for these materials during the planning phase.

Modern motion picture film has an acetate base or a polyester base with emulsion. Pre-1950 film could have a nitrate base or an acetate base. Acetate is sometimes called "safety film." This is usually printed along the edge of the film.

Nitrate film is flammable if it has deteriorated. It is fairly stable if intact and stored appropriately. Motion picture and photograph archives that have nitrate film should store this film in a separate location, below 32° Fahrenheit, with lots of air circulation. Mark on the floor plans where nitrate film is located. If undamaged in the disaster and in a safe, stable environment, leave it alone. If damaged during the disaster, contact the fire department for appropriate disposal, for it is categorized as a hazardous material. Consult a conservator before discarding the nitrate film to determine if it can be copied or salvaged.

Microfilm comes in a variety of types: silver halide, diazo, or vesicular. Master negatives and positives are usually made on silver halide. Master positives and negatives should be stored off-site at a depository such as Iron Mountain National Underground Storage in Pennsylvania. Masters are the most valuable version because they are the original copies of microfilm, especially if they were created during "brittle books" programs or if the original hard-copy books were destroyed after filming. If masters are stored on-site, identify these during the prioritization phase and rank for recovery.

Microfilm or microfiche for everyday use is made on diazo or vesicular film. Both are fairly stable and can handle some exposure to water, although 72 hours is the maximum recommended without professional reprocessing. If the master negative or positive is intact, discard the use copy and make a new one. If not, then reprocess the use copy.

Slides are merely pieces of film that have been cut into individual frames and mounted in cardboard or plastic. If the slide collection is housed in plastic sleeves or sheets that are wet, remove the slides from their housing as quickly as possible or immerse in water (for up to three days). Hang the slides to dry. Flatten and mount after they are dry. If you do not have time to do this and the collection does not have monetary value, freeze the pages. If the slides were frozen, discuss the side effects of thawing or vacuum freeze-drying with a photograph conservator. These suggestions for stabilization and treatment are suitable for negatives processed after 1950. Consult a photograph conservator for pre-1950 processes.

## Deterioration of Film

Most post-1950 film is composed of three layers: the base, the binder, and the emulsion. Other terms for these layers are support, interlayer, and image-bearing layer, respectively.

The base can be made of polyester, acetate, or nitrate. Polyester and acetate are the two most common types. United States firms ceased manufacture of nitrate film by 1958, later in Europe.

The emulsion, or image-bearing layer, usually has microscopic particles of silver that are chemically changed during exposure to light, processing, and, later, storage and atmospheric pollutants. High humidity can also damage the image, or emulsion layer. The silver particles are what create the image on the film.

The binder, or interlayer, is a very thin layer of adhesive called gelatin that attaches the emulsion to the base. When the binder deteriorates, the emulsion will flake or slide off the base. The binder is susceptible to moisture and environmental changes. If slightly moist, the emulsion will stick to whatever it touches.

Color film is composed of the same layers. The image-bearing layer contains dyes. These are very susceptible to damage due to light and storage and environmental conditions. The color fades and changes as the film ages.

## Reactions of Film to Water

Some modern films react slowly to water; others begin decomposition immediately. After 72 hours there is a greater risk of the emulsion flaking or sliding off. It is essential that you keep the photographs wet until you are ready to handle them. If allowed to dry on their own, the emulsion of the photograph or film will stick to whatever it is touching. Once this happens, it is almost impossible to separate them. Freeze the film if you are unable to stabilize it within 72 hours. Do not freeze photographs without discussing this with a photograph conservator. It is best to remove all film from sleeves, folders, and binders, as the emulsion will stick to the paper or Mylar. You will need to keep track of which photograph or slide goes with which sleeve, otherwise the provenance and description of the item are lost.

Soot, smoke, and pollution are all types of particulate matter. These small particles become trapped under and in emulsion. Particulate matter and pollution are not always removable and may stain, oxidize, and scratch the image on the film. Mold can form under the emulsion, eating away at the gelatin and destroying the images.

## Stabilizing and Drying Film-Based Materials

Before drying or treating film-based materials, remove all items from paper or Mylar sleeves and folders to prevent sticking of emulsion to surfaces. This should be done before the items dry. If the negatives, film, or photographs are stuck together, there are no guarantees that soaking them in water won't separate the base from the emulsion. Do not pull or force apart. It is important to maintain the order of the film, sleeves, and containers, as many items do not have contents indicated on film.

If you have older photographs and film-based materials in your collection, it is a good idea to talk with a photograph conservator before treating water-damaged photographs. A preliminary consultation should take place while surveying the collection during the planning phase of your disaster response plan.

## Drying Options

- Vacuum freeze-dry film-based materials only if they have no monetary or artifactual value, as treatment may leave nonglossy patches on the surface. Do not use the vacuum thermal-drying process as it may cause the photograph to flake and distort.
- Dehumidification and air drying are suitable treatments. Do not worry if photographs or negatives curl when drying. A conservator can help you flatten or humidify them later.

### Small Collections of Wet Photographs, Negatives, and Microfilm

- Hang to dry. Use plastic clothespins on monofilament to dry negatives, post-1950 photographs, and microfiche.
- Reprocess all motion picture film and most silver halide microfilm to reestablish the correct chemical balance.

## Slides

- Remove from mounts to prevent warping of image and mold and mildew growth under frames. Cardboard mounts are susceptible to warping and distorting when drying. It is easier to remount than deal with the side effects of warped slides. Transfer the intellectual information from the slide mounts before discarding the water-damaged mounts.

# Magnetic Tape—Handling and Drying Methods

Two factors make magnetic tapes difficult to handle and dry. First, magnetic materials are very fragile and susceptible to external damage. Second, special equipment is necessary to copy the original and to determine if the data are intact. Of all the different formats and materials, there is still little information available for recovering damaged magnetic tapes in all their various formats.

Magnetic tape was developed after World War II and became an industry standard for instantaneous recording of sound. The industry branched out in the last sixty years to create audiotape and videotape, both reel-to-reel and cassette. Computer tapes and computer diskettes came later. Today flash drives, SD memory cards, and other removable data storage devices are the most common magnetic media.

Removable data storage devices are found in all areas and departments of libraries and other cultural institutions. They are the most forgotten aspect and information resource when organizations are creating disaster response and recovery plans. The removable data storage devices contain important day-to-day records of the business aspects of the institution, including payroll and invoicing. Magnetic tapes may contain the OPAC, internal circulation, and cataloging systems, as well as databases. Software may have been modified to the needs of the institution and may be difficult to reproduce. Documentation may be in paper or computerized form. When a disaster strikes, this information is usually needed for the business side of the institution to survive. Your institution stores many different types of magnetic media in offices, archives, records centers, and information technology and computer services departments.

Much has been written by contingency planners on how to get the data up and running.[2] However, when it comes to drying, cleaning, and reading the damaged data, little information is available to help deal with the situation.

All magnetic tapes are composed of three layers of different materials—the base, the binder, and the emulsion—very similar to photographs. The base is either polyester or acetate. Both are fairly stable and have their own unique preservation and deterioration problems. You differentiate between polyester and acetate in the following manner: polyester stretches when pulled; acetate breaks cleanly. There is sometimes an antistatic back coating, which can cause its own preservation problems when it becomes brittle or ages at a different rate than the base. The binder is often urethane. It holds the layer that has the signal embedded in it. The binder layer adheres the signal or emulsion layer to the base. The signal is encoded by magnetizing the oxides.

The major difference between videotape, audiotape, and computer tape is the way the information is encoded into the magnetized oxide particles. Each AV format must be played on the appropriate equipment to decipher and read the data. Because of the rapid development of these media, recording and playback equipment become obsolete quickly. After a few years, it may be difficult to obtain the equipment necessary to access the older data. Companies that specialize in the recovery of magnetic materials collect and maintain the old machines. Even so, recovered data should be transferred to the newest or most stable format available.

Magnetic tapes are sensitive to changes in the environment. Videocassettes and audiocassettes may last for years, accumulating little particles of dust and dirt until they are no longer playable. Before that point, the tape should be replaced or copied onto the same or a newer format. The life span for much of this material is approximately ten years. By that time, the magnetic signal will deteriorate, the picture or sound will not be audible, or the tape itself will deteriorate. Poor storage and environmental conditions accelerate the deterioration of the tape and its magnetic signal.

The optimum or ideal environment for magnetic media is 50° to 60° Fahrenheit with a maximum of 30 percent to 40 percent relative humidity.[3] If this environment cannot be achieved, then strive for standard working conditions of 68° to 70° Fahrenheit with a maximum of 50 percent to 55 percent relative humidity. Relative humidity should not drop below 30 percent. As with paper and photographs, a stable, constant environment is best. Fluctuations in temperature and relative humidity will exacerbate the deterioration of the components of magnetic tape.

Vulnerabilities of magnetic tape abound. Temperature and humidity cause all types of preservation and playback problems. High temperatures can increase the distortion of sound, data, or image, as well as the physical tape. High temperatures can cause sticking when winding and rewinding and encourage layer-to-layer adhesion. High humidity encourages the deterioration of the binder layer, shedding of the signal or emulsion layer, and clogging of equipment when the tape layers flake off.

On the other hand, temperatures that are too low can cause tapes to loosen on their spools and can change the dimensions of tapes, thereby encouraging distortion and timing errors. If tapes are cold, allow time for the tapes to acclimate to new temperatures before winding, playing, or repairing. Low humidity encourages the attraction of debris and dust particles to tape, increases static electricity on tapes and in machines, and inhibits playing of tapes.

### Damaging Conditions

Magnetic tape is extremely sensitive to heat. Diskettes, removable data storage devices, film, and magnetic media distort and become unreadable at 125° Fahrenheit. By contrast, paper does not start to smolder until 350° Fahrenheit.

Frequent changes in temperature can cause oozing or a white deposit on the tape. Playing a tape with white deposits will damage the tape irreparably, as the deposits will stick to the play heads.[4] This white deposit must be removed by a professional. Do not attempt to remove it. Send the tape to a videotape or audiotape cleaning or restoration firm.[5]

Mold and mildew are also enemies of magnetic tape. Mold will eat away the binder layer, obstructing the readability of magnetic signals and distorting images or signals on the tape. Care must be taken not to seal a tape in a plastic bag or container that does not permit air exchange.

### Drying Methods

During or immediately after a disaster involving water, remove all magnetic media to a dry, secure area. Tapes should be removed from their boxes and containers to prevent mold growth and deterioration of the magnetic signal. If the tape is not wet, remove the tape to another location, being careful to retain the title or identifying information. Disinfect the containers, dry thoroughly, and let them sit 48 hours to prevent trapping moisture. Store magnetic media in

a clean, smoke- and particulate-free environment. Clean the containers and replace the tapes. Tape is extremely sensitive to pollution; this includes solvents, particulate matter, cigarette smoke, and dust. After the containers have dried, and been labeled if necessary, replace the tape.

If magnetic tape is wet, remove all excess water from the container and treat it as indicated above. Dry the outside of the open reels first. Cassettes can be opened and all external surfaces dried. Air dry all tape under the direction of a conservator. If the tape dries without treatment, it will adhere to whatever it touches, resulting in permanent loss of sound, image, or data. If the tape is wound tightly and properly upon the spool, no water should be present between layers. The danger here is that moisture will cause the adhesives to release or the layers of tape to come apart. In addition, mold could begin to grow on the tape surfaces. Do not attempt to play tapes as a means of drying them. If there are a lot of tapes, a professional magnetic tape cleaning and restoration firm may be better suited for this cleaning project. Do not use tape machines to dry or clean tapes, unless they are designed to do so.

When all tapes and containers are dry, have the tapes cleaned professionally or on a special tape-cleaning machine. One such machine is called an RTI cleaner and is available from RTI-Tek Media (see appendix B). It is designed for use with commercially produced videotapes only.

Unique items or noncommercial videotapes should be identified during the prioritization phase and ranked for recovery. Clean and transfer water-damaged or moldy magnetic tapes by contracting with a conservator or professional specializing in magnetic tape. Commercial and nonunique tapes should be replaced if they are water damaged.

## Compact Discs (CDs) and DVDs—Handling and Drying Methods

CDs, DVDs, and other optical storage devices in all their formats are present in all libraries and archives. We receive files on them, and transfer or burn files to them. Research on longevity and the effects of the environment on these media is still in its infancy. It is clear that there is limited longevity, and that the physical medium is fragile and easily damaged. Researchers are still testing how long data, visuals, sounds, or signals will remain encoded on discs. The current estimates are still 10 to 25 years if there are no severe scratches or nicks that affect the encoding.

Information on preservation, environmental and storage needs of discs, and recovering water-damaged CDs and DVDs is still scarce. Researchers write about tests and real-life experience with this format while discussing digital preservation issues. CDs and DVDs and optical video, laser discs, and interactive multimedia permutations are commonplace in cultural institutions. Preservation, handling, and recovery guidelines are fairly straightforward. Copy or migrate data from old CDs to new, store under normal environmental conditions, and avoid damaging the label side and cracking the hub

CDs come in some of the following formats: CD-ROM (Read-Only Memory); CD-I (Interactive); CD-WORMs (Write Once, Read Many times); Photo-CD (these are CD-WORMs with photographs encoded to various scales); and CD (usually denotes audio only). Optical formats include video or laser discs, which are 12-inch platters with visual images or densely encoded programming information; and optical discs, which come in a variety of sizes from 5 to 10 inches and usually contain office records with or without images. Three-inch compact discs are available, but not common in the United States. DVDs are also called Digital Versatile Discs or Digital Video Discs. (According to the literature, DVD is not an acronym.)

All these optical discs are variations of the same format and should be treated the same way. It is important to note that, with the exception of optical discs, commercially produced CDs and DVDs, when damaged, should be replaced if not playable. Recorded or burned CDs, DVDs, and optical discs that contain unique information should be treated carefully. They are generally irreplaceable, and the print materials that were input to create the disc may be fragile or brittle and so are stored away from daily use after scanning was completed.

All compact and optical discs are composed of five layers: the label, an acrylic that is often silk-screened onto the CD; the sealcoat, which protects the metal and pit layers; the metal layer, made of aluminum, copper, silver, or sometimes gold; the pits, which hold the encoded signals; and polycarbonate (substrate), which seals the layers together, preventing deterioration of the metal and pits and protecting the metal from scratches.

The label layer is directly on top of the metal, which holds the pits. Thus, the label is the most vulnerable layer of the CD.

Optical discs that are encoded on both sides are usually housed in cartridges, and are very vulnerable to damage. Do not remove them from their cartridge unless wet. Avoid fingerprints, smudges, and dust on the surface of optical discs. This can cause reading errors and distortions.

The physical difference between DVDs and CDs is that DVDs can be encoded on both sides. Two-sided DVDs are made of two layers, bonded together to make a disc that is the same thickness as the CD.[6]

Optical discs are fairly stable and, for the most part, will remain unaffected by normal temperatures. For longevity and seldom-used collections, optimal or ideal environmental conditions are 68° Fahrenheit with 45 percent relative humidity. As with all formats, it is best to keep the temperature and relative humidity stable. Fluctuations in temperature could cause the polycarbonate to crack. Avoid freezing optical discs or subjecting them to dramatic changes in temperature. CDs are also susceptible to high temperatures as the polycarbonate may soften at 212° Fahrenheit (100° centigrade).

Avoid exposing CDs to particulate matter and pollution as they can inhibit the signal and erode the polycarbonate. Avoid storing CDs near solvents, such as janitorial supplies, ozone, and paint, all of which can corrode the polycarbonate.

## Damaging Conditions

Optical discs are susceptible to water, mold, and mildew. If the polycarbonate surface is damaged or not sealed appropriately, moisture can become trapped and begin to corrode the metal encoding surface. If moisture or mold is invasive enough, it will make the disc unreadable.

Clean surfaces with dry, lint-free cotton cloth. Never spray cleaning solutions directly on discs. Clean discs from the center out, using a motion that is perpendicular to the grooves to avoid damaging and scratching the polycarbonate surface. Disinfect and dry all wet or soot-damaged containers. Allow them to dry for 48 hours. Store discs in a dry, clean, pollution- and particulate-free environment.

Because DVDs can be coded on both sides, if they are water- or soot-damaged, extra care must be taken to remove the debris and dirt from the surface. Try not to touch the surface at all by handling the DVDs by the center hole and the edge. Clean gently as you would a CD.

# Phonograph Records—Handling and Drying Methods

Modern LPs are made of vinyl or plastic that is flexible and fairly stable. Older phonograph records can be made of acetate, shellac, glass, metal, cardboard, or any combination thereof. They range in size from 7 to 20 inches in diameter. The most common sizes are 10, 12, and 16 inches. Records can vary within each size as much as ¾ inch and can be up to ½ inch thick.

The primary preservation issues to deal with are warping, mold from poor environmental conditions, scratches from abrasion, incorrect playback equipment, and cleaning.

## Storing LPs

Phonograph records should be stored perpendicular to the shelf, with the same type and size stored together. Protect records with paper or inert plastic sleeves. The sleeved records can be stored in cardboard record sleeves, boxes, or just in the sleeve. Try to avoid wrinkles in the plastic as these can permanently distort the playing surface. Records are very heavy and can damage each other if packed too tightly on the shelf or in a box.

## Environmental Conditions

- The ideal environmental conditions are 68° Fahrenheit with a relative humidity of 45 percent.
- Keep the environment stable.
- Avoid all particulate matter and pollution.

## Water-Damaged LPs 1970s–1990s

The following seven procedures deal primarily with vinyl recordings. Recordings made before 1970 are more susceptible to damage from water, mold, and rough handling. Contact a conservator for advice and training during the planning phase, if you have a large collection of LPs.

1. Remove all discs from paper or plastic sleeves upon exposure to moisture or water. This prevents additional growth of mold and mildew and decreases decay and damage to plastics and vinyl.

2. If discs are vinyl (1970s–1990s), clean and remove water with a clean lint-free cotton cloth. This cloth can be dampened with slightly soapy water (one teaspoon mild soap such as Ivory or Kodak Fotoflo 200 to 1 gallon lukewarm distilled water. Do not use tap water—it contains impurities that can create deposits of crystals in the grooves) or use LP Discwasher solution sparingly. Never spray solutions directly onto LPs.

3. Move cloth in a circular manner counterclockwise along the grooves in the disc.

4. Clean both sides of the record gently with a lint-free cotton cloth and air dry in a rack so the discs are perpendicular to a surface. Be certain the paper label is completely dry before placing discs in new sleeves.

5. Call a conservator if the LPs are not plastic or vinyl (that is, from 1969 or earlier).

6. Label record sleeves.

7. Replace records in new sleeves when completely dry. (Paper sleeves should not have plastic lining.)

Most vinyl records will not be damaged by a minimal amount of water. The greatest dangers to vinyl records are mold from not drying them thoroughly and that the labels might come off when exposed to water.

Cleaning machines could be used after the records are dry. The most common are made by Nitty Gritty Record Care Products and Keith Monks Record Cleaning Machine (see appendix B). Their machines use alcohol-based cleaners that remove dust, dirt, and mold. Alcohol-based cleaners (including LP Discwasher) should not be used on acetate and shellac records.

# Works of Art on Canvas and Paper—Handling and Drying Methods

The following four steps must be taken when drying and stabilizing works of art on canvas and paper.

1. Contact an art conservator during the prioritization and planning phase, when these items are identified, located on the floor plan, and ranked for recovery.

2. The paintings should be removed to a separate location to avoid additional damage.

3. Paper backing should be opened and removed from any of the paintings that are wet. You can remove the paintings from the frames if the paintings are wet, allowing them to dry on all sides. Do not remove paintings from the stretchers. A conservator can flatten warped paintings that are mounted on stretchers.

4. Check the backs of these paintings for indications of mold or mold stains.

Discuss stabilization techniques with an art conservator before freezing or drying works of art on canvas or paper.

# Mold

Mold is constantly present in the air and on most objects. It is most evident in locations where there is a high relative humidity or when there has been water damage. Its presence, particularly the smell, is sometimes masked by odors of wet items, such as acoustic tiles.

Mold should be treated seriously. It is highly infectious and will spread throughout furnishings, materials, and the building. Mold will irritate people who have allergies, asthma, and immune deficiencies.

Mold and mildew will grow between 40° and 100° Fahrenheit when conditions are right. Mold likes a moist environment and the dark, as seen by mold in a refrigerator or basement.

Different types of mold like to grow on different materials. Some like trees and wood; others like leather or the glues and starch found in books; and others like gelatin and paper pulp. In most instances, a variety of mold species will be visible on a "moldy" object. Three major types of mold are found in buildings: allergenic, mycotic, and toxic. Most tests will reveal allergenic mold varieties. An example of mycotic mold is *Candida.* A toxic variety of mold is *Stachybotrys chartarum,* also known as *Stachybotrys atra.* This type of toxic mold is in the headlines when discovered in public buildings and schools.

Allergenic mold will trigger allergies and asthma. Coughing, sneezing, and discomfort are the most common symptoms. People working around mold, especially those with allergies, should protect themselves by wearing respirators, gloves, and disposable or washable clothing.

Working around mold can cause people to develop sensitivities and then allergies to the mold. Therefore, health and safety precautions are advised for all employees. In addition, all air in areas where moldy materials are stored or being cleaned should be vented to the outside. Air-handling systems should not be recycling this moldy air.

The presence of *Stachybotrys atra* is a sign that there is excess moisture or water within the building. It is sometimes found behind walls, sometimes in mechanical and HVAC rooms. *Stachybotrys atra* loves materials that are high in cellulose, and it requires high humidity to grow. Not all black molds are *Stachybotrys atra.* If you do find *Stachybotrys atra,* consult with an industrial hygienist about testing and removal of the active mold. The source of the excess moisture should be identified and eliminated prior to initiating the removal of the mold from the building. Removing the mold without eliminating the excess moisture is pointless; the mold will just return.[7]

Control of the environment and moisture are key factors in dealing with and controlling mold. High relative humidity and hygroscopic materials will encourage mold growth. Hygroscopic materials include furniture, carpets, works of art on canvas and paper, textiles, acoustic tiles, paper, books, and wood. Moisture barriers are not always useful for controlling mold, for they may not let the moisture out, therefore allowing mold to grow. Examples of moisture barriers are latex paint, wall coverings, and plastic sheeting. The moisture condenses on the cooler side and encourages mold growth.

## *Effects of Mold*

### Cellulose or Paper-Based Materials

Mold eats away at cellulose materials, weakening the fibers and destroying the form. Paper becomes stained. Books will swell in areas where mold has infected them. Mold is attracted by increased moisture content. The normal moisture content of paper should be between 6 percent and 8 percent. Below this, paper becomes brittle. Above 8 percent, paper is too wet and encourages mold to grow. Mold will grow on all areas of books and papers. Different species or varieties of mold are attracted to starch, adhesives, cellulose, leather, or cloth. Different colors and textures of mold indicate different species.

The goal of removing and "eliminating" mold is to keep it from germinating and thereby infecting the entire collection or building. Controlling the environment and eliminating sources of "food" will inhibit mold growth.

### Film-Based Materials

Mold is attracted to film-based materials such as photographs, negatives, microfilm/microfiche, and motion picture film. The mold will grow on the surface of photographs and these other materials, eating away the images.

To prevent mold growth, keep the rH below 50 percent. If mold starts to grow, clean off and store items under low rH conditions.

Mold also likes fingerprints and body oils and salts. Avoid touching photographs and negatives with bare hands. The mold will grow in traces of fingerprints and continue to damage the photograph surfaces.

If mold infects slides, remove them from mounts before drying and cleaning. Replace the mounts when the slides dry.

A method to prevent mold growth on film-based materials is to store them in frost-free refrigerators. Eliminate all sources of condensation in the refrigerator, or mold will grow without control. Store in low temperatures and rH. Use dehumidification if necessary.

The following are ideal temperature and relative humidity ranges for the storage of film-based materials:

*Black-and-white film:* 50° to 70° Fahrenheit (± 2°); 20 percent to 30 percent relative humidity, with a maximum of 50 percent relative humidity

*Color film:* 15° to 35° Fahrenheit (± 2°); 20 percent to 30 percent relative humidity, with a maximum of 50 percent relative humidity

### Magnetic or Tape-Based Materials

Mold will infect magnetic and tape-based materials. The mold is attracted to the binder or adhesive that attaches the layers of tape together. A white sticky residue is a sign of mold infection. Store magnetic and tape-based media in a low rH environment to prevent mold growth. Mold should be removed by professional tape restoration firms to prevent loss of image, sound, or information.

## Controlling Mold

To control additional growth in a building and on a collection, determine what caused the mold.

- Check the temperature and relative humidity. The temperature should be below 72° Fahrenheit, preferably below 70° Fahrenheit. The relative humidity should be below 60 percent; the ideal rH is 45 percent to 50 percent.
- Dark, moist areas are prime locations for mold growth. Turning on the lights can slow growth.
- Check air circulation. Stagnant air and moist conditions will also trigger mold growth.
- Check intake, heating, and cooling ducts for obstructions to air flow.
- Check heating-exchange coils. This is a prime location for mold growth. Mold on the coils will spread throughout a building via the ductwork. Clean coils with disinfectant.
- Check air ducts. Clean any infected ducts. A fungicide or microbial cleanser can be used under controlled conditions, with approval by a conservation or preservation officer.
- Fix or eliminate the mold problem at the source. Treating only the symptoms guarantees another infection of mold.
- Isolate the infected materials in a room or area. Ventilate air to the outside to prevent spreading mold into the air ducts.

## Change the Environment

- Increase air circulation and decrease humidity.
- Dehumidification is the best method. Opening windows if the rH is lower outside is a possibility.
- Measure the relative humidity using a hygrograph or a datalogger. Measurements should be taken several times a day. Hygrographs record temperature and rH on paper that tracks changes over a period of one week or month. Dataloggers are electronic temperature and relative humidity recorders that measure changes in the environment over long periods of time. Both devices will provide justification for fixing serious environmental problems in a building.
- Remove mold from books and objects. Vent all the air to the outside, both in the area with the mold infection and where you are removing mold.
- Clean and disinfect the room, shelves, and any wood or metal containers. Use Lysol, Clorox, or a

disinfectant. Try not to reintroduce mold into air ducts. Use protective clothing, gloves, and respirators when cleaning. Clean or discard all clothing after exposure to mold.

- Odors can be removed by opening baking soda or placing charcoal in the room. Do not use these items directly on books!

- Ozone is not suitable for eradication or control of mold because of its side effects and unpredictability. See the materials on ozone, later in this section.

## Cleaning Dirty and Moldy Books

Dry all materials before cleaning. Moldy materials that cannot be treated immediately should be frozen. Freezing mold does not kill or eradicate it but merely stops mold growth. Take the following six steps to clean dirty and moldy books.

1. Hold book shut at front edge.

2. Vacuum mold from
   - top edge of book, moving from spine to edge
   - bottom edge from spine to edge
   - front edge from top to bottom

3. Vacuum
   - front cover
   - back cover
   - spine

4. Open front cover and vacuum inner edge near fold (hinge area).

5. Open back cover and vacuum inner edge near fold (hinge area).

6. Repeat the process using a "dry chemical sponge."

Dry chemical sponges are made of pure latex or rubber, not cellulose. Do not get dry chemical sponges wet. Do not use any liquid to eliminate mold; it will cause mold to grow again. Do not put treated materials into sealed containers, boxes, or plastic; this can encourage mold growth.

Before returning cleaned materials to the regular collection, take the following steps:

- Look through the books and make certain no mold, soot, and dirt remains.

- Put books in a stable, dry environment.

- Monitor books for reappearance of mold.

- Return books to their original location after the environment is stable and the relative humidity is back to 45 percent to 60 percent (± 2 percent). These materials are very susceptible to mold.

- Monitor previously infected areas throughout seasonal changes to determine that mold remains arrested.

## Mold in Buildings

A major cause of sick building syndrome is the presence of mold in the HVAC system. The mold is carried throughout the structure by the fans blowing air across a moldy condensation coil, heat exchange coil, or even moldy ducts. This contaminated air is circulated again and again until it becomes a serious health issue.

External walls and joints contribute to mold growth. The moisture condenses near these cooler walls and can encourage the growth of mold. Keeping air flow active and increasing the temperature of the air near these external surfaces can control mold. Decreasing the moisture content of the air is also important.

Poor environmental conditions are perfect for encouraging mold growth. When a building is air-conditioned, there is a good chance for mold. Just because there is air-conditioning does not mean that there is humidity control. If the air-conditioning is up too high, surfaces can become too cold and the moisture content too high. At this point, water will condense on the surfaces and encourage mold growth. To prevent this, decrease the number of "cold" spots by increasing the air flow and the temperature. Condensation on windows is a key indicator of an imbalance in the environment. These conditions are ripe for a mold infection.

Check air ducts, heating and cooling ducts, and intake ducts to make certain air flow is not obstructed.

Treat the cause and the symptoms, not just the symptoms, of poor indoor air quality.

- Clean all infected areas.

- Eliminate outside and building factors that encourage mold or condensation.

- Stabilize the environment.

- Monitor areas for repeat infection.

# Ozone

## *Effects on Materials in Cultural Institutions and Uses for Disaster Recovery*

In the aftermath of the Mississippi River flood in the Midwest in 1993, and during several mold eradication jobs, a number of inquiries were made about the effects of ozone and what it can and cannot do.

Since 1993, there have been some new studies on the effects of ozone on natural, organic, and cellulose materials, as well as on people. Most research on ozone examines its effects on the atmosphere. The creation and use of ozone indoors, and its side effects, were researched before the 1980s. Some of the new studies look at the effects of ozone during disaster recovery and in conjunction with indoor air/environmental quality. Ozone-generating machines, also described as "energized oxygen" and "pure air" machines, are sometimes used to eliminate odors from soot-, fire-, or mold-damaged cellulose materials. This includes all paper formats, textiles, art on canvas and paper, wood, and photographs. In addition, ozone's effects on film-based materials such as microfilm, motion picture film, and magnetic tape were examined.

## *Background*

Ozone found in the atmosphere is a very stable and powerful element. It screens out ultraviolet light and absorbs some harmful radiation. Ozone exists primarily as a gas. It has a pungent odor, most noticeable when electrical appliances spark.

Machines create ozone by passing an electric charge through oxygen. This is what occurs in the ozone generators or precipitators. Ozone is also a byproduct of photocopiers and laser printers. This ozone is highly reactive and, therefore, very unstable. The extra oxygen molecule looks for other molecules in the room to attach to and creates some harmful, highly reactive compounds that damage materials.

Ozone is normally present in the atmosphere in concentrations of .03 parts per million (ppm). However, when generated artificially in concentrations greater than 1 ppm, ozone is toxic to people and animals. Ozone decreases lung capacity and function, aggravates asthma, and irritates mucous membranes, causing coughing and chest pains and increasing susceptibility

to respiratory infection. The Occupational Safety and Health Administration (OSHA) regulates regular exposure up to 0.1 ppm; exposure in short duration is permitted, up to a maximum of 0.3 ppm.

Some scientists use ozone's powerful oxidizing properties for sterilizing water and purifying air. Ozone can be used for sterilizing food, but "effective bactericidal concentrations may be irritating and toxic to humans."[8] Many disaster response/drying companies generate ozone and use it as a deodorizer. To date, no government agency has approved the use of ozone generators in an occupied space.[9]

## *Uses and Effects*

Ozone is highly effective for deodorizing materials after a fire or mold damage. It actually seeks out and attacks the odor-causing molecules, changing their molecular composition and, thus, neutralizing the smell. Similar changes occur when sprays are used to counteract odors.

The problem with ozone that is generated is that it is highly reactive. This ozone seeks out unsaturated organic compounds such as soot, mold, and molecules that create odors and bonds with them. This means that the ozone changes molecular bonds and creates a new compound. Many of these compounds act as bleaches and are very caustic. When natural or organic materials are exposed to ozone, the inherent chemical reactions already going on inside the item will begin to accelerate. Even with minimal exposure, ozone ultimately destroys organic, natural, and cellulose materials.

Libraries, archives, museums, and historical societies are full of cellulose and natural and organic materials. Most paper created between 1860 and 1980 is acidic. Chemical reactions occur constantly, causing the paper to deteriorate, lose strength, and become very brittle. When ozone is generated for use in deodorizing the cellulose and paper-based materials, it tends to bond with the reactive chemicals already present and accelerate the aging process. Even a minimum amount of exposure to ozone will cause these materials to become more acidic.

Ozone speeds up the invisible and deadly reactions in paper, creating more sulfur dioxide and hydrogen peroxide and accelerating the acidic process. Ozone will cause paper to turn brown and become brittle. Eventually, the paper will become so brittle it will flake to the touch. Preservation and conservation activities in cultural institutions are designed to delay and retard the deterioration of cellulose and film-based materials. Using ozone to eliminate mold and soot odors may eradicate all advances in preservation efforts.

When ozone comes in contact with photographs and film, it is even more deadly. Ozone increases the rate of oxidation of silver, destroying the images on film-based materials. It reacts even more quickly with color film than black and white. In strong concentrations, ozone can cause the images to flake off the film. The chemicals that once interacted to create and stabilize photographic images bond with ozone to cause the photograph to continue to develop. The same reactions occur when microfilm and motion picture film are exposed to ozone. In addition, ozone will react with the materials that make up magnetic media, causing the layers to deteriorate.

To make matters worse, as mentioned earlier, ozone is generated by photocopiers and laser printers.[10] Although the output of ozone is filtered and regulated by OSHA, these machines should not be present in rooms where large collections of cellulose materials are stored, especially film-based materials.

Compact discs and laser or optical discs are also adversely affected by ozone. Ozone can bond with elements to create solvents that cause the protective polycarbonate layer to deteriorate, ultimately destroying the signal or data encoded upon these discs.

The five most disturbing issues about ozone follow:

1. There is no way to know what chemicals and molecules are nearby to bond with.
2. There is no way to determine what the ozone will make when it bonds with other molecules.
3. Ozone can bond to create toxic or carcinogenic chemicals, or it can be harmless and dissipate into the atmosphere.
4. There is no way to predict ozone's behavior.
5. Air flow, temperature, and bonding elements must be factored into the high reactivity and unpredictability of ozone.

### *Uses with Damaged Materials*

Despite all the warnings against using ozone, some disaster response/drying companies use it. Keep the following issues in mind before authorizing the use of ozone.

■ Ozone, as noted above, is incredibly effective for removing the odor from soot-, smoke-, and mold-damaged materials. The ozone actually seeks out and attacks these odors, creating new chemicals that are sometimes caustic and sometimes benign. Ozone does act as a bleaching and disinfecting agent.

■ Ozone can be used to deodorize an empty building. Its use in office buildings, factories, and warehouses is possible, providing the precautions below are taken. Do not use in buildings when people are present. The ozone should be evacuated completely from the building or enclosed area before people enter.

Ozone should not be used on any items of lasting value found in cultural institutions. In high concentrations, ozone may remove mold, but these concentrations are deadly for the materials. Ozone should not be used with cellulose materials, as it causes them to become brittle and decompose. Paintings, textiles, paper, film, furniture, and leather are all organic materials. Ozone is highly dangerous to use with these items.

Minimal exposure to ozone is recommended, no more than three hours total. Remember, it is not for use with cellulose, natural, organic, or film-based materials.

## Insects and Pests

After a disaster, it is particularly important to keep an eye out for insects and other pests such as mice, bats, birds, and other small animals. If there is a break in the building envelope or a change in the environment, your institution may become infected with insects and pests. But insects and pests may be present even without a disaster, so when surveying the building and performing routine maintenance and housekeeping, keep an eye out for them.

Let's start with insects. The most common types of insects in libraries, archives, and museums are cockroaches, silverfish, book mites, and termites. They are attracted to damp places such as basements and mechanical rooms. Anywhere moisture might collect, insects and mold will not be far away. Insects like to eat the starch and adhesives in book covers and leave droppings on books. Termites will eat into paper and cardboard and make nests that are difficult to remove and will ultimately destroy the objects they nest in and damage the physical structure of the building. After a disaster that involves water, it is extremely important to stabilize the environment as quickly as possible and to remove any standing water. Most insects like environments between 68° and 86° Fahrenheit and relative humidity between 60 and 80 percent.[11] Control of the environment and good housekeeping are the keys to controlling insects, just as you control mold growth. Use of insecticides, fumigants, and other chemicals should be the last control method you select. Contact a conservator before using any chemicals.

The small animals, such as field mice, birds, and bats, may come inside because it is warm and there are great nesting materials in paper, books, and boxes. You are most likely to find birds and bats in an attic; mice and other rodents in basements, loading docks, and other sheltered areas of a building. When you survey the physical building, look for evidence of pests and have a professional eliminate them and their access to the building.

# Disaster Response and Contingency Planning

- ■ It is important to have a plan, any plan. There must be some notion of where staff will work, how data will be accessed, and how customers will find employees.

- ■ Testing is imperative. Test the data, test the recovery, and test the telecommunications.

- ■ Activate your disaster response team and get the operations up and running as soon as you can. Activate the disaster response plan now.

- ■ Provide emotional counseling and assistance to employees to help them deal with the crisis.

- ■ Don't wait until the dust clears; call the remote location and declare that emergency. Some remote data centers had hundreds of businesses call with a "declared disaster."

## NOTES

1. This should have been determined and the collections identified during the prioritization for recovery phase.

2. Articles pertaining to restoring computer operations are found in the bibliography at the end of this book.

3. Jim Lindner, president of VidiPax, interview by author, New York City, 1994. For additional information, refer to the bibliography.

4. This is known as "sticky shed syndrome."

5. There is a list of companies that provide this service in appendix B.

6. Definitions for various optical disc formats, including their construction, durability, and storage capacity, can be found at http://whatis.techtarget.com.

7. Information about *Stachybotrys atra* is abundant. The best sources for information are the Centers for Disease Control and the Environmental Protection Agency. Several print and Internet sites are listed in the bibliography under "Indoor Air Quality" and in the general resources. In particular, see the fact sheet from the CDC available at www.cdc.gov/mold/stachy.htm.

8. "Ozone," in *McGraw-Hill Encyclopedia of Science and Technology*, 7th ed. (New York: McGraw-Hill, 1992), 17:435.

9. U.S. Environmental Protection Agency, "Ozone Generators" (Washington, DC, 2001), p. 1, or www.epa.gov/iaq/pubs/ozonegen.html. More information is available through the National Institute for Occupational Safety and Health at www.cdc.gov/niosh/topics/ozone.

10. Torben Bruun Hansen and Bente Andersen, "Ozone and Other Air Pollutants from Photocopying Machines," *American Industrial Hygiene Association Journal* 47, no. 10 (1986): 659–65.

11. "Integrated Pest Management," *NEDCC News* 8, no. 1 (Winter 1998): 4; and Beth Lindblom Patkus, preservation consultant, "Integrated Pest Management," Preservation Leaflet 3.10 (2007), www.nedcc.org/resources/leaflets/3Emergency_Management/10PestManagement.php.

# Appendix A

## Checklists and Forms

# 1. Elements of a Disaster Response Plan

This checklist outlines the four sections of disaster response planning and recovery. Use it to make certain all the components are accounted for. Add to this list or modify it to reflect the needs of your institution and your specific disaster response plan. Use the elements as the table of contents for your plan. Just attach page numbers to each section or category.

Make a basic response plan with phone numbers the first page of your disaster response manual for easy reference and contact. Post the daytime numbers for the disaster response team at phones for swift response.

For a quick and dirty plan, use the checklist for the three response phases in conjunction with the list of activities in the subsection "What If the Disaster Happens before You Have a Plan?" in the introduction.

## Prevention

☐ Survey building and collection for potential damage and hazards.

☐ Check fire, smoke, and door alarms, and exit signs.

☐ Mark collections that are water- and heat-sensitive. Make certain they are stored in areas that have the least potential for destruction.

☐ Monitor indoor air quality.

☐ Examine remote storage facilities.

☐ Plan for construction and renovation projects.

☐ Create list of consultants and conservators who can deal with the damaged format (get alternative names).

## Planning

☐ Select disaster response team and alternative staff members.

☐ Assign responsibilities for each of the response phases.

☐ Set priorities for recovery of each of the collections (by format, type, department, floor, or building).

☐ Plan for large and small disasters.

☐ Plan for damage to computers and digital resources.

☐ Plan for loss of access to collections, buildings, materials.

☐ Plan for loss of telecommunications, wireless, and Internet access.

☐ Review insurance coverage and update as needed. Determine what is not covered, and time, situation, and money limitations. Set update schedule for annual review.

☐ Establish communications policy.

☐ Contact disaster response companies and consultants for walk-through and discussion of their roles in potential disasters.

☐ Work with facilities and security to discuss their roles during potential disaster.

☐ Education—train disaster response team; explain responsibilities to rest of staff.

☐ Practice response phases—evaluate plan and revise.

## Response: Three Phases

1. Immediate response to notification that there is a disaster.
   ☐ Gather the team.
   ☐ Alert outside professionals of the disaster.
   ☐ Determine if the building should be closed and for how long.

2. Assess the scope of damage.
   ☐ Call in outside assistance.
   ☐ Organize recovery steps based upon prioritization (developed or assigned in planning phase).
   ☐ Set up communications—internal and external.

3. Begin to deal with items that fall into primary prioritization/recovery categories.
   ☐ Reassign/reallocate staff as needed.
   ☐ Deal with emotional issues.

## Recovery

☐ Restore primary services—skeleton staff.

☐ Restore primary functions—skeleton functions with available staff.

☐ Return to normal—most staff back to regular duties.

☐ Evaluate response procedures and revise disaster response plan.

## 2. Disaster Response Team Contact Information

| Name | Phone |
|------|-------|
|  |  |
|  |  |
|  |  |
|  |  |
|  |  |
|  |  |
|  |  |
|  |  |
|  |  |
|  |  |
|  |  |
|  |  |
|  |  |
|  |  |

**Emergency Meeting Place** is located at

_____

_____

Alternative operating location: _____

Street address: _____

Contact name and phone number: _____

Directions (or append map): _____

# 3. Emergency Contact List—Services

**Institution's insurance company:** _____

Contact person: _____

Policy number: _____

Phone number: _____

**Alarm or security company:** _____

Phone number: _____

Account number/password: _____

Contact person: _____

**Power company:** _____

Emergency phone number: _____

Account number: _____

**Gas company:** _____

Emergency phone number: _____

Account number: _____

**Water company:** _____

Emergency shutoff number: _____

Account number: _____

| Phone company | Emergency phone number | Account number |
|---|---|---|
| Local | | |
| Long distance | | |
| Voicemail | | |
| Cellular or pager service | | |
| Internet service provider | | |

**Information systems/specialist:** _____

Phone number: _____

| Computer vendor company | Phone number | Contact person |
|---|---|---|
| | | |
| | | |

**Office space rental company:** _____

Contact person: _____

Phone number: _____

Location: _____

**Office suite/services company:** _____

Contact person: _____

Phone number: _____

Location: _____

**Construction trailer rental:** _____

Phone number: _____

| Disaster response service providers | Phone number | Contact person |
|---|---|---|
| Servpro Drying Company | 800-909-7189 | |
| Belfor | 800-856-3333 | |
| Polygon Group | 800-422-6379 | |
| BMS Catastrophe Services | 800-433-2940 | |
| | | |
| | | |
| | | |

# 4. Phase I: Activate Plan—Gather Disaster Response Team

Activate emergency purchase orders and contingency fund

Document actions and expenditures

Insurance company contacted at _____

    Contact name and phone number: _____

    _____

    Claim number: _____

Floor plans assembled and as-built blueprints located

    Contact person:_____

Visual documentation by digital, film, or video camera

Indicate areas to be photographed on Phase II—Assessment forms:

_____

_____

_____

Utilities shut off at _____ o'clock by _____ .

# 5. Phase II: Assessment—External Structural Damage

### Documenting the Damage—Create One Chart per Building

Perform and document a building structure survey and collection survey noting damaged and undamaged materials. (This should be updated daily for the first week, weekly after that.)

| External structure | Type of damage | Action ordered date | Contracted or self-performed | Estimated cost (PO#) / insurance coverage | Action completed date |
|---|---|---|---|---|---|
| Walls | | Cover holes | | | |
| Windows | | Board up | | | |
| Roofs | | Cover holes | | | |
| Foundations | | Protect from water | | | |
| Doors | | Board up | | | |
| Security guard | | | | | |
| Grounds | | | | | |
| | | | | | |
| | | | | | |
| | | | | | |
| | | | | | |

Alert security about structural damage and open doors/windows to guard/monitor.

# 6. Phase II: Assessment—Internal Structural Damage

### Documenting the Damage—Create One Chart per Floor or Department

| Internal structure | Type of damage | Action ordered date | Contracted or self-performed | Estimated cost (PO#) / insurance coverage | Action completed date |
|---|---|---|---|---|---|
| Carpets | | Remove or dry all wet areas | | | |
| Ceiling tiles | | Remove all wet tiles | | | |
| Curtains / blinds | | | | | |
| Furniture | | | | | |
| Internal walls | | | | | |
| Office equipment | | | | | |
| Plumbing | | | | | |
| Mechanical equipment | | | | | |
| | | | | | |
| | | | | | |

Indicate damaged areas on drawings of floor plans.

Contact person and phone number for contractual work: _____

_____

## 7. Phase II: Assessment—Contents and Furniture

### *Documenting the Damage—Create One Chart per Floor or Department*

| Equipment | Serial # | Type of damage | Repair or replace | Cost (PO#) / insurance coverage | Date of completion |
|---|---|---|---|---|---|
| Copier | | | | | |
| Fax | | | | | |
| Telephone | | | | | |
| Desk | | | | | |
| Chair | | | | | |
| | | | | | |
| | | | | | |
| | | | | | |
| | | | | | |

Indicate damaged areas on drawings of floor plans.

Contact person and phone number for contractual work: _____

_____

_____

# 8. Phase II: Assessment—Collections

## *Documenting the Damage—Create One Chart per Floor or Department*

| Department or type of collection (by shelf, row, or call number) | Type of damage | Replace or repair | Contract service or internal work | Cost (PO#) / insurance coverage | Date of completion |
|---|---|---|---|---|---|
| Books | | | | | |
| | | | | | |
| | | | | | |
| | | | | | |
| | | | | | |
| Bound periodicals | | | | | |
| | | | | | |
| | | | | | |
| AV materials | | | | | |
| | | | | | |
| Photographs | | | | | |
| | | | | | |
| | | | | | |
| Artwork | | | | | |
| | | | | | |
| | | | | | |

Indicate damaged areas on drawings of floor plans.

Contact person and phone number for contractual work: _____

Off-site storage location and contact information for collections:

_____

_____

_____

# 9. Phase II: Assessment—Computers

## *Documenting the Damage—Create One Chart per Floor or Department*

| Computer components | Serial # | Type of damage | Replace or repair | Contracted or internal work | Cost (PO#) / insurance coverage | Date completed |
|---|---|---|---|---|---|---|
| Monitor | | | | | | |
| CPU or tower | | | | | | |
| | | | | | | |
| Ethernet or IP address | | | | | | |
| Wireless node or router | | | | | | |
| | | | | | | |
| Server | | | | | | |
| | | | | | | |

Indicate damaged areas on drawings of floor plans.

Contact person and phone number for contractual work: _____

Off-site storage location and contact information for computers:

_____

_____

_____

## 10. Phase III: Rescue and Recovery

List contractors and contact information for repair of external damage:

_____

_____

_____

List contractors and contact information for repair of internal structural damage:

_____

_____

_____

List contractors and contact information for storage of furniture, equipment, and collections:

_____

_____

_____

## 11. Phase III: Rescue and Recovery—
## Assignment of Disaster Response Team Responsibilities

| Responsibility | Team member | Backup |
|---|---|---|
| Moving collections | | |
| Packing collections (supervision) | | |
| Inventory of damaged collections (for drying) | | |
| Inventory of stored collections | | |
| Volunteers | | |
| Communications and assignment of staff | | |
| Liaison with contractors and insurance | | |
| | | |
| | | |

## 12. Phase III: Rescue and Recovery— Reallocation of Staff within Building

| Name and home contact information | Reassigned (list responsibility) | Hours to work |
|---|---|---|
|  |  |  |
|  |  |  |
|  |  |  |
|  |  |  |
|  |  |  |

## 13. Phase III: Rescue and Recovery— Reallocation of Staff outside of Building

| Name and contact information | Where assigned (what branch or library) | Cost of salary or unemployment | Hours to work |
|---|---|---|---|
|  |  |  |  |
|  |  |  |  |
|  |  |  |  |
|  |  |  |  |
|  |  |  |  |

## 14. Phase III: Rescue and Recovery— Returning to Normal

| Task | Scheduled for | Date completed |
|---|---|---|
| Visual inspection of external building structure | | |
| Visual inspection of internal building and collection areas | | |
| Return of equipment and furniture | | |
| Return and reinstallation of computers | | |
| Return of collections | | |
| Shelf reading, shifting, etc. | | |
| Library reopens for patrons | | |
| Press releases for reopening celebration sent | | |
| Staff recognition for work on disaster response | | |
| Documentation of changes in procedures | | |
| Evaluation of efficiency of disaster response plan | | |
| Revision of plan | | |
| | | |
| | | |

# 15. Phase III: Rescue and Recovery— Communications

☐ Inform staff—library closed (change emergency line and website information)

Where to report: _____

When to report: _____

☐ Inform vendors and suppliers—library closed

Phone number: _____

Fax number: _____

E-mail address: _____

☐ Temporary location

☐ Do not deliver

☐ Inform public—library closed (change recording on library info line)

☐ Returns

Where to return items if at all: _____

Contact number: _____

☐ Press releases to:

Radio

Newspapers

Television

Website

# 16. Prioritization for Recovery Checklist

Use mission statement and collection development policies as guidelines.

### First Priority

Valuable/permanent papers

Irreplaceable items—rare books, etc.

Artwork and framed materials

Cannot get wet—pre-1950 photographs, clay-coated paper

Objects, etc.

Textiles

Circulation system

Registrar's records

### Second Priority

Expensive to replace/repair—rare books/ manuscripts

Essential to workings/function of institution, library, or information center

Core collection

Masters of microfilm (should be stored off-site)

Digital masters

OPAC/computer services, hardware, software, data

### Third Priority

Supplements core collection

Heavily requested items

Government documents

Indexes, major reference tools, CD-ROM indexes

### Fourth Priority

Standing orders/annual replacements and updates

Nice to have but not essential to mission of institution

Duplicate microfilm/microfiche—otherwise replace

Items duplicated by microfilm/microfiche— periodicals, government documents

Items duplicated by digital and online resources

### Fifth Priority

Disposable items

Items replaceable with other formats

### Other Items of Importance

Computer files should be backed up daily, if not more often

Contact manager

List of vendors and suppliers

Inventory should be stored off-site. Copies on server or network drives

Inventory of artwork stored off-site, plus pictures and provenance

Inventory of textiles, clothing, etc., stored off-site with pictures and provenance

# 17. Vital and Permanent Records Checklist

Indicate where these items are stored.

Contracts

_____

_____

Articles of incorporation, certificates, licenses, or legal papers

_____

_____

Titles, deeds, and mortgages

_____

_____

Stock records

_____

_____

Bylaws

_____

_____

Resolutions

_____

_____

Ownership and lease papers

_____

_____

Insurance papers

_____

_____

Board of directors'/trustees' minutes in microform copy (should be stored off-site)

_____

_____

# 18. Recovery Decisions and Priorities Checklist

If there is no plan in place or the prioritization for recovery phase was not completed, the following are guidelines of how different materials can be stabilized and some basic treatments.

If collections are not wet, quickly cover the stacks with plastic to prevent additional water damage, increase the temperature and the air flow, and decrease the relative humidity. Remember to remove the plastic as soon as the environment is stable or move the materials to a dry location.

### Plain Paper*
☐ Attend to within 72 hours.

### Clay-Coated Paper, Including Thermal-Fax and Self-Carboned Paper
☐ Remove from water and treat or freeze within 1–6 hours of exposure to water. *Only if wet.*

### Microfilm/Microfiche
☐ Attend to within 72 hours or
☐ Keep wet and send for reprocessing.

### Motion Picture Film, Post-1950 Negatives, Slides, and Post-1950 Photographs
☐ Attend to within 72 hours.
☐ Hang to dry.
☐ Keep wet or
☐ Freeze quickly.

### Pre-1950 Photographs and Negatives
☐ Contact photograph conservator before treating or freezing.

### CD-ROM, DVD, and Optical Discs
☐ Remove from water.
☐ Treat immediately.
☐ Dry and clean appropriately.

### Magnetic Tape (Audio or Video)
If unique and wet
☐ Remove from water.
☐ Treat immediately.
☐ Send for drying, cleaning, and copying.

If exposed to dust, soot, or particulate matter
☐ Dry first, then clean.

If not unique (commercial tape) and wet
☐ Discard and replace.

If not wet
☐ Clean tape.
☐ Place in dry, clean boxes.

### Computer Tapes without Backup Copies
☐ Remove from water.
☐ Treat immediately.
☐ Identify:
    Format
    Computer type
    Amount of space used on tapes
☐ Send for drying and copying.

If exposed to dust, soot, or particulate matter
☐ Dry first, then clean.

### Diskettes and Removable Data Storage Devices without Backup Copies
Treat immediately.
☐ Dry.
☐ Clean.
☐ Copy.

### Hardware
Drives (if exposed to dust, soot, or particulate matter)
☐ Dry, clean, and recertify.

Keyboards
☐ Replace.

---

* After drying, paper may have expanded and will require additional storage space or rebinding when returned to the collection.

Monitors (depends upon value)

☐ Clean or

☐ Replace.

Servers

☐ Clean or

☐ Replace.

LANs and servers, peripherals and wireless notes

☐ Clean or

☐ Replace.

Unique or obsolete hardware (depends upon insurance)

☐ Upgrade or

☐ Clean.

***Office Equipment
(fax, photocopier, printers, etc.)***

☐ Dry, clean, and recertify.

# 19. Paper Records Recovery Decision Checklist

Depending upon prioritization for recovery decisions, mission statement, and collection development policies, evaluate by collection, not item-by-item. Some of these items may be replaced with like kind or digital formats.

Vital and permanent records

☐ Must retain original or legal surrogate.*

☐ Dry and clean.

Daily and retrospective records and paper materials

☐ Remove from wet location.

☐ Dry and clean as necessary.

☐ Pack file folders in document storage boxes.

☐ Label boxes with contents and location.

For small quantities (less than 300 volumes or 10 linear/cubic feet), treat in-house if you have the manpower and time, otherwise freeze and freeze-dry.

☐ Decrease temperature and relative humidity in drying room.

☐ Increase air movement.

☐ Spread papers out or support vertically.

☐ Paper may curl and wrinkle when drying.

☐ Watch for mold growth.

For large quantities (more than 300 volumes or 10 linear/cubic feet)

☐ Freeze immediately.

☐ Ship to freeze-drying facility as soon as possible.

☐ May be directed to ship in refrigerator/freezer trucks.

☐ Freeze-drying takes 4–6 weeks depending upon quantity of materials and amount of moisture.

☐ Have mold removed if necessary.

☐ Loose papers should be returned in new folders if needed.

---

* Legal surrogates are documents that are scanned as PDF images and certified as originals onto optical/compact disc, websites, microforms, or some xerographic processes. Check with legal counsel for the most recent court decisions.

## 20. Clay-Coated Paper Recovery Decision Checklist

Is coated paper wet?

*If no*

- ☐ Remove to dry location or
- ☐ Cover to prevent getting wet.

If yes, is it a priority to recover?

*If no*

- ☐ Discard.

*If yes*

- ☐ Must attend to very quickly (within 1–6 hours) or it will become solid block.*
- ☐ Keep wet until ready to interleave or
- ☐ Freeze and then freeze-dry.
- ☐ Interleave with sheets of double-sided wax paper or freezer paper, and
- ☐ Start drying procedures as soon as possible.

Note: Whether freeze-drying or dehumidifying, the success rate for coated paper is 50 percent.

---

* Inks are often embedded in clay and text may float off paper when soaked in water.

# 21. Books and Bound Materials Recovery Decision Checklist

Evaluate using mission statement and collection development policies. Treat by collection, not item-by-item. Some of these items may be replaced with like kind or digital formats.

### Valuable or irreplaceable?

☐ If no, consider replacing with newer format.

☐ If yes, pack wet books flat or spine down in one-(1) cubic-foot boxes, and

☐ Freeze to stabilize physical deterioration and arrest mold.

### Standing order

☐ Wait for new issue.

### Replaced on regular basis

☐ Discard.

### Reference title and materials

☐ Replace with new version or digital format.

Not all materials are available in digital format; consult collection development or acquisitions professionals before discarding.

### Periodical

If already own microfilm copy or have digital access,

☐ Discard.

If no,

☐ Purchase online or digital access or

☐ Consider using document delivery service for low-use items.

Not all materials are available in digital format; consult collection development or acquisitions professionals before discarding.

### Indexes

☐ Purchase online access to newer volumes.

☐ Dry and clean or

☐ If destroyed, purchase older volumes as needed.

Not all materials are available in digital format; consult collection development or acquisitions professionals before discarding.

### For small quantities or damp materials (less than 300 volumes or 10 cubic feet)

☐ Air dry or dehumidify.

☐ Check for mold and clean as needed.

☐ Check physical structure.

☐ Rebind or recase if necessary.

### For large quantities or wet materials (more than 300 volumes or 10 cubic feet)

☐ Freeze.

☐ Ship for freeze-drying as instructed by company. (Takes four to six weeks to dry depending upon moisture content and quantity of materials.)

☐ Remove mold as needed.

☐ Check physical structure.

☐ Rebind or recase if necessary.

# 22. Microforms Recovery Decision Checklist

Wash dirt off surface with clean water if necessary.

### Dry

- ☐ Remove to dry location or
- ☐ Cover to prevent from getting wet.

### Wet duplicate, vesicular, or diazo

- ☐ Discard and replace using copy from master copy.

### Wet original or master (should be stored off-site)

- ☐ If yes, recover.
- ☐ Remove from paper boxes or sleeves.
- ☐ Send film for reprocessing—keep wet during shipment.
- ☐ Hang fiche to dry.
- ☐ Place in new boxes and sleeves.

### Wet-jacketed fiche

- ☐ Remove from water and treat immediately or it will stick together permanently.
- ☐ Remove film from sleeves.
- ☐ Hang to dry.
- ☐ Insert into new sleeves or jackets.
- ☐ Label accordingly.

# 23. Software and Data Recovery Decision Checklist

### Backup version in dry, safe location?

☐ Load software and data using most recent backup versions.

### Need original software?

☐ Send to be dried and copied onto new removable data storage device, server, or tape.

☐ Load copied version into "recertified" computer or network server.

☐ Import data.

☐ Discard the original.

### Time to upgrade commercial program?

☐ Purchase new version of software or new format.

☐ Load onto computer.

☐ Import data.

☐ Discard the original, out-of-date software.

## 24. Computer Equipment Recovery Decision Checklist

Check the recovery priority for equipment.

### Dry

☐ Remove to dry, safe location.

### Wet

☐ Check recovery priority.

### Upgrade scheduled?

☐ Replace according to needs and insurance coverage.

### No insurance

☐ Open covers.

☐ Do not let ceiling tiles, soot, and dirt drop inside.

☐ Let inside dry.

☐ Recertify equipment.

### Fire-damaged

☐ Open covers.

### Soot or dirt inside

☐ Have disaster recovery firm dry, clean, and restore and recertify equipment to pre-loss condition.*

☐ Replace parts as necessary.

---

* Some disaster response companies provide cleaning and recertification services for computer equipment. Belfor, 2425 Blue Smoke Court South, Fort Worth, TX 76105 (800-856-3333), is one company that provides these services. See listings of companies that provide these services in appendix B.

# 25. Checklist for Determining Drying Method

☐ Type of materials that are wet

☐ Amount of time exposed to water or very high humidity

☐ Quantity of materials that are wet or water-damaged

☐ Value or restrictions on access

If more time is needed to make decisions or raise money, freeze and store the materials.

Check with a conservator before freezing:

Artwork

Pre-1950 photographic processes

Leather or vellum

Furniture

Pre-1950 phonograph records and cylinders

Textiles

Museum objects

Note: Do not freeze magnetic tape, optical discs, or removable data storage devices.

# 26. Environmental Conditions for Air Drying Books and Paper Files Checklist

### Temperature

☐ As cold as possible

☐ No temperatures above 72° Fahrenheit

High temperatures will decrease the life of paper and photographic materials, causing irreparable and irreversible aging and secondary damage, such as release of adhesives and distortion of bindings.

### Humidity

☐ As low as possible, not below 30 percent rH.

☐ Moisture content of paper should read 6 percent to 8 percent when dry. Very dry air can cause paper and film to become brittle.

For very hygroscopic materials such as leather, vellum, textiles, furniture, and framed works of art on canvas:

☐ Very slowly reduce humidity to prevent additional distortion and to prevent structural damage.

☐ Contact conservators who specialize in these formats before treating or stabilizing.

Before accepting dried materials back from the disaster response or drying company:

☐ Stabilize temperatures in the institution to prevent absorption of excess moisture and to prevent a mold infection, and clean the area and get it ready for shelving materials.

☐ Confirm HVAC is recalibrated to preservation standards.

# 27. Current Suggested Temperature and Relative Humidity for Cultural Institutions

Ideal ranges for:

Open stacks, public access areas: 68° to 72° Fahrenheit; relative humidity 45 percent to 60 percent

Closed stacks and low-use areas: 65° to 68° Fahrenheit; relative humidity 45 percent to 55 percent

Black-and-white film and photographs: 45° to 60° Fahrenheit; relative humidity 35 percent to 50 percent

Color film requires colder temperatures below 32° Fahrenheit; with a relative humidity of 30 percent to 45 percent. Check with a photograph or film conservator.

Maximize air flow to prevent mold growth.

Note: If the collection was exposed to mold in the past, then maintain a lower relative humidity to prevent mold growth. Monitor the collection regularly for mold infections.

# 28. Cleaning Books Checklist

☐ Dry all dirty, sooty, and moldy materials before cleaning or removing mold.

☐ Moldy materials that cannot be treated immediately should be frozen. Freezing mold does not kill or eradicate it, but merely stops mold growth.

☐ Hold book shut at front edge.

☐ Vacuum mold from

> top edge of book moving from spine to edge,
>
> bottom edge from spine to edge, and
>
> front edge from top to bottom.

☐ Vacuum

> front cover,
>
> back cover, and
>
> spine.

☐ Open front cover and vacuum off inner edge near fold (hinge area).

☐ Open back cover and vacuum off inner edge near fold (hinge area).

☐ Repeat process using "dry chemical sponge" made of pure latex or rubber sponge, not cellulose.

> *Do not* get the sponge wet.
>
> *Do not* use any liquid to eliminate mold; it will cause mold to grow again.
>
> *Do not* put treated materials into sealed containers, boxes, or plastic; this can encourage mold growth.

When the cleaning process has been completed, before returning the materials to the rest of the collection:

☐ Look through the book and make certain no mold, soot, and dirt remain.

☐ Put in stable, dry environment.

☐ Monitor for reappearance of mold.

☐ Return to original location after the environment is stable and the relative humidity is back to 45 percent to 60 percent (± 2 percent). These materials are very susceptible to mold.

☐ Monitor previously infected areas throughout seasonal changes to determine that mold remains arrested.

## 29. Checklist for When Materials Are Returned from the Contractor

☐ Have file folders been labeled correctly?

☐ Are materials filed in their original order in document storage boxes?

☐ Are cartons labeled with proper identifying information? Include name of institution, number of items, location taken from, box number, and type of material.

☐ Check contents against inventory sheets.

☐ Are items dry and clean?

Note: Contact disaster response/drying company immediately if there is a problem.
Report to the insurance company immediately any problems with returned collections.

# 30. Building Survey Checklist

### Fire exits

☐ Visible and clearly marked

☐ Exit signs and doors not blocked

☐ Alarms on the doors work

☐ Alarms ring in central security office

Security people call _____ in an emergency.

### Emergency and fire alarms

☐ Ring and strobe in the immediate vicinity

☐ Ring and strobe throughout the building

☐ Ring or light up in a central security office

Security people call _____ in an emergency.

### Emergency lighting

☐ Batteries work

☐ Batteries were replaced on _____

### Fire extinguishers

☐ Locations for all marked on the floor plan

☐ Type indicated on the floor plan

☐ Fire extinguishers checked on _____

### Fire alarm call boxes

☐ Locations for all marked on the floor plan

☐ Type indicated on the floor plan

### Smoke and heat alarms

☐ Meet the appropriate needs of the collections in those areas

☐ Alarms ring _____

Emergency evacuation drill practiced on _____

Alarms tested on _____

## 31. Fire Extinguisher Information List

| Location | Rating or Type: ABC or A? | Last Inspection |
|----------|---------------------------|-----------------|
|          |                           |                 |
|          |                           |                 |
|          |                           |                 |
|          |                           |                 |
|          |                           |                 |
|          |                           |                 |
|          |                           |                 |
|          |                           |                 |
|          |                           |                 |
|          |                           |                 |

# 32. Remote Storage Facilities Checklist

Owned by institution

☐ Map and directions with identification of main and auxiliary entrances appended.

Collections owned by institution only?

☐ yes

☐ no

Shared/regional facility?

☐ yes

☐ no

Contact information for other institutions:

_____

_____

Entire building rented?

Name of lessor: _____

_____

_____

Emergency contact and phone number: _____

_____

_____

_____

Designated space contracted from _____

_____

_____

Emergency contact and phone number:

_____

Specific liaison from the institution and phone number:

_____

_____

_____

Building survey of remote storage facility:

☐ Sprinklers present

☐ Fire and smoke alarms

☐ Utilities

in separate area

run near or over collections

☐ Floor plan appended

Collection-type survey of remote storage facility:

☐ Low-use collections

☐ Archives and paper record storage

☐ Data and magnetic media

☐ All of the above

☐ Priority level: _____

☐ Create floor plans identifying and locating the utilities, collection locations with their associated priorities for recovery, and emergency exits.

☐ Identify personnel who are familiar with the remote storage facility collections and the building layout. These persons should be able to gain access to the building after hours (usually the head of the remote storage facility and the second in command).

Head of remote storage facility and phone number:

_____

_____

Assistant and phone number:

_____

_____

Dates or frequency of inspection of the remote facility and the collections:

_____

_____

_____

# 33. Computer Backup Tape and Data Storage Facilities Checklist

☐ How often are tapes taken to "remote" storage? _____

☐ Digital or remotes data backup frequency: _____

☐ Record storage or data storage—off-site

    Where are tapes stored?_____

    How are tapes stored? _____

    Environmental conditions: _____

☐ Security

    On-site

    In transit

☐ Contact procedures

    1-hour retrieval: _____

    24-hour retrieval: _____

☐ Who is authorized to have physical access to data? _____

☐ Last visit to storage facility: _____

☐ Record storage or data storage on remote server in building

    Where are tapes stored? _____

    How are tapes stored? _____

    Environmental conditions: _____

☐ Security?

    yes

    no

    Emergency phone number: _____

☐ Who has physical access to data? _____

☐ Alarm system

    Smoke

    Fire

    Water

☐ Fireproof cabinets

    Rating: _____

# 34. Telecommunications and Phone-Dependent Services Checklist

### Fax

- ☐ Set up an account with a service provider.
- ☐ Use e-mail if available.

### Voice and e-mail

- ☐ Write out routines for how to access the various information providers from an outside number on switchboard.
- ☐ Determine when each department is scheduled to have its system backed up and accessible (based on prioritization for recovery).
- ☐ Inform customers, colleagues, and suppliers of new fax, Internet and IP address, e-mail addresses.
- ☐ Designate one or two lines for incoming calls.

### Internet service provider

- ☐ Write down user name, phone number for office, alternative access, and technical support.
- ☐ Outline alternative access procedures, including configuring browser and e-mail service.
- ☐ Define who has access to change and move Internet accounts and IP addresses.

### Website host

- ☐ Write out account, e-mail, and URL access information.
- ☐ Define who has access to change and move website.
- ☐ Provide phone number for web developer, web hosting service.

### Wireless access

- ☐ Write out simple instructions for use without preprogrammed scripts.
- ☐ Cable modem (DSL and ISDN lines if applicable).
- ☐ Retrieve copy of operating software with drivers.
- ☐ Reinstall software.

# 35. Computers and Data—Hardware Checklist

Create a separate list for each system or location.

For replacement and insurance purposes, keep track of what equipment is where.

Location: _____

Phone number: _____

| ID or serial number | Computer type | Memory | RAM | Peripherals | Operating system |
|---|---|---|---|---|---|
|  |  |  |  |  |  |
|  |  |  |  |  |  |
|  |  |  |  |  |  |
|  |  |  |  |  |  |
|  |  |  |  |  |  |
|  |  |  |  |  |  |
|  |  |  |  |  |  |
|  |  |  |  |  |  |

## 36. LANs and Servers Checklist

| Location or department | Serial number/ model number | Components | Network type | Minimum requirements |
|---|---|---|---|---|
|  |  |  |  |  |
|  |  |  |  |  |
|  |  |  |  |  |
|  |  |  |  |  |
|  |  |  |  |  |
|  |  |  |  |  |

## 37. Printers Checklist

| Location or department | Serial number | Type | Model number | Computer port or IP address |
|---|---|---|---|---|
|  |  |  |  |  |
|  |  |  |  |  |
|  |  |  |  |  |
|  |  |  |  |  |
|  |  |  |  |  |
|  |  |  |  |  |

## 38. Battery Backup or UPS (Uninterruptable Power Supply) Checklist

| Location or department | Serial number/ model number | Hours of power | Model number | Attached to which LAN, network, or computers |
|---|---|---|---|---|
|  |  |  |  |  |
|  |  |  |  |  |
|  |  |  |  |  |
|  |  |  |  |  |
|  |  |  |  |  |
|  |  |  |  |  |

## 39. Software Checklist—Commercial Software

Keep track of what is owned and where it is located for backup, replacement, and insurance purposes.

| Type of program | Program name and version number | Serial number | Site license number for how many users | Technical help number or URL |
|---|---|---|---|---|
| Operating system |  |  |  |  |
| Software |  |  |  |  |
|  |  |  |  |  |
|  |  |  |  |  |
| Browser |  |  |  |  |
|  |  |  |  |  |
| Downloaded software |  |  |  |  |

Note: Not all computer software companies have a replacement policy for programs lost to fire or flood. Earlier versions are usually not available. Proof of ownership via serial and license number may be required for assistance.

## 40. Software Checklist—Customized and Proprietary Software

Keep track of what is owned and where it is located for backup, replacement, and insurance purposes.

| Type of program | Program name and version number | Last modification date | Documentation stored | Technical help number or URL |
|---|---|---|---|---|
| Operating system | | | | |
| Software | | | | |
| | | | | |
| | | | | |
| Browser | | | | |
| | | | | |
| Downloaded software | | | | |

Note: Not all computer software companies have a replacement policy for programs lost to fire or flood. Earlier versions are usually not available. Proof of ownership via serial and license number may be required for assistance.

## 41. Software Checklist—Software Documentation

Keep track of what is owned and where it is located for backup, replacement, and insurance purposes.

| Type of program | Location of physical server or network or digital data | Location of manuals or documentation |
|---|---|---|
| | | |
| | | |
| | | |
| | | |
| | | |
| | | |
| | | |

Note: Not all computer software companies have a replacement policy for programs lost to fire or flood. Earlier versions are usually not available. Proof of ownership via serial and license number may be required for assistance.

# 42. Backup Routines Checklist

Suggested backup routines, off-site data storage requirements,
hardware and software needs.

***Backup routines***

Method

☐ full

☐ incremental

Frequency

☐ daily

☐ other

Off-site storage: _____

_____

Number of tapes or amount of space per backup: _____

_____

Second person trained in backup routine: _____

_____

# 43. Computer Backup Information Checklist

Indicate where each item is located.

Manuals: _____

_____

_____

Software licenses and current program versions: _____

_____

_____

Hardware configurations and requirements: _____

_____

_____

LAN configuration and requirements: _____

_____

_____

Server configuration and requirements: _____

_____

_____

Data files (stored off-site): _____

_____

_____

# Associations, Organizations, and Companies

## Disaster Response Assistance and Referrals

American Association of Museums
  1225 I Street NW, Suite 400
  Washington, DC 20005
  Phone: 202-289-1818
  Fax: 202-289-6578
  www.aam-us.org

American Institute for Conservation of Historic and Artistic Artifacts (AIC)
  1717 K Street NW, Suite 301
  Washington, DC 20006
  Phone: 202-452-9545
  Fax: 202-452-9328
  www.conservation-us.org
  *Request referral for conservators.*

American Red Cross, Disaster Services National Headquarters
  430 17th Street NW
  Washington, DC 20006
  Phone: 202-639-3500
  www.redcross.org

AMIGOS Library Services, Inc.
  Imaging and Preservation Services Manager
  14400 Midway Road
  Dallas, TX 75244-3509
  Phone: 972-851-8000 or 800-843-8482
  Fax: 972-991-6061
  www.amigos.org

Association of Records Managers and Administrators, Inc. (ARMA)
  4200 Somerset Drive, No. 215
  Prairie Village, KS 66208
  Phone: 913-341-3808 or 800-422-2762 (U.S. and Canada)
  Fax: 913-341-3742
  www.arma.org

Canadian Conservation Institute (CCI)
  1030 Innes Road
  Ottawa, Ontario K1B 4S7
  Canada
  Phone: 613-741-4390
  www.cci-icc.gc.ca

---

The lists in this appendix are not comprehensive; nor does inclusion imply an endorsement.

Conservation Center for Art and Historical Artifacts
(CCAHA)
    264 South 23rd Street
    Philadelphia, PA 19103
    Phone: 215-545-0613
    Fax: 215-735-9313
    www.ccaha.org

European Commission on Preservation and Access,
Royal Netherlands Academy of Arts and Sciences
    Kloveniersburgwal 29
    P.O. Box 19121
    NL-1000 GC Amsterdam
    Netherlands
    Phone: +31-20-551 08 39
    Fax: +31-20-620 49 41
    E-mail: ecpa@bureau.knaw.nl
    www.knaw.nl

Heritage Preservation
(formerly NIC—National Institutions for the
Conservation of Cultural Property)
    1730 K Street NW, Suite 566
    Washington, DC 20006-3836
    Phone: 202-634-1422 or 888-388-6789
    Fax: 202-634-1435
    www.heritagepreservation.org

Institute of Museum and Library Services (IMLS)
    1100 Pennsylvania Avenue NW
    Washington, DC 20506
    Phone: 202-6066-5836
    www.imls.gov

International Centre for the Study of the Preservation
and the Restoration of Cultural Property (ICCROM)
    13, Via di San Michele
    1-00153 Rome, Italy
    E-mail: oci@iccrom.org
    www.iccrom.org

International Council of Museums (ICOM)
    Maison de l'UNESCO
    1 rue Miollis
    F-75732 Paris
    CEDEX 15, France
    Phone: +33-1-4734-0500
    Fax: +33-1-4306-7862
    http://icom.museum

International Federation of Library Associations (IFLA)
    P.O. Box 95312
    2509 CH The Hague
    Netherlands
    Phone: +31-70-3140884
    Fax: +31-70-3834827
    E-mail: IFLA@ifla.org
    www.ifla.org

Lyrasis (a merger of SOLINET, PALINET, and NELINET)
    Preservation Services
    1438 West Peachtree Street NW, Suite 200
    Atlanta, GA 30309-2955
    Phone: 404-592-4804 or 800-999-8558
    Fax: 404-892-7879
    E-mail: marlee.givens@lyrasis.org
    www.lyrasis.org

National Archives and Records Administration
    8601 Adelphi Road
    College Park, MD 20740-6001
    700 Pennsylvania Avenue NW
    Washington, DC 20408
    Phone: 866-325-7208
    www.nara.gov

National Park Service (NPS)
    1849 C Street NW
    Washington, DC 20240
    Phone: 202-208-6843
    www.nps.gov

    Technical Preservation Services at NPS/
      Historic Preservation
      www.nps.gov/history/hps/tps/

Northeast Document Conservation Center (NEDCC)
    Preservation Field Services
    100 Brickstone Square
    Andover, MA 01810-1494
    Phone: 978-470-1010
    Fax: 978-475-6021
    www.nedcc.org

OCLC Online Computer Library Center, Inc.
6565 Frantz Road
Dublin, OH 43017-0702
Phone: 614-764-6000 or 800-848-5878 (U.S. and
Canada)
Fax: 614-764-6096
www.oclc.org

*OCLC provides some disaster response services, including priority to get rewired, reload data, and rent or lease computer equipment to replace damaged OCLC terminals. If the library is still using catalog cards, OCLC will replace them for a minimal cost.*

Regional Alliance for Preservation
www.rap-arcc.org/index.php

*National cooperative providing preservation resources and assistance with disaster response*

Society of American Archivists
527 South Wells Street, 5th floor
Chicago, IL 60607-3922
Phone: 312-922-0140
Fax: 312-347-1452
www.archivists.org

Special Libraries Association (SLA)
1700 Eighteenth Street NW
Washington, DC 20009-2514
Phone: 202-234-4700
Fax: 202-265-9317
www.sla.org

*Seek referral for a consultant to help rebuild collections, computer systems, temporary librarians, and online information providers.*

## Water-Damaged, Film-Based Collections

American Film Institute
2021 North Western Avenue
Los Angeles, CA 90027
Phone: 323-856-7600
Fax: 323-467-4578
www.afi.com/index.asp

Association of Moving Image Archivists
8949 Wilshire Boulevard
Beverly Hills, CA 90211
Phone: 310-550-1300
Fax: 310-550-1363
www.amianet.org

Canadian Conservation Institute (CCI)
1030 Innes Road
Ottawa, Ontario K1B 4S7
Canada
Phone: 613-741-4390
www.cci-icc.gc.ca

Image Permanence Institute
Rochester Institute of Technology
70 Lomb Memorial Drive
Rochester, NY 14623-5604
Phone: 585-475-5199
Fax: 585-475-7230
www.rit.edu

National Archives of Canada
395 Wellington Street
Ottawa, Ontario K1A 0N4
Canada
Phone: 613-995-5138 or 866-578-7777
(Canada and U.S.)
Fax: 613-995-6274
www.archives.ca

Northeast Document Conservation Center (NEDCC)
Preservation Field Services
100 Brickstone Square
Andover, MA 01810-1494
Phone: 978-470-1010
Fax: 978-475-6021
www.nedcc.org

*Conservation treatment available from NEDCC and other regional conservation centers.*

## Commercial Companies That Will Reprocess Microfilm

Contact companies about specific services before adding them to your list.

Kodak Disaster Recovery Services
    Eastman Kodak Company
    1700 Dewey Avenue
    B65, Door 0, Room 340
    Rochester, NY 14650-1819
    Attn.: Howard Schwartz 800-EKC-TEST (352-8378)

UMI
    300 North Zeeb Road
    P.O. Box 1346
    Ann Arbor, MI 48106-1346
    Phone: 800-521-0600, ext. 2619
    www.umi.com

## Magnetic Tape—Cleaning and Restoration Firms

Chace Productions
    201 South Victory Boulevard
    Burbank, CA 61502-2349
    Phone: 818-842-8346
    Fax: 818-842-8353
    www.chace.com
    *Sound and audio restoration*

John Polito
    Audio Mechanics
    6735 Forest Lawn Drive, No. 200
    Los Angeles, CA 90068
    Phone: 818-846-5525
    Fax: 818-846-5501
    E-mail: john@audiomechanics.com
    www.audiomechanics.com
    *Sound restoration and remastering*

OnTrack Data International, Inc.
    9023 Columbine Road
    Eden Prairie, MN 55347
    Phone: 952-937-5161 or 800-872-2599
    Fax: 952-937-5750
    www.ontrackdatarecovery.com
    *Magnetic media, computer tapes, hard drives, and diskettes*

Tek Media Supply Company (a subsidiary of the RTI Group)
    4700 Chase
    Lincolnwood, IL 60712-1689
    Phone: 847-677-3000 or 800-323-7520
    Fax: 847-677-1311 or 800-784-6733
    www.rtico.com/tekmedia/
    *Cleaning, inspection, and repair supplies for AV: film, tapes, and discs*

### Information Resources

National Center for Film and Video Preservation at the American Film Institute
    2021 North Western Avenue
    Los Angeles, CA 90027
    Phone: 323-856-7600
    Fax: 323-467-4578
    www.afi.com

## Water-Damaged Phonograph Records

### Sources of Information

Association for Recorded Sound Collections (ARSC)
    c/o Peter Shambarger, Executive Director
    P.O. Box 543
    Annapolis, MD 21404-0543
    www.arsc-audio.org

### Sound Recordings

Conservation Division
    Library of Congress
    101 Independence Avenue
    Washington, DC 20540-4530
    Phone: 202-707-5213
    Fax: 202-707-3434
    www.loc.gov/preserv/

National Library of Canada
    Recorded Sound and Video Collection
    Music Division
    395 Wellington Street
    Ottawa, Ontario K1A 0N4
    Canada
    Phone: 613-996-7510
    Fax: 613-952-2895
    www.nlc-bnc.ca

Seth B. Winner
Seth Winner Sound Studios, Inc.
2055 Whalen Avenue
Merrick, NY 11566-5320
Phone: 516-771-0028
Fax: 516-771-0028
E-mail: Seth.B.Winner@worldnet.attnet
*Audio restoration engineer and archivist, sound restorations, classical music archives*

Steven Smolian—Smolian Sound
1 Wormans Mill Court
Frederick, MD 21701
Phone: 301-694-5134
www.soundsaver.com

## Cleaning Machines and Supplies for Dry Phonograph Records

Discwasher
c/o Recoton Corporation
2950 Lake Emma Road
Lake Mary, FL 32746-6240
Phone: 800-732-6866
Fax: 407-333-1628
www.discwasher.com

Keith Monks Record Cleaning Machine
c/o Digital Audio Restoration
P.O. Box 672
Don Mills, Ontario M3C 2T6
Canada
Phone: 416-444-3444 (10 to 10 ET)
Fax: 416-444-3550
www.audio-restoration.com/monks5.htm

Nitty Gritty Record Care Products
4650 Arrow Hwy., No. F4
Montclair, CA 91763
Phone: 909-625-5525
www.nittygrittyinc.com

## Mold and Indoor Air Quality Issues

Indoor Air Quality Information Clearinghouse
(IAQ INFO)
U.S. Environmental Protection Agency
P.O. Box 37133
Washington, DC 20013-7133
Phone: 703-356-4020 or 800-438-4318
Fax: 703-356-5386

Information Sources
Aerotech Laboratories, Inc. (a division of EMLab P&K)
2020 West Lone Cactus Drive
Phoenix, AZ 85027
Phone: 800-651-4802
Fax: 623-780-7695
www.aerotechpk.com

National Institute for Occupational Safety and Health
(NIOSH)
Education and Information Division Publications Dissemination
4676 Columbia Parkway
Cincinnati, OH 45226-1988
Phone: 800-356-4674
Fax: 513-533-8573
E-mail: pubstaft@cdc.gov
www.cdc.gov/niosh/homepage.html

U.S. Environmental Protection Agency, National Center for Environmental Publications (NSCEP)
P.O. Box 42419
Cincinnati, OH 42419
Phone: 800-490-9198
Fax: 513-489-8695
www.epa.gov/ncepihom

## Disaster Recovery Companies

For local companies that remove standing water and dry small areas in buildings, see the Yellow Pages under "Fire and Water Damage Restoration."

Belfor USA Group, Inc.
2425 Blue Smoke Court West
Fort Worth, TX 76105
Phone: 817-535-6793 or 800-856-3333
Fax: 817-536-1167
www.belforusa.com

*Freeze-drying, cleaning, and mold removal from print and nonprint materials, as well as decontamination and repair of electronic and mechanical equipment*

BMS CAT
303 Arthur Street
Fort Worth, TX 76107
Phone: 800-433-2940
www.bmscat.com

Commercial Drying Technologies
1520 Route 37 West
Toms River, NJ 08757
Phone: 732-323-0149 OR 800-318-0764
www.cdtcompanies.com

*Provides integrated water-damage recovery solutions. Water-damage recovery/restoration utilizing highly mobile/high-volume desiccant dehumidification. Service for northeastern United States.*

Document Reprocessors
40 Railroad Avenue
Rushville, NY 14544
Phone: 585-554-4500
Fax: 585-554-4114
OR
1384 Rollins Road
Burlingame, CA 94010
Phone: 650-401-7711
Fax: 650-401-8711
www.documentreprocessors.com

Polygon Group
Headquarters and 24-Hour Emergency
15 Sharpner's Pond Road, Building F
North Andover, MA 01845
Phone: 800-422-6379
Fax: 978-655-8511
www.polygongroup.us

NBD International, Inc.
P.O. Box 1003
241 Myrtle Street
Ravenna, OH 44266
Phone: 330-296-0221 or 800-929-3398
Fax: 330-296-0292 or 800-783-3802
www.nbdint.com

*Water- and smoke-damage recovery of audio- and videotape; computer tapes, diskettes, and CD formats; and vinyl records. Also provides water- and smoke-damage recovery of paper-based materials.*

Servpro Drying Companies
575 Airport Road
Gallatin, TN 37066
Phone: 615-451-0200 or 800-SERVPRO (737-8776)
Fax: 615-451-0291
www.servpro.com

## Contingency Planning and Response Companies with Hot or Cold Sites

IBM Corporation
1 New Orchard Road
Armonk, New York 10504-1722
Phone: 914-499-1900
IBM Business Continuity and Resiliency Services
Phone: 800-IBM-7080
www-935.ibm.com/services/us/en/it-services/
business-continuity-and-resiliency-services
.html

SunGard Availability Services
680 East Swedesford Road
Wayne, PA 19087
Phone: 800-468-7483
Alert and Disaster Hotline: 866-722-1313
www.sungardas.com

## Suppliers: Special Services and Products for Disaster Response and Prevention

American Power Conversion
132 Fairgrounds Road
West Kingston, RI 02892
Phone: 800-726-0610
www.apc.com

*Uninterruptible power supply, surge suppressors*

Blackberry
c/o Research in Motion
295 Phillip Street
Waterloo, Ontario N2L 3W8
Canada
Phone: 519-888-7465 or 877-255-2377
Fax: 519-888-7884
http://us.blackberry.com

Ebac Industrial Products
700 Thimble Shoals Blvd, Suite 109
Newport News, VA 23606-2575
Phone: 757-873-6800
Fax: 757-873-3632
www.ebacusa.com

*Dehumidifiers—rental*

FedEx Custom Critical or FedEx Express Freight
3875 Airways, Module H3
Department 4634
Memphis, TN 38116
Phone: 800-332-0807
http://customcritical.fedex.com

*24-hour emergency trucking and freight service*

Iron Mountain, National Underground Storage Inc.
745 Atlantic Avenue
Boston, MA 02111
Phone: 800-935-6966
www.ironmountain.com

*Remote storage of data, archives, microfilm and digital data, some disaster recovery support*

Polygon Group
Headquarters and 24-Hour Emergency
15 Sharpner's Pond Road, Building F
North Andover, MA 01845
Phone: 800-422-6379
Fax: 978-655-8511
www.polygongroup.us

*Dehumidifiers—rental*

ProText
PO Box 864
Greenfield, Massachusetts 01302
Phone: 301-320-7231
Fax: 301-320-7232
www.protext.net

*Boxes, supplies, and ready-made kits for disaster recovery*

Remote Backup Systems, Inc.
Memphis, TN
Phone: 901-405-1234 or 800-519-7643
www.remote-backup.com

*Remote backup services and systems*

SafeWare
6500 Busch Boulevard, Suite 233
Columbus, OH 43229
Phone: 800-800-1492
www.safeware.com/Home.aspx

*Computer insurance*

Servpro Drying Companies
575 Airport Road
Gallatin, TN 37066
Phone: 615-451-0200 or 800-SERVPRO (737-8776)
Fax: 615-451-0291
www.servpro.com

*Local franchises rent dehumidifiers and floor fans.*

## *Basic Supplies*

To get started and to keep on hand

Plastic sheeting to protect collections and equipment from water

Tape and waterproof markers

Rubber boots and gloves for protection from water

Flashlights with batteries or solar powered/hand crank flashlights

Disposable camera with film—or disposable digital camera

Office supplies: paper, pencils, waterproof pens

Phone lists of staff and local assistance

# Bibliography

Disaster response continues to grow as a field that affects more than our cultural institutions. This bibliography is divided into three parts. The first is a basic bibliography that contains books, articles, and online resources for responding to and preparing for disasters. The second part lists publications by topic to answer specialized questions and to design response plans for specialized materials. The third part is a general bibliography containing additional readings on a wide variety of disaster response topics and is not inclusive. Some citations refer to other bibliographies. Use the citations to educate the disaster response team and staff members of your institution.

## Basic Articles and Books on Disaster Response

Conservation Center for Art and Historical Artifacts—Technical Bulletins. www.ccaha.org/publications/technical-bulletins.

Federal Emergency Management Agency (FEMA). *Emergency Management Guide for Business and Industry.* Washington, DC: FEMA, 2010. Available at www.fema.gov/business/guide/index.shtm.

Fleischer, S. Victor, and Mark J. Heppner. "Disaster Planning for Libraries and Archives: What You Need to Know and How to Do It." *Library and Archival Security* 22 (December 2009): 125–40.

Halsted, Deborah D., Richard Jasper, and Felicia Little. *Disaster Planning: A How-to-Do-It Manual for Librarians.* New York: Neal-Schuman, 2005.

Library of Congress. Preservation Directorate. *Emergency Preparedness* (April 2010). Includes planning advice, insurance, risk management, and recovering a variety of water-damaged formats. www.loc.gov/preserv/emergprep/prepare.html.

Matthews, Graham, Yvonne Smith, and Gemma Knowles. *Disaster Management in Archives, Libraries and Museums.* Burlington, VT, and Farnham, England: Ashgate, 2009.

McCarthy, Diedre. *Historic Preservation Response Methodology: Based on the Hurricane Katrina Model.* Cultural Resource GIS Facility, Heritage Documentation Programs. Washington, DC: National Park Service, 2009. www.nps.gov/history/hdp/crgis/HPRM-Katrina%20PRINT.pdf.

*Preservation of Library and Archival Materials: A Manual.* Continuously updated. Andover, MA: Northeast Document Conservation Center, 1999–. See especially the section on emergency management. Available at www.nedcc.org/resources/leaflets.list.php. NEDCC 24/7 Emergency Assistance and disaster response materials, www.nedcc.org/disaster/disaster.php.

*A Primer on Disaster Preparedness, Management, and Response: Paper-Based Materials.* Washington, DC: National Archives and Records Administration, Library of Congress, Smithsonian Institution and National Park Service, 1993. Distributed by the participating agencies. Available at www.archives.gov/preservation/emergency-prep/disaster-prep-primer.html and www.nps.gov/museum/publications/primer/primintro.html.

Walsh, Betty. "Salvage of Water-Damaged Archival Collections: Salvage at a Glance." *WAAC Newsletter* 10, no. 2 (May 1988): 2–5.

———. "Salvage Operations for Water-Damaged Archival Collections: A Second Glance." *WAAC*

*Newsletter* 19, no. 2 (May 1997). Available at http://cool.conservation-us.org/waac/wn/wn19/wn19-2/wn19-206.html.

———. "Salvage at a Glance" [the recovery decision chart that goes with the articles above]. Available at http://cool.conservation-us.org/waac/wn/wn19/wn19-2/wn19-207.html.

Wilkinson, Frances C., Linda K. Lewis, and Nancy K. Dennis. *Comprehensive Guide to Emergency Preparedness and Disaster Recovery.* Association of College and Research Libraries. Chicago: American Library Association, 2010.

## Audiovisual and Film-Based Materials

*Care of Photographic Materials.* Ottawa: Canadian Conservation Institute, 1996. www.cci-icc.gc.ca/crc/notes/index-eng.aspx.

Fortson, Judith. "Microforms" and "Magnetic Media and Other Disks." In *Disaster Planning and Recovery,* 66–69, 70–75. New York: Neal-Schuman, 1992.

Hendriks, Klaus. "Storage and Care of Photographs." In *Conservation Concerns: A Guide for Collectors and Curators,* edited by Konstanze Bachmann. Washington, DC: Smithsonian Institution, 1992.

Norris, Debra Hess. *Disaster Recovery: Salvaging Photograph Collections.* Philadelphia: Conservation Center for Art and Historical Artifacts, 1998. Also available at http://ccaha.punkave.net/uploads/media_items/technical-bulletin-salvaging-photographs.original.pdf.

Reilly, James M. *Care and Identification of Nineteenth-Century Photographic Prints.* Kodak Publication no. 0-2S. Rochester, NY: Eastman Kodak, 1986, reprinted 2009.

Rempel, Siegfried. *The Care of Photographs.* New York: N. Lyons Books, 1987.

Ritzenthaler, Mary Lynn, and Diane Vogt-O'Connor. *Photographs: Archival Care and Management.* Chicago: Society of American Archivists, 2006. See especially pp. 268–69.

Wilhelm, Henry, and Carol Brower. *The Permanence and Care of Color Photographs: Traditional and Digital Color Prints, Color Negatives, Slides and Motion Pictures.* Grinnell, IA: Preservation, 1993. www.wilhelm-research.com.

## Magnetic Media, Optical Discs, and Computers

Arps, Mark. "CD-ROM: Archival Considerations." In *Preservation of Electronic Formats and Electronic Formats for Preservation,* edited by Janice Mohlhenrich. Ft. Atkinson, WI: Highsmith, 1993. See especially pp. 83–108.

Byers, Fred R. *Care and Handling of CDs and DVDs: A Guide for Librarians and Archivists.* Pub. 121 (October 2003). Washington, DC: Council on Library and Information Resources, 2003. www.clir.org/pubs/abstract/pub121abst.html.

Child, Margaret, comp. *Directory of Information Sources on Scientific Research Related to the Preservation of Sound Recordings, Still and Moving Images and Magnetic Tape.* Washington, DC: Commission on Preservation and Access, 1997. Available at www.clir.org/pubs/reports/child/child.html.

"Folk Heritage Collections in Crisis." Pub. 96. Washington, DC: Council on Library and Information Resources, 2001. Available at www.clir.org/pubs/reports/pub96/contents.html.

Hunter, Gregory. *Preserving Digital Information.* New York: Neal-Schuman, 2000.

Iraci, Joe. *Longevity of Recordable CDs and DVDs.* CCI Notes 19/1. Ottawa: Canadian Conservation Institute, 2010. www.cci-icc.gc.ca/publications/ccinotes/enotes-pdf/19-1_e.pdf.

Mohlhenrich, Janice, ed. *Preservation of Electronic Formats and Electronic Formats for Preservation.* Ft. Atkinson, WI: Highsmith, 1993.

Moore, Reagan, Arcot Rajasekar, and Richard Marciano. *Collection-Based Persistent Archives.* San Diego Supercomputing Center. Available at www.sdsc.edu/NARA/Publications/OTHER/Persistent/Persistent.html.

Paton, Christopher Ann. "Whispers in the Stacks: The Problem of Sound Recordings in Archives." *American Archivist* 53 (Spring 1990): 274–80.

Pohlmann, Ken C. *The Compact Disc Handbook.* 2nd ed. Computer Music and Digital Audio Series, vol. 5. Madison, WI: A-R Editions, 1992.

Saffady, William. "Stability, Care and Handling of Microforms, Magnetic Media and Optical Disks." *Library Technology Reports* (January–February 1991). Entire issue.

Van Bogart, John W. C. *Magnetic Tape Storage and Handling*. Washington, DC: Commission on Preservation and Access; St. Paul, MN: National Media Laboratory, 1995. www.clir.org/pubs/abstract/pub54.html.

————. "Recovery Data in the Wake of Hurricane Marilyn." *NML BITS* (National Media Lab) 5, no. 2 (November 1995): 1, 8.

Zimmerman, Robert. "Shelf Lives and Videotape." *Fortune* (October 18, 1993): 99.

## Information Sources

National Center for Film and Video Preservation at the American Film Institute

2021 North Western Ave.
Los Angeles, CA 90027
Phone: 323-856-7600
www.afi.com

National Media Laboratory, now Imation Government Services Program

Imation Corp.
1 Imation Way
Oakdale, MN 55128-3421
Phone: 651-704-4000
www.imation.com/en-us/

## *Phonograph Records*

Bamberger, Rob, and Sam Brylawski on behalf of the National Recording Preservation Board. *The State of Recorded Sound Preservation in the United States: A National Legacy at Risk in the Digital Age*. Pub. 148. Washington, DC: Council on Library and Information Resources, August 2010.

Marco, Guy A., and Frank Andrews, eds. *Encyclopedia of Recorded Sound in the United States*. New York: Garland, 1993.

McWilliams, Jerry. *Preservation and Restoration of Sound Recordings*. Nashville, TN: American Association for State and Local History, 1979. See especially pp. 22–43.

Nelson-Strauss, Brenda. "Preservation Policies and Priorities for Recorded Sound Collections." *Notes* (December 1991): 425–45.

Paton, Christopher Ann. "Annotated Selected Bibliography of Works Relating to Sound Recordings and Magnetic and Optical Media." *Midwestern Archivist* 16, no. 1 (1991): 31–47.

Pickett, A. G., and M. M. Lemcoe. *Preservation and Storage of Sound Recordings*. Washington, DC: Library of Congress, 1959.

"Sound Recordings" (special issue). *Library Trends,* July 1972.

Ward, Alan. *Manual of Sound Archive Administration*. Brookfield, VT: Gower, 1990.

## *Indoor Air Quality and Mold*

Chamberlain, William R. "Fungus in the Library." *Library and Archival Security* 4, no. 4 (1982): 35–55.

Image Permanence Institute. "Mold Is Not Your Friend." *Climate Notes Newsletter,* no. 9 (September 2010). https://www.imagepermanence institute.org/resources/newsletter-archive/v9/mold-not-friend.

Nyberg, Sandra. *The Invasion of the Giant Spore*. SOLINET Preservation Program, leaflet no. 5, 1987, updated 2003. http://cool.conservation-us.org/byauth/nyberg/spore.html.

Patkus, Beth Lindblom. "Emergency Salvage of Moldy Books and Paper." In *Technical Leaflet— Emergency Management*. Andover, MA: Northeast Document Conservation Center, 2007. www.nedcc.org/resources/leaflets/3Emergency_Management/08SalvageMoldyBooks.php.

Price, Lois Olcott. *Mold*. CCAHA Technical Series, no. 1. Philadelphia: Conservation Center for Art and Historic Artifacts, 1993–96.

Strang, Thomas J. K., and John E. Dawson. *Controlling Museum Fungal Problems*. Technical Bulletin no. 12. Ottawa: Canadian Conservation Institute, 1991.

Thomson, Garry. *Museum Environment*. London: Butterworths, 1986.

U.S. Environmental Protection Agency and U.S. Department of Health and Human Services. *Building Air Quality: A Guide for Building Owners and Facility Managers*. Washington, DC: Superintendent of Documents, 1991, 1998. www.epa.gov/iaq/largebldgs/baqtoc.html.

Wellheiser, Johanna G. *Nonchemical Treatment Processes for Disinfestation of Insects and Fungi in Library Collections*. International Federation of Library Associations (IFLA) Publications, no. 60. Munich; New York: K. G. Saur, 1992.

## Ozone

Fink, Ronald G. "Ozone Uses in Disaster Restoration Business." *Disaster Recovery Journal* (Spring 1998): 94–95.

National Institute for Occupational Safety and Health. Occupational Safety and Health Administration. 29 CFR 1910, subpart Z.

Thomson, Garry. *The Museum Environment.* 2nd ed. In association with International Institute for Conservation of Historical and Artistic Works. London; Boston: Butterworths, 1986.

U.S. Environmental Protection Agency. *Mold Remediation in Schools and Commercial Buildings.* EPA 402-K-01-001, March 2001. Available at www.epa.gov/mold/index.html.

———. *Mold Resources.* [List of resources and articles.] Washington, DC, 2001–02. Available at www.epa.gov/mold/moldresources.html.

———. *Ozone Generators That Are Sold as Air Cleaners: An Assessment of Effectiveness and Health Consequences.* Washington, DC, 2001. Available at www.epa.gov/iaq/pubs/ozonegen.html.

Whitmore, P. M., and G. R. Cass. "The Ozone Fading of Traditional Japanese Colorants." *Studies in Conservation* 33 (1988): 29–40.

## Resources

Conversations with Professor Arnold Feingold, SUNY, Stony Brook, New York; Professor Yair Zarmi, Ben Gurion University, Beer Sheva, Israel; Professor Robert Dezafra, SUNY, Stony Brook, New York; Larry Wood, Disaster Recovery Services, Ft. Worth, Texas; Rick Kemper, Aegis Environmental Management Inc., Cincinnati, Ohio; Vernon Will, Ohio Historical Society, Columbus, Ohio; Doug Nishimura, Image Permanence Institute, Rochester, New York.

## Selected General Bibliography

Ahenkorah-Marfo, Michael, and Edward Mensah Borteye. "Disaster Preparedness in Academic Libraries: The Case of the Kwame Nkrumah University of Science and Technology Library, Kumasi, Ghana." *Library and Archival Security* 23, no. 2 (2010): 117–36.

Alire, Camila. *Library Disaster Planning and Recovery Handbook.* New York: Neal-Schuman, 2000.

American Institute of Certified Public Accountants. *Disaster Recovery Planning.* Technical Consulting Practice Aid, no. 15. New York: American Institute of Certified Public Accountants, 1991.

American National Red Cross. *How Do I Deal with My Feelings?* Available in numerous languages at www.redcross.org/services/disaster/keepsafe/howdo.pdf.

Artim, Nick. "Cultural Heritage Fire Suppression Systems: Alternative to Halon 1301." *WAAC Newsletter* 15, no. 2 (May 1993).

Bader, Nancy. "Run for Coverage: When Disaster Strikes, It Pays to Have a Plan." *Your Company* (Summer 1993): 14–15.

Ballman, Janette. "Merrill Lynch Resumes Critical Business within Minutes of Attack." *Disaster Recovery Journal* (Fall 2001): 26–28.

Balloffet, Nelly. *Library Disaster Handbook: Planning, Recovery, Resources.* Highland, NY: Southeastern New York Library Resources Council, 1992.

Barlak, K. "Emotional Coping Mechanisms in Times of Disasters." *New Jersey Libraries* 28, no. 3 (Summer 1995): 13, 15.

Barstow, Sandra. "Library Security After the Renovation: How Much Is Enough?" *Library and Archival Security* 23, no. 1 (March 2010): 37–48.

Bates, Regis L., Jr. *Disaster Response for LANS: A Planning and Action Guide.* New York: McGraw-Hill, 1994.

———. *Disaster Response Planning: Networks, Telecommunications, and Data Communications.* New York: McGraw-Hill, 1992.

Baum, Kristin. "Interpreting Deluge: A Story of Collections and Response from the 2008 Iowa Floods." *The Bonefolder: An E-Journal for the Bookbinder and Book Artists* 5, no. 2 (Spring 2009): 48–53.

Bigley, Tom. "Backup for Safe Keeping." *InfoWorld* (October 15, 1990): 67–81.

Boudette, Neal E. "A Piece of the Rock for Computers: Recovery Firms Protect against 'Data Disasters.'" *Industry Week* (November 7, 1988): 85.

Burgess, Dean. "The Library Has Blown Up!" *Library Journal* (October 1, 1989): 59–61.

Byers, T. J. "PC World's Guide to Painless Backups." *PC World* (September 1990): 217–22.

Carlsen, Soren. "Effects of Freeze Drying on Paper." Preprint from the 9th International Congress of "Internationale Arbeitsgemeinschaft der Archiv-, Bibliotheks- und Graphikrestauratoren" (International Association of Archive, Book and Paper Conservators or IADA), Copenhagen, August 15–21, 1999. Full text available at http://cool .conservation-us.org/iada/ta99_115.pdf.

Cerullo, Michael J., R. Steve McDuffie, and L. Murphy Smith. "Planning for Disasters." *CPA Journal* (June 1994): 34–38.

Chandler, Robert C. "How to Communicate during the Six Stages of a Crisis." White paper. Glendale, CA: Everbridge, 2009. http://everbridge.com/ crisislifecycle.

Chase, Deborah. "Disaster Recovery Systems: A Specialized Form of Insurance." *Inform* 3 (April 1989): 32–35.

Clolery, Paul. "When Disaster Strikes: Keep Your Practice Running." *Practical Accountant* 21 (May 1993): 24–28.

Coleman, Randall. "Six Steps to Disaster Recovery." *Security Management* 37 (February 1993): 61–62.

Collingwood, Harris. "Message Therapy." *Working Woman* (February 1997): 26–29, 53, 55.

Conroy, Cathryn. "Accidents Will Happen: Formulating a Recovery Plan in Case of Disasters, Mishaps, and Hard Luck Might Save Business." *CompuServe* (September 1993): 30–33.

Cooper, Joanne Kimbler. "Sick Buildings: Some Fresh Remedies." *Business First of Columbus— Environmental Report* (May 17, 1993): 20A–24A.

Courtney, Philip E. "LA Earthquake Prompts Recoveries." *Enterprise Systems Journal* (March 1994): 98–99, 102.

Cox, Jack E., and Robert L. Barber. "Preparing for the Unknown: Practical Contingency Planning." *Risk Management* 43 (September 1996): 14–20.

Cunha, George. "Disaster Planning and a Guide to Recovery Resources." *Library Technology Reports* (September/October 1992): 533–624.

Davis, Mary B., Susan Fraser, and Judith Reed. "Preparing for Library Emergencies: A Cooperative Approach." *Wilson Library Bulletin* (November 1991): 42–44, 128.

Deering, Ann. "Online Disaster Management Resources." *Risk Management* 43 (September 1996): 12.

DiLandro, Daniel. "2009 Flood on Buffalo State Campus and Disaster Recovery." *WNYLRCWatch Newsletter.* http://wnylrcwatch.org/newsletter/ ?p=2144.

"Disaster Planning: A Necessity for All Firms." *Small Business Report* 12, no. 7 (July 1987): 34–41.

Dobb, Linda S. "Technostress: Surviving a Database Crash." *Reference Services Review* (Winter 1990): 65–68.

Doig, Judith. *Disaster Recovery for Archives, Libraries, and Records Management Systems in Australia and New Zealand.* Wagga Wagga, New South Wales: Centre for Information Studies, 1997.

Dougherty, Meghan, and Heather Seneff. "Updating Disaster Planning for the Digital Age." *Visual Resources Association Bulletin* 35, no. 1 (Spring 2008): 49–54.

Ebling, R. G. "Establishing a Safe Harbor: How to Develop a Successful Disaster Recovery Program." *Risk Management* 43 (September 1996): 53–54.

Edwards, B., and J. Cooper. "Testing the Disaster Recovery Plan." *Information Management and Computer Security* 3, no. 1 (1995): 21–27.

Ellis, Judith, ed. *Keeping Archives.* 2nd ed. Melbourne: Thorpe in association with the Australian Society of Archivists, 1993.

England, Claire, and Karen Evans. *Disaster Management for Libraries: Planning and Process.* Ottawa: Canadian Library Association, 1988.

Ernst and Young, Entrepreneurial Division. "Hot Sites Help Firms Avoid Computer Meltdown." *Business First of Columbus* (March 15, 1993): 37.

Eulenberg, Julia Niebuhr. *Handbook for the Recovery of Water-Damaged Business Records.* Prairie Village, KS: ARMA International, 1986.

Federal Emergency Management Agency (FEMA). *Emergency Management Guide for Business and Industry.* Washington, DC: FEMA, [n.d.]. Available at www.fema.gov/business/.

Field, Susan Copony. "Fire in the University of Georgia Libraries." *DttP* 36, no. 3 (Fall 2008): 20–26.

*Fire Protection Handbook.* 20th ed. Boston: National Fire Protection Association, 2008.

Fitzgerald, K. J. "Security and Data Integrity for LANs and WANs." *Information Management and Computer Security* 3, no. 4 (1995): 27–33.

Flesher, Tom. "Special Challenges over Extended Distance." *Disaster Recovery Journal* (Winter 2002): 54.

Florian, Mary-Lou E. *Heritage Eaters: Insect and Fungi in Heritage Collections.* London: James and James, 1997.

Forde, Helen. *Preserving Archives. Principles and Practice in Records Management and Archives Series.* London: Facet, 2007. See especially chapters 5, 7, and 12.

Fortson, Judith. *Disaster Planning and Recovery: A How-to-Do-It Manual for Librarians and Archivists.* How-to-Do-It Manuals for Libraries, no. 11. Edited by Bill Katz. New York: Neal-Schuman, 1992.

Fox, Lisa L. "Management Strategies for Disaster Preparedness." *ALA Yearbook of Library and Information Services* 14 (1989): 1–6.

———. "Risk Management for Libraries." *ALA Yearbook of Library and Information Services* 15 (1990): 218–19.

Gagnon, Robert M. "Water Mist Fire Suppression Systems Theory and Applications." *FireWatch* 1997. Available at www.nafed.org/resources/library/wmist.cfm.

Galbraith, Thomas, with Ann-Louise Seago. "Conservation of Manuscripts and Books: Considerations on Insurance and Risk Reduction" *Feliciter* 55, no. 2 (2009): 54–55.

Gallagher, J. N. "Preparation, Communication Are Key to Emergency Procedures." *Real Estate Forum* 51 (June 1996): 44.

Gauthier, Michael R. "Managing Information: How to Avoid a Computer Catastrophe." *Business Month* (May 1989): 81–82.

Gauthier, Ronald. "Three Years after Katrina." *Library Journal* 133, no. 14 (September 1, 2008): 46.

George, S. C. "Library Disasters: Are You Prepared?" *College and Research Libraries News* 56, no. 2 (February 1995): 80, 82–84.

Gibson, Steve. "To Keep Your PC Running Smoothly, Let the Power Flow." *PC World* (September 24, 1990): 32.

Gilbert, Evelyn. "Disaster Plans Called Key to Museum Loss Control." *National Underwriter: Property and Casualty/Risk and Benefits Management* 96 (May 4, 1992): 23–25, 50–51.

Gilderson-Duwe, Caroline, comp. *Disaster Recovery Supplies and Suppliers.* Madison: Wisconsin Preservation Program (WISPPR), 1995.

Green, Sonya L., and Thomas H. Tepper. "The Importance of Disaster Planning for the Small Public Library." *Public Library Quarterly* 25, no. 3/4 (2006): 47–59.

Hall, Matthew. "Off-Site Storage Helps Firms Clean Up Their Act." *Business First of Columbus* (August 8, 1994): 17.

———. "Trade Center Offers Emergency Lessons." *Business First of Columbus* (June 7, 1993): 15, 18.

Hammaker, Robert, Robert Irvine, and Karl Brimner. "Managing the Mental Health Role in Disasters: An Alaska Experience." *Disaster Recovery Journal* (Spring 1998): 16–22.

Hankins, Joseph. "Choosing the Right Automatic Sprinkler." *Disaster Recovery Journal* (April–June 1992): 56–60.

Hargrave, Ruth (project director). *Cataclysm and Challenge: Impact of September 11, 2001 on Our Nation's Cultural Heritage.* Washington, DC: Heritage Preservation and Heritage Emergency National Task Force, 2002. Available at www.heritagepreservation.org/PDFS/Cataclysm.pdf.

Harrington, Gary. "Flood! or, Disasters Always Happen on the Weekend." *Southwestern Archivist* 16, no. 4 (Winter 1993): 1–5.

———. "Flood Recovery in Oklahoma City." *Conservation Administration News* 54 (July 1993): 10–11.

Harris, Jamey L. "Locking Down a University Library: How to Keep People Safe in a Crisis." *Library and Archival Security* 23, no. 1 (March 2010): 27–36.

Harris, K., and J. Fenn. "Emerging Technologies to Minimize Disruptions: Checklist." *Research Note Technology: Advanced Technologies and Applications* (September 2001). Available at www.gartner.com/reprints/backweb/101212.html.

Harrison, H. P. "Emergency Preparedness and Disaster Recovery of Audio, Film, and Video Materials." *IASA Journal* (November 1995): 82–85.

Harvey, Ross. *Preservation in Libraries: A Reader.* Topics in Library and Information Studies. London; New York: Bowker; K. G. Saur, 1993. (Contains reprints of articles and chapters.)

———. *Preservation in Libraries: Principles, Strategies, and Practices for Librarians.* Topics in

Library and Information Studies. London; New York: Bowker; K. G. Saur, 1993. (Contains reprints of articles and chapters.)

Heath, Robert L., and H. Dan O'Hair. *Handbook of Risk and Crisis Communication.* New York: Routledge, 2009.

Hendriks, Klaus B., and Brian Lesser. "Disaster Preparedness and Recovery: Photographic Materials." *American Archivist* 46, no. 1 (Winter 1983): 52–68.

Heritage National Task Force. *Field Guide to Emergency Response.* Washington, DC: Heritage Preservation, 2006.

Higginbotham, Barbra Buckner, and Judith W. Wild. "It Ain't Over 'til It's Over: The Process of Disaster Recovery." *Technicalities* 16, no. 5 (May 1996): 12–13.

———. "Practical Preservation Practice—Managing Emergencies: Small Construction Projects." *Technicalities* 16, no. 9 (October 1996): 1, 12–14.

———. *Preservation Program Blueprint.* Chicago: American Library Association, 2001.

Hirsch, Steven A. "Disaster! Could Your Company Recover?" *Management Accounting* 71, no. 9 (March 1990): 50–52.

Hirst, Donna. "The Iowa City Flood of 2008: A Librarian and IT Professional's Perspective." *Information Technology and Libraries* 27, no. 4 (December 2008): 5–8.

Hoffman, Eva. "Protecting Yesterday for Tomorrow." National Association of Fire Equipment Distributors, 1999. Available at www.nafed.org/Library .html.

Hoffman, T. "Publisher Does Disaster Planning by the Book." *Computer World* 30 (May 20, 1996): 74.

Holderman, Eric. "Disaster Wiki: Get Ready Now to Harness Social Media!" *Disaster Resource Guide Quarterly* (June 2010). www.disaster-resource .com.

"Hospital Cures PBX Failures with Surge Protection." *Communications News* (April 1994): 10–11.

Inland Marine Underwriters Association, Arts and Records Committee. *Libraries and Archives: An Overview of Risk and Loss Prevention.* New York: Inland Marine Underwriters Association, 1993.

"Integrated Pest Management." *NEDCC News* 8, no. 1 (Winter 1998): 4–5.

Jessup, Wendy Claire. *Integrated Pest Management: A Selected Bibliography.* Falls Church, VA: Wendy Jessup, 1997. Available at http://cool.conservation -us.org/byauth/jessup/ipm.html.

Kahn, Miriam. *Disaster Prevention and Response for Computers and Data.* Columbus, OH: MBK Consulting, 1994.

———. *Disaster Prevention and Response for Special Libraries: An Information Kit.* Washington, DC: Special Libraries Association, 1995. (Note: The print version is no longer available from SLA. It is available in full text at www.sla.org/content/ resources/inforesour/sept11help/disip/infokit.cfm.)

———. "Disaster Prevention or Protecting Your Business." In *The RBS Book,* edited by Rob Cosgrove. Memphis, TN: Data Precision, 1994.

———. "Fires, Earthquakes, and Floods: How to Prepare Your Library and Staff." *Online* 18, no. 3 (May 1994): 18–24.

———. *First Steps for Handling and Drying Water-Damaged Materials.* Columbus, OH: MBK Consulting, 1994.

———. "Mastering Disasters: Emergency Planning for Libraries." *Library Journal* 118, no. 21 (December 1993): 73–75.

Kahn, Miriam, and Barbra Higginbotham. "Disasters for Directors: The Role of the Library or Archive Director in Disaster Preparedness and Recovery." In *Advances in Preservation and Access,* vol. 2. Edited by Barbra Higginbotham. Medford, NJ: Learned Information, 1995.

Kiely, Helen U. "The Effect of Moisture on Paper." American Writing Paper Company, 1927. Available at http://cool.conservation-us.org/byauth/kiely/ moisture.html.

Kirvan, Paul. "NYBOT Recovers with Backup Trading Floor." *Contingency Planning and Management* (January/February 2002): 49–50.

Kuyk, Charlie. "Resolving Business Interruption Claims." *Columbus CEO* (March 2002): 39–40.

Laiming, Susan, and Paul Laiming. "Insurance: Minimizing Your Loss and Managing Risk." *Bottom Line* 2, no. 1 (1988): 14–16.

Learn, Larry L. "Diversity: Two Are Not Cheaper Than One! A Look at Facilities Disaster Avoidance." *Library Hi Tech News* (January/February 1992): 17–22.

LeBoeuf, Mary Cosper. "Disasters Strike, Public Libraries Prevail: The Impact of Hurricanes Katrina and Rita on Louisiana Public Libraries." *Louisiana Libraries* 68, no. 4 (Spring 2006): 3–7.

Lemley, Don. "Precautions and Safe Practices for Records Storage Systems." *Records Management Quarterly* (April 1992): 24–27.

Lepczyk, Tim. *Zombie Emergency Preparedness.* blog (January 25, 2011). http://digitaldunes.blogspot .com/2011/01/emergency-response-zombies-and -risks-to.html. While this is a tongue-in-cheek posting, the disaster response and prevention advice is sound.

Lewis, Steven, and Richard Arnold. *Disaster Recovery Yellow Pages.* Ashton, MD: Edwards Information, 2011. www.edwardsinformation.com.

Lull, William P., with the assistance of Paul N. Banks. *Conservation Environment Guidelines for Libraries and Archives in New York State.* Albany: New York State Library, 1990.

Lunde, Diane B., and Patricia A. Smith. "Disaster and Security: Colorado State Style." *Library and Archival Security* 22, no. 2 (July–December 2009): 99–114.

———. "Staff Training for Disaster Response." *Colorado Libraries* 34, no. 4 (2008): 29–31.

Marley, Sara. "Learning from Disaster." *Business Insurance* 27 (June 7, 1993): 3–4.

Maslen, C. "Testing the Plan Is More Important Than the Plan Itself." *Information Management and Computer Security* 4, no. 3 (1996): 26–29.

Matthews, Graham, Yvonne Smith, and Gemma Knowles. "The Disaster Control Plan: Where Is It At?" *Library and Archival Security* 19, no. 2 (July–December 2004): 3–23.

Mayer, John H. "Disaster Prone." *Client/Server Computing* (October 1996): 47–52.

McCrady, Ellen. "Mold: The Whole Picture." Parts 1–4. *Abbey Newsletter* 23, no. 4–7 (1999). Available at http://cool.conservation-us.org/byorg/abbey/.

McGinty, John. "Insuring Libraries against Risk." *Library and Archival Security* 21, no. 2 (2008): 177–86.

Miller, R. Bruce. "Contingency Planning Resources." *Information Technology and Libraries* (June 1990): 179–80.

———. "Libraries and Computers: Disaster Prevention and Recovery." *Information Technology and Libraries* (December 1988): 349–58.

Mitroff, Ian I., L. Katherine Harrington, and Eric Gai. "Thinking about the Unthinkable." *Across the Board* 33 (September 1996): 44–48.

Moore, Pat. "Safeguarding Your Company's Records." *Risk Management* 43 (September 1996): 47–50.

Morris, John. *The Library Disaster Preparedness Handbook.* Chicago: American Library Association, 1986.

Murray, Toby. *Basic Guidelines for Disaster Planning in Oklahoma.* Tulsa, OK: University of Tulsa, 1985.

———. *Bibliography on Disasters, Disaster Preparedness, and Disaster Recovery.* Tulsa, OK: University of Tulsa Preservation Department, 1994.

———. "Don't Get Caught with Your Plans Down." *Records Management Quarterly* (April 1987): 12–41 (bibliography 18–30, 41).

Myatt, Paul B. "Business Resumption Planning: An ROI Opportunity." *Enterprise Systems Journal* (November 1994): 83–88, 92.

Myree, Simone. "Fire Suppression and Water Mist Systems." *Library and Archival Security* 21, no. 2 (July–December 2008): 169–76.

National Parks Service. Museum Management Program. Department of the Interior. *NPS Museum Handbook.* Washington, DC: Government Printing Office, 2006. Available at www.cr.nps.gov/ museum/publications/handbook.html.

Nelton, Sharon. "Prepare for the Worst." *Nation's Business* 81 (September 1993): 20–28.

New York City Department of Health. *Guidelines on Assessment and Remediation of Fungi in Indoor Environments.* New York: New York City Department of Health, Bureau of Environmental and Occupational Disease and Epidemiology, 2008. Also available at http://nyc.gov/html/doh/html/epi/ moldrpt1.shtml.

New York State Program for the Conservation and Preservation of Library Research Materials. *Disaster Preparedness: Planning Resource Packet.* Albany: University of the State of New York, State Education Department, New York State Library Division of Library Development, 1988.

———. *Environmental Controls Resource Packet.* Albany: University of the State of New York, State

Education Department, New York State Library Division of Library Development, 1990.

Newman, William F. "Sky-High Disaster Management." *Security Management* (January 1994): 26–30.

Nichols, Don. "Back in Business." [Case study.] *Small Business Reports* (March 1993): 55–63.

Nishimura, Doug. "Fire Suppression Systems." *ConsDist.Lst* 20 (October 1993). Available online in CoOL Archives at http://cool.conservation-us.org.

Norton, Judith. "Disaster Planning Resources" [part of a special issue: Emergency and disaster preparedness and response]. *OLA Quarterly* 14, no. 4 (Winter 2008): 23–26.

Nyberg, Sandra. *The Invasion of the Giant Spore.* SOLINET Preservation Program, leaflet no. 5, November 1987. The updated version is available at http://cool.conservation-us.org/byauth/nyberg/spore.html.

O'Connell, Mildred. "Disaster Planning: Writing and Implementing Plans for Collections-Holding Institutions." *Technology and Conservation* 8 (Summer 1983): 18–24.

Ogden, Sherelyn. "An Introduction to Fire Detection, Alarm, and Automatic Fire Sprinklers." Technical Leaflet—Emergency Management—Section 3, Leaflet 2. Andover, MA: Northeast Document Conservation Center, 2007. Also available at www.nedcc.org/resources/leaflets/3Emergency_Management/01ProtectionFromLoss.php.

Olson, Nancy B. "Hanging Your Software Up to Dry." *College and Research Libraries News* 47, no. 10 (November 1986): 634–36.

Osborne, Larry N. "Those (In)destructible Disks; or, Another Myth Exploded." *Library Hi Tech* 27 (1989): 7–10, 28.

Pacey, Antony. "Halon Gas and Library Fire Protection." *Canadian Library Journal* (February 1991): 33–36.

Paradine, T. J. "Business Interruption Insurance: A Vital Ingredient in Your Disaster Recovery Plan." *Information Management and Computer Security* 3, no. 1 (1995): 9–17.

Payton, Annie Malessia, and Theodosia T. Thields. "Insurance and Library Facilities." *Library and Archival Security* 21, no. 2 (2008): 187–93.

Pelland, D. "Disaster Management Reaches Mid-Size Firms: Planning to Survive." *Risk Management* 43 (September 1996): 10.

Piotrowicz, Lynn M., and Scott Osgood. *Building Science 101: A Primer for Librarians.* Chicago: American Library Association, 2010.

Post, Deborah Cromer. "Fire Protection Systems." *Security World* (March 1981): 30–32.

Ragsdale, K. W., and J. Simpson. "Being on the Safe Side." *College and Research Libraries News* 57, no. 6 (June 1996): 351–54.

Ray, Emily. "The Prague Library Floods of 2002: Crisis and Experimentation." *Libraries and the Cultural Record* 41, no. 3 (Summer 2006): 381–91.

Reference and User Services Association. "Guidelines for Resource-Sharing Response to Natural and Man-Made Disasters." *Reference and User Services Quarterly* 50, no. 2 (Winter 2010): 197–98.

Reilly, James M., Douglas W. Nishimura, and Edward Zinn. *New Tools for Preservation: Assessing Long-Term Environmental Effects on Library and Archives Collections.* Council on Library and Information Resources Pub. 59. Washington, DC: Commission on Preservation and Access, 1995. www.clir.org/pubs/abstract/pub59.html.

Rentschler, Cathy, and Pamela Burdett. "Mock Disaster at Stetson Law Library Prepares Staff for a Real One." *Florida Libraries* 49, no. 1 (Spring 2006): 13–15.

Resnick, Rosalind. "Protecting Computers and Data." *Nation's Business* 81 (September 1993): 26.

Rice, Donna B. "First Response to Disasters for Small Museums and Libraries." *PNLA Quarterly* 70, no. 3 (Spring 2006): 4, 13–18.

Rightmeyer, S. P. "Disaster Planning; or, The 'What Next' Attitude." *New Jersey Libraries* 28, no. 3 (Summer 1995): 3–18.

Roberts, Barbara O. "Speaking Out: Establishing a Disaster Prevention/Response Plan: An International Perspective and Assessment." *Technology and Conservation* (Winter 1992–93): 15–17, 35–36.

Robertson, Guy. "People, Paper, Data: Disaster Planning for Libraries." *Disaster Recovery Journal* 10, no. 1 (Winter 1997): 38–43.

Rothstein, Philip J. "Up and Running; How to Insure Disaster Recovery." *Datamation* (October 15, 1988): 86–96.

Sanders, Robert L. "Planners and Fire Fighters: A Records Management Synthesis." *Records Management Quarterly* (April 1992): 50–59.

Seal, Robert A. "Risk Management for Libraries." *ALA Yearbook of Library and Information Services* 14 (1989): 218–21.

———. "Risk Management for Libraries." *ALA Yearbook of Library and Information Services* 13 (1988): 294–98.

Shelly, Rose Ann. "How the GSA (General Services Administration) Responds to Emergencies." *Communications News* (April 1994): 20–23.

Silverman, Randy. "The Seven Deadly Sins of Disaster Recovery." *Public Library Quarterly* 25, no. 3/4 (2006): 31–46.

———. "Toward a National Disaster Response Protocol." *Libraries and the Cultural Record* 41, no. 4 (Fall 2006): 497–511.

Smith, Kenneth. "When Timing Is Everything: Disaster Recovery Timing and Business Impact." *Enterprise Systems Journal* (January 1994): 72–76.

Smith, Richard D. "Disaster Recovery: Problems and Procedures." *IFLA Journal* 17 (1991): 13–24.

Souter, Gavin. "Active Disaster Plan Thanked for Swift Recovery." *Business Insurance 27* (June 7, 1993): 6, 10.

St. Lifer, Evan, and Michael Rogers. "Corporate Libraries Recover from Trade Center Bombing." *Library Journal* (April 1, 1993): 18–19.

Stagnitto, Janice. "The Shrink Wrap Project at Rutgers University." *Special Collections and Archives AIC Book and Paper Group Annual* 12 (1993): 56–60. Available at http://cool.conservation-us.org/coolaic/sg/bpg/annual/v12/bp12-13.html.

Stephan, Elizabeth. "Recovering from Disaster." *Mississippi Libraries* 70, no. 3 (Fall 2006): 55.

Stephenson, Mary Sue. *Planning Library Facilities: A Selected, Annotated Bibliography.* Metuchen, NJ: Scarecrow, 1990.

Stigall, Lisa. "Hurricanes Close Libraries but the Service Doesn't Stop." *Louisiana Libraries* 68, no. 3 (Winter 2006): 45.

Stratton, Lee. "A Fungus among Us." *Columbus Dispatch* (January 6, 2002): 01I.

———. "Mold Causing Stink for Builders, Insurance Companies." *Columbus Dispatch* (January 6, 2002): 01I.

Sutherland, J. Warren. "Computerized Contingency Planning Can Aid RMs (Risk Managers)." *National Underwriters: Property and Casualty/Risk and Benefits Management* 97 (May 17, 1993): 11, 25.

Tanzillo, Kevin. "How Users Survived the 1994 L.A. Quake." *Communications News* (April 1994): 12–14.

*Technical Support/Special Report: Disaster Recovery.* Official magazine of the National Systems Programmers Association, October 1990.

Thenell, Jan. *The Library's Crisis Communications Planner: A PR Guide for Handling Every Emergency.* Chicago: American Library Association, 2004.

Thomas, Marica, and Anke Voss, eds. *Emergency Response Planning in College Libraries.* CLIP Note 40, College Library Information Packet Committee, College Libraries Section, Association of College and Research Libraries. Chicago: American Library Association, 2009.

Tillson, Timothy B. "Post-Disaster Recovery." *Small Business Reports* 15, no. 2 (February 1990): 46–50.

Tremain, David. "Notes on Emergency Drying of Coated Papers Damaged by Water." Canadian Conservation Institute, n.d. Available at http://cool.conservation-us.org/byauth/tremain/coated.html.

Ungarelli, Donald L. "National Statistics—Fire Losses for 1987." *Library and Archival Security* 9, no. 2 (1989): 50–53.

U.S. Centers for Disease Control, National Institute for Occupational Safety and Health. *Indoor Environmental Quality.* www.cdc.gov/niosh/topics/indoorenv/mold.html.

U.S. National Archives and Records Administration. *Records Emergency Information.* www.archives.gov/preservation/records-emergency/.

Van Mill, Susan, and Al Gliane. "Insurance and Disaster Recovery Planning: Business Income Coverage and Claims Preparation." *Disaster Recovery Journal* (Spring 1998): 89–90.

*Vital Records and Records Disaster Mitigation and Recovery: An Instructional Guide.* National Archives and Records Administration Instructional Guide Series. College Park, MD: National Archives and Records Administration, Office of Records Administration, 1996. Available at http://cool.conservation-us.org/bytopic/disasters/misc/vitalrec/.

Vossler, Janet L. "The Human Element of Disaster Recovery." *ARMA Quarterly* (January 1987): 10–12.

Wall, Kay L. "Lessons Learned from Katrina: What Really Matters in a Disaster." *Public Library Quarterly* 25, no. 3/4 (2006): 189–98.

Wallace, Michael. *The Disaster Recovery Handbook: A Step-by-Step Plan to Ensure Business Continuity and Protect Vital Operations, Facilities, and Assets.* New York: American Management Association, 2004.

Walsh, Betty. "Salvage of Water-Damaged Archival Collections: Salvage at a Glance." *WAAC Newsletter* 10, no. 2 (April 1989): 2–5. http://cool.conservation-us.org/waac/wn/wn10/wn10-2/wn10-202.html.

———. "Salvage Operations for Water-Damaged Archival Collections: A Second Glance." *WAAC Newsletter* 19, no. 2 (May 1997). Available at http://cool.conservation-us.org/waac/wn/wn19/wn19-2/wn19-206.html. The updated salvage chart is available at http://cool.conservation-us.org/waac/wn/wn19/wn19-2/wn19-207.html.

Waters, Peter. *Procedures for Salvage of Water-Damaged Library Materials.* Washington, DC: Library of Congress, 1975.

Watson, Tom. "After the Fire: Everett Community College Library Is Back in Business." *Wilson Library Bulletin* (November 1988): 63–65.

Welch, J. "On-Screen Disaster Provides Vital Lessons." *People Management* 2 (May 16, 1996): 9.

Wellheiser, Johanna G., and Jude Scott. *An Ounce of Prevention: Integrated Disaster Planning for Archives, Libraries, and Record Centres.* 2nd ed. Lanham, MD: Scarecrow and Canadian Archives Foundation, 2002.

Welsh, Elizabeth. "Fire Suppression Using Micromist." *ConsDist.Lst* 28 (September 1993). Available online in CoOL Archives at http://cool.conservation-us.org/byform/mailing-lists/cdl/.

Western New York Library Resources Council (WNYLRC). *Western New York Disaster Preparedness Manual for Libraries and Archives.* 3rd ed. Buffalo, NY: Western New York Library Resources Council, 2003. www.wnylrc.org/documentView.asp?docid=35.

Wettlaufer, B. "Preparing a Library Disaster Plan." *Library Mosaics* 6, no. 6 (November–December 1995): 8–10.

Whiting, Rick. "Spoilt for Choice." *Client/Server Computing* (October 1996): 40–44.

Wiener, Judith A. "The Element of Surprise: Preparing for the Possibility of Hazardous Materials within Archival Collections." *Journal of Archival Organization* 5, no. 4 (2007): 33–49.

Wilson, J. Andrew. "Fire Fighters: An Automatic Fire Suppression System Is among Your Museum's Best and Safest Forms of Insurance." *Museum News* (November–December 1989): 68–72.

Wolf, Alisa. "Wake-Up Call: Fire at the U.S. Treasury Building." *NFPA Journal* 90, no. 6 (November–December 1996): 52–57.

## Journals

CLIR Issues
> Council on Library and Information Resources
> Commission on Preservation and Access
> 1755 Massachusetts Avenue NW, Suite 500
> Washington, DC 20036
> Phone: 202-939-4750
> Fax: 202-939-4765
> www.clir.org

*Disaster Recovery Journal* (free trade publication)
> 1862 Old Lemay Ferry
> Arnold, MO 63010
> Phone: 636-282-5800
> www.drj.com

*Enterprise Systems Journal* (free trade publication)
> c/o Cardinal Business Media, Inc.
> www.esj.com

*Records Management Quarterly*
> Association of Records Management and Administrators, Inc.
> 11880 College Blvd., Suite 450
> Overland Park, KS 66210
> Phone: 913-341-3808 or 800-422-2762
> Fax: 913-341-3742
> www.arma.org

## Internet Addresses and Websites

American Fire Sprinkler Association (AFSA; automatic fire sprinklers)
> www.sprinklernet.org

CoOL: Conservation On-Line
> http://cool.conservation-us.org

Federal Emergency Management Agency (FEMA)
www.fema.gov

"Florence 40 Years after the Flood" (pictures, photos, and stories of the conservation efforts during the flood and afterward)
www.mega.it/allu/eng/ealluvho.htm

National Association of Fire Equipment Distributors (selection and design of alarm and suppression systems)
122 S. Michigan Ave., Suite 1040
Chicago, IL 60603
Phone: 312-461-9600
Fax: 312-461-0777
www.nafed.org

National Fire Protection Association (NFPA)
1 Batterymarch Park
Quincy, MA 02169-7471
Phone: 617-770-3000
www.nfpa.org/Home/index.asp

Ready.Gov (part of FEMA; a national public service advertising campaign launched in 2003 to provide public awareness of the need to plan for disasters in homes and businesses)
*Ready* Campaign
Federal Emergency Management Agency
500 C St., SW
Washington, DC 20472
www.ready.gov

# *Index*